Informal Logic

Informal Logic

A HANDBOOK FOR CRITICAL ARGUMENTATION

Douglas N. Walton

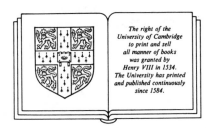

The right of the
University of Cambridge
to print and sell
all manner of books
was granted by
Henry VIII in 1534.
The University has printed
and published continuously
since 1584.

Cambridge University Press

Cambridge

New York   Port Chester   Melbourne   Sydney

Published by the Press Syndicate of the University of Cambridge
The Pitt Building, Trumpington Street, Cambridge CB2 1RP
40 West 20th Street, New York, NY 10011, USA
10 Stamford Road, Oakleigh, Melbourne 3166, Australia

First published 1989
Reprinted 1989, 1991

Printed in the United States of America

Library of Congress Cataloging-in-Publication Data
Walton, Douglas N.
Informal logic: a handbook for critical argumentation / Douglas
N. Walton.
p. cm.
Bibliography: p.
Includes index.
ISBN 0-521-37032-9.   ISBN 0-521-37925-3 (pbk.)
1. Logic   2. Reasoning   I. Title.
BC177.W324 1989   88-30762
168 – dc 19   CIP

British Library Cataloguing in Publication Data
Walton, Douglas N.
Informal logic: a handbook for critical
argumentation.
1. Argument
I. Title
168

ISBN 0-521-37032-9 hardback
ISBN 0-521-37925-3 paperback

Contents

Preface   *page* ix
Acknowledgments   xiii

1 Argument as reasoned dialogue   1

   1.1 Types of argumentative dialogue   3
   1.2 Components of argumentative dialogue   9
   1.3 Persuasion dialogue (critical discussion)   11
   1.4 Negative rules of persuasion dialogue   16
   1.5 Some major informal fallacies   19
   1.6 The critical perspective   23

2 Questions and answers in dialogue   27

   2.1 Presuppositions of questions   28
   2.2 Complex questions   31
   2.3 Have you stopped beating your spouse?   35
   2.4 Reasonable dialogue   39
   2.5 Arguments from ignorance   43
   2.6 Replying to a question with a question   49
   2.7 Begging the question   52
   2.8 Question–answer rules in dialogue   54

3 Criticisms of irrelevance   60

   3.1 Allegations of irrelevance   61
   3.2 Global irrelevance   64
   3.3 Question–answer relevance   67
   3.4 Setting an agenda for a discussion   71
   3.5 Varieties of criticisms of irrelevance   75
   3.6 Summary   77

4 Appeals to emotion   82

   4.1 *Argumentum ad populum*   84
   4.2 The argument from popularity   87

4.3	Problems with appeals to popularity	90
4.4	Threatening appeals to force	93
4.5	Further *ad baculum* problems	97
4.6	Appeals to pity	101
4.7	Overt, pictorial appeals to pity	103
4.8	Summary	105
5	Valid arguments	108
5.1	Deductive validity	108
5.2	Identifying arguments	110
5.3	Validity as a semantic concept	114
5.4	Valid forms of argument	117
5.5	Invalid arguments	121
5.6	Inconsistency	124
5.7	Composition and division	128
5.8	Summary	131
6	Personal attack in argumentation	134
6.1	The abusive *ad hominem* argument	135
6.2	The circumstantial *ad hominem* argument	141
6.3	The attack on an arguer's impartiality	149
6.4	Nonfallacious *ad hominem* arguments	154
6.5	Replying to a personal attack	159
6.6	Critical questions for an *ad hominem* argument	163
6.7	Important types of error to check	165
6.8	Some cases for further discussion	168
7	Appeals to authority	172
7.1	Reasonable appeals to authority	173
7.2	Three common errors in citing expert opinions	178
7.3	Expert testimony in legal argumentation	181
7.4	How expert is the authority?	184
7.5	Interpreting what the expert said	189
7.6	Argumentation scheme for appeal to expert opinion	192
7.7	Critical questions for the appeal to expert opinion	194
8	Inductive errors, bias, and fallacies	198
8.1	Meaningless and unknowable statistics	200
8.2	Sampling procedures	204

8.3	Insufficient and biased statistics	206
8.4	Questionable questions and definitions	208
8.5	The *post hoc* argument	212
8.6	Six kinds of *post hoc* errors	215
8.7	Bias due to defining variables	222
8.8	*Post hoc* criticisms as raising critical questions in an inquiry	224
8.9	Strengthening causal arguments by answering critical questions	228
8.10	Summary	234

9 Natural language argumentation 239

9.1	Ambiguity and vagueness	240
9.2	Loaded terms and question-begging language	243
9.3	Equivocation	250
9.4	Arguments based on analogy	253
9.5	Argumentative use of analogy	256
9.6	Criticizing arguments from analogy	260
9.7	Slippery slope arguments	263
9.8	Subtle equivocations	269
9.9	Variability of strictness of standards	274
9.10	Conclusions	277

| Bibliography | 282 |
| Index | 287 |

Preface

The purpose of this handbook is to furnish the reader with the basic methods of critical analysis of arguments as they occur in natural language in the real marketplace of persuasion on controversial issues in politics, law, science, and all aspects of daily life. This is very much a practical (applied) subject, because each argument is, to some extent, unique. The technique of applying the general guidelines of criticism for each type of argumentation scheme to each case requires practical skills of good judgment and judicious interpretation in identifying the argument and sorting out the main thread of the argument from the discourse it is contained in. These are pragmatic skills requiring prior identification of the type of dialogue in which an argument occurs.

Logical semantics is an important subject in its own right. It is the construction of consistent and complete theories based on semantical constants and the use of variables. Chapter 5 is about semantics. But the eight other chapters are mainly about the pragmatics of argumentation. For the most part, applying critical rules of good argument to argumentative discourse on controversial issues in natural language is an essentially pragmatic endeavor. It is a job requiring many of the traditional skills associated with the humanities – empathy, a critical perspective, careful attention to language, the ability to deal with vagueness and ambiguity, balanced recognition of the stronger and weaker points of an argument that is less than perfectly good or perfectly bad, a careful look at the evidence behind a claim, the skill of identifying conclusions, sorting out the main line of argument from a mass of verbiage, and the critical acumen needed to question claims based on expert knowledge in specialized claims or arguments. Thus the terms 'informal logic' and 'critical argumentation' are well suited to the subject matter and methods of this handbook.

A basic requirement of critical argumentation is that any argument that a critic attempts to evaluate must be set out and sympathetically appreciated in the context of dialogue in which the argument occurs. This means that we must sometimes contend with lengthy and complex arguments, and we must sometimes probe in depth the unstated parts of argument, the arguer's position and commitments as indicated by the evidence of the text, and the question that the argument was supposed to answer. This requirement means that if a criticism is to be made of an argument, or if the argument is to be called weak, erroneous, or even fallacious, substantial justification for the reasonableness of the criticism must be given in the form of documented evidence from the actual wording and context of the given argument. This dialectical type of approach to the study of arguments means that it is crucial to bring out the question–answer context of an argument in all reasoned criticism and analysis of arguments. Thus every argument is conceived along the lines of a challenge–response model of interactive dialogue, in which two people "reason together." Some of the most important types of contexts of argumentation are profiles of sequences of question–answer dialogue on disputed subjects. Thus generally the theory of informal logic must be based on the concept of question–reply dialogue as a form of interaction between two participants, each representing one side of an argument, on a disputed question.

As Erik Krabbe (1985) has indicated, the concept of critical argument analysis as a dialogue logic deserves to be the cornerstone of the emerging theories of argumentation, now the subject of so much interest. In recent times, the attention to the classical logic of propositions and its extensions has begun to shift, through the need for a practical approach to the study of arguments, toward a pragmatic conception of reasonable dialogue as a normative structure for argument. This shift has been signaled by the appearance of many new practically oriented textbooks but also by scholarly work in this emerging field. Two new important journals have recently come out – *Informal Logic* and *Argumentation*. And the Association for Informal Logic and Critical Thinking, as well as the International Society for the Study of Argumentation, have been founded. As well, in June 1986 the First International Conference on Argumentation was held in Amsterdam. These trends point toward a welcome shift to the practical in logic and a resurgence of interest in the study of argumentation generally.

Whatever happens in the next few years in the theory of argumentation study, it is clear that a new approach to logic and argument has already begun to be taught in logic classes around the world. Although that new logic is, or should be, based on new theoretical foundations including abstract structures of formal dialogues and pragmatic structures of discourse analysis, it is a subject that has moved much closer to many of the traditional aims of the humanities through a more practical approach to the study of particular arguments in natural language.

Acknowledgments

This work was supported by a Killam Research Fellowship, a Fellowship from the Netherlands Institute for Advanced Study in the Humanities and Social Sciences, and a research grant from the Social Sciences and Humanities Research Council of Canada. The techniques used were much refined and improved by discussions with Frans van Eemeren and Rob Grootendorst during workshops and discussions at the University of Amsterdam and also by many discussions with Erik Krabbe during a five-month period of joint research on a related project at NIAS in 1987–8.

Another important stimulus was the International Conference on Argumentation in Amsterdam in June 1986. Among the colleagues whose papers, conversations, or correspondences were particularly helpful in shaping ideas in the present work, I would like to thank Francisca Snoeck Henkemans, Tjark Kruiger, Johan Kaufmann, John Woods, Bob Binkley, Jim Mackenzie, William Mann, Henry W. Johnstone, Jr., Dick Epstein, Max Cresswell, Michael Wreen, Christoph Lumer, Tony Blair, John Hoaglund, Ralph Johnson, Michael Schmidt, Trudy Govier, John Biro, Ed Damer, Maurice Finocchiaro, Alan Brinton, and Michel Meyer. I would like to express my grateful appreciation to Amy Merrett for word processing of the text and figures of the manuscript.

1

Argument as reasoned dialogue

The goal of this book is to help the reader use critical methods to evaluate impartially and reasonably the strengths and weaknesses of arguments. The many examples of arguments studied in this text are familiar, yet controversial specimens from such sources as political debates, legal arguments, international disputes of foreign policy, scientific controversies, consumer decision-making questions, ethical problems, and health issues. Any argument, including contexts of lively debate, conflict of opinion, reasoned persuasion, questioning, criticism, or cross-examination, can be usefully analyzed by the methods that follow.

It is to be emphasized that the methods of this undertaking are essentially practical. They come as much or more under the topic of what is properly called logical pragmatics, as opposed to (semantical) logical theory. Logical theory traditionally has tended to emphasize semantic relationships, that is, relationships between sets of true or false propositions (the subject matter of Chapter 2 in this book). Logical pragmatics has to do with the use of these propositions by an arguer to carry out a goal of dialogue in reasoning with a second participant in the dialogue. One common and important type of goal is to convince or persuade another arguer with whom the first arguer is engaged in reasoned dialogue. In logical theory, an argument is a set of propositions, nothing more or less. And all that matters is the truth or falsehood of these propositions. The wider context of dialogue is not taken into account. In logical pragmatics, an argument is a claim that, according to appropriate procedures of reasonable dialogue, should be relevant to proving or establishing the arguer's conclusion at issue.

Logical theory, then, is centrally concerned with the propositions that make up an argument. Logical pragmatics is concerned with the reasoned use of those propositions in dialogue to carry out a goal, for example, to build or refute a case to support one's side of a contentious issue in a context of dialogue. It is concerned with what is done with those propositions in a context of dialogue, what use is made of them, to convince another arguer. Logical pragmatics is a practical discipline, an applied art.

The distinction between semantics and pragmatics can be picturesquely illustrated by the following anecdote:

Example 1.0

A seaman drafted to our ship just before we sailed from Halifax had never seen his new captain, who at sea often went hatless and wore a nondescript jacket.

The new man had just begun a forenoon watch on the gun deck when the captain came along. The skipper suddenly stooped and picked up a butted cigarette. He thrust the butt at the seaman and demanded: "I want to know who the hell owns this damned thing."

The new hand considered for a moment, then said slowly to the rankless, hatless officer: "I'd say you do, mate. You found it."[1]

In this case, the seaman's answer to the other man's question was perfectly reasonable and appropriate, except that the context of dialogue was wrong. In this instance, the questioner happened to be the captain. And the acceptable procedures of dialogue for responding to questions from the captain can be very different from responses appropriate for replying to a fellow shipmate. From what the seaman took to be the context of dialogue, his answer was semantically appropriate. But the context of dispute was not that of ownership of the cigarette butt as found property. From the pragmatic point of view, therefore, the seaman's response was highly inappropriate, and he misunderstood the purpose of the question entirely. Had he known that his questioner was the captain, he would of course have known at once that the context of dialogue required the question to have a very different meaning. The captain wanted to know who was responsible for dropping a cigarette butt on deck. And the seaman would have known that an affirmative answer in this context of dialogue was an admission of guilt for a culpable offense.

The problem here was to know what the argument was about. The captain thought it was about the issue of keeping the ship clean.

---

1 Jack Wilson, as told to Dave McIntosh in *Legion Magazine*. Reprinted in *Readers Digest*, November 1986, p. 39.

The seaman thought the argument was about ownership of a found object. The misunderstanding posed a pragmatic problem.

A typical problem of logical pragmatics is that in a given argument various important factors of the context of dialogue can be unclear, vague, ambiguous, and generally problematic to pin down. It may not be clear what the real issue is supposed to be. It may not even be clear what the argument is. But before an argument, or what looks like an argument, can be evaluated as strong or weak, good or bad, it may be a nontrivial job to pin down just what the argument is or may be taken to be. Much of the work of logical pragmatics lies in this preliminary phase of clearing up or clarifying what the argument is.

Of course, it is well known that applying any theory to real, complex objects as they occur in ordinary experience and issue is a project that has certain problems unique to this type of practical endeavor. And so it is with practical logic. Each raw, given argument must be approached with care, and the best use made of the evidence that is given, if it is to be reasonably evaluated. From the pragmatic point of view, any particular argument should be seen as being advanced in the context of a particular dialogue setting. Sensitivity to the special features of different contexts of dialogue is a requirement for the reasoned analysis of an argument.

1.1 TYPES OF ARGUMENTATIVE DIALOGUE

Dialogue is a sequence of exchanges of messages or speech acts between two (or more) participants. Typically, however, dialogue is an exchange of questions and replies between two parties. Every dialogue has a goal and requires cooperation between the participants to fulfill the goal. This means that each participant has an obligation to work toward fulfilling his own goal in the dialogue and also an obligation to cooperate with the other participant's fulfillment of his goal. The basic reason that any argument can be criticized as a bad argument always comes down to a failure to meet one of these basic obligations.

One context of dialogue is the *personal quarrel*, characterized by aggressive personal attack, heightened appeal to emotions, and a desire to win the argument at all costs. The quarrel is characterized by bitter recriminations, a loss of balanced perspective, and, afterwards, most often a regret for excessive personal attacks that were not meant or deserved. The quarrel is no friend of logic and frequently represents argument at its worst. The goal of the quarrel is for each arguer to attack or "hit" his opponent at all costs, using any means, whether reasonable, fair, or not. Thus the quarrel is characterized by the fallacious *ad hominem* attack (attack against the person, rather than the argument) and by emotional arguments that would not be judged relevant by more reasonable standards of argument.

The quarrel represents the lowest level of argument. Reasonable standards of good argument should be designed to prevent argument from deteriorating into the personal quarrel. Most of the logical lessons to be drawn from the quarrel turn out to be pathological. The quarrel too often represents the bad argument, the heated argument, the medium of fallacies, vicious attacks, and one-sided criticisms that should be avoided or discouraged by reasonable dialogue. When an argument descends to the level of the quarrel, it is usually in deep trouble.

Another context of dialogue is the *(forensic) debate*. The forensic debate is more regulated than the quarrel. In a debate there are judges or referees who determine, perhaps by voting, which side had the better argument. The debate is regulated by rules of procedure that determine when each arguer may speak, and how long each may speak. In some cases, a debate may be judged by an audience who may take a vote at the conclusion of the debate, and the majority of voters then determines who won the debate.

The forensic debate is more congenial to logical reasoning than the personal quarrel is, because the outcome is decided by a third party who is not subject to the personal attacks that may be contained in the arguments. Also, some debates are controlled by rules that disallow the more severe forms of personal attack and other aggressive or fallacious tactics. But the rules of the forensic debate are often very permissive and may allow all kinds of fallacious arguments. Sometimes very damaging personal allegations are allowed in questions, and the answerer may be hard pressed to respond to extremely aggressive questions while still answering the question. Such fallacious moves may not only be tolerated, but even be praised as good tactics of debating.

Clearly, the debate is a step above the personal quarrel, from the point of view of logic.[2] However, the basic purpose of the forensic debate is to win a verbal victory against your opponent by impressing the audience (or referee) of the debate. This means that fallacious arguments and personal attacks are a good idea if they help you to win the argument. In other words, a successful argument, in the context of a debate, is not necessarily a reasonable argument from the standpoint of logic. It may be good strategy to *appear* to have a reasonable argument, but really having a reasonable argument is not the main thing. The main thing is to win the debate. Consequently, the standards of good forensic debate do not necessarily or reliably represent good standards of reasonable argument.

A third context of argument is that of *persuasion dialogue*,[3] also sometimes called *critical discussion*. In this type of dialogue, there are two participants, each of whom has a thesis (conclusion) to prove. The main method of persuasion dialogue is for each participant to prove his own thesis by the rules of inference from the concessions of the other participant.[4] If you and I are engaged in persuasion dialogue, my goal is to persuade you of my thesis. And hence my obligation should be to prove that thesis from premises that you accept or are committed to. Your obligation is to prove your thesis from premises that I accept or am committed to (Figure 1.0).[5]

The goal of persuasion dialogue (critical discussion) is to persuade the other party of your thesis (conclusion, point of view), and the method is to prove your thesis.[6] However, two kinds of proof may be involved. *Internal proof* by a participant means proof by inferring a proposition from the other participant's concessions in the dialogue. This is the primary method of persuasion dialogue.

Persuasion dialogue can also be facilitated by bringing in external scientific evidence. *External proof* entails the introduction of "new

2 For more on the quarrel and debate as models of argument, see Woods and Walton (1982, ch. 1).
3 See Walton (1984). The notion of reasonable dialogue as a regulated game was first systematically analyzed by Lorenzen (1969) and Hamblin (1970).
4 Proving from the concessions of the other participant is not the only type of reasonable dialogue. However, it is a very important one for the purposes of practical logic. Theoretical models of this type of dialogue in reasoned argument are outlined in Hintikka (1981) and Barth and Krabbe (1982).
5 See Krabbe (1985).
6 The concept of a critical discussion is outlined in van Eemeren and Grootendorst (1984).

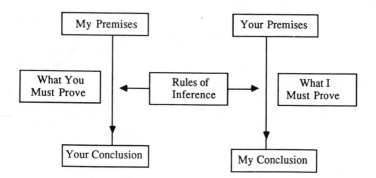

Figure 1.0. Obligations of persuasion dialogue (critical discussion).

facts" into the argument by appealing to scientific evidence or the expert opinion of a third party or group of expert sources.[7] Guidelines for the use of external proof in persuasion dialogue are studied in Chapters 7 and 8. Once a proposition is advanced by one participant on the basis of external proof and accepted by the other participant, it can then be appealed to as a premise suitable for an internal proof.

Although the primary obligation of a participant in persuasion dialogue is to prove his thesis from the other participant's concessions, a secondary obligation to cooperate with the other participant's attempts to prove his thesis also exists. This obligation requires giving helpful and honest replies to the other participant's questions, in order to allow him to extract commitments from the first participant in dialogue that can then be used as premises in his arguments.[8]

Argument in persuasion dialogue is based on the concessions of the other party, and a participant is free to concede any proposition he cares to. But in another type of dialogue, called the *inquiry,* premises can only be propositions that are known to be true, that have been established as reliable knowledge to the satisfaction of all parties to the inquiry.

7 Van Eemeren and Grootendorst (1984, p. 167) refer to an intersubjective testing procedure in dialogue as a method whereby the participants agree on how they will determine what is acceptable as evidence in an argument.
8 This idea is brought out very clearly in the model of dialogue analyzed by Hintikka (1981).

An example of an inquiry would be the Warren Commission Report on the death of John F. Kennedy, which attempted to determine the known facts relevant to the assassination and thereby produce a proof of an established conclusion. By contrast, a persuasion dialogue might typically be on an issue like "Is socialism the best form of government?" in which the goal is not conclusive proof of one side of the issue or the other, but an evaluation of the persuasiveness of the arguments on both sides.[9] Such arguments can reveal important convictions and reasons for personal commitments on an issue, even if the goal is not to establish conclusive proof based on premises known to be true.

The basic goal of the inquiry is to acquire increments of knowledge, and therefore the inquiry is an essentially *cumulative* type of dialogue, meaning that retraction of commitment is not anticipated. The inquiry, too, is based on an initial position, but the position here is a certain degree of lack of knowledge that must be overcome. Thus the inquiry seeks out *proof*, or the establishment of as much certainty as can be obtained by the given evidence. Evidential priority is the key feature of the inquiry, for the inquiry is strongly directed toward deriving conclusions from premises that can be well established on solid evidence. This contrasts with persuasive dialogue, in which the best one can hope for is plausible commitment to an opinion based on reasoned (but not conclusive) evidence.

In the inquiry, the participants are supposed to be neutral investigators of an objective truth, to the extent that this is possible. The inquiry is a cooperative rather than an adversarial context of dialogue.[10] Logical proof is important in the inquiry, but the method may vary with the subject matter or area of the inquiry. Inquiry most often purports to be "scientific" and "factual" in its methods and standards.

In *negotiation dialogue*, the primary goal is self-interest and the method is to bargain. Bargaining makes no pretensions to be an objective inquiry into the truth of a matter. Indeed, negotiation, in

9 This function of dialogue that reveals concealed commitments is brought out in the analysis of Walton (1984, ch. 5).

10 Reasonable evaluation of any argument always involves the given data of a text of discourse to be analyzed. Common but unstated presumptions of the arguer and the evaluator also play a role in the evaluation. A theory of discourse analysis that shows the relation of the dialogue to the text is given in van Eemeren and Grootendorst (1984).

contrast to persuasive dialogue, need not involve commitment to the truth of propositions, or convictions that ideals are based on strong arguments. In negotiation, opinions about what is true, or convictions about what is believable, are not centrally at stake and may even be contravened by a good negotiator. The concessions in bargaining are not commitments in the same sense as they are in persuasive dialogue, but trade-offs that can be sacrificed for gains elsewhere. The position now becomes a bargaining position. Logical proof is not important in bargaining dialogue, for this type of dialogue is completely adversarial. This type of dialogue is frankly based on personal gain and makes no pretense of being neutral or objective, or of being an inquiry into truth. Coalitions may be made with partners, but the objective is always self-interest in "making a good deal."

The negotiation type of dialogue is called the *interest-based conflict* by Moore (1986, p. 74), who describes it as "competitive cooperation" where "the disputants are collaborating to compete for the same set of goods or benefits" in conditions of "perceived or actual scarcity." In this situation, gains for one participant may mean losses for another. The dialogue is a kind of trading of concessions to the satisfaction of both participants.

Some cases of argumentative discourse combine two or more of these types of dialogue. For example, a divorce dispute may begin as a competition to determine which party is to obtain custody of the children. However, if the dialogue turns to a consideration of the issue of which party is best suited to look after the children, the dialogue may cease to be an interest-based bargaining dialogue and become a persuasion dialogue. This shift in the context of dialogue could be highly constructive and beneficial. It may betoken a shift from the individual interests of the husband and wife to a wider consideration of what is best for everyone, including the children. Often a shift from the negotiation model to the persuasion model is a good step.

Although the persuasion, inquiry, and bargaining types of dialogues are the most basic for the purpose of studying the fundamental kinds of reasoned criticism in argumentation, there are many other types of dialogue. One is the *information-seeking* type of dialogue, in which one party has the goal of finding information that the other party is believed to possess. Another is the *action-seeking* type of dialogue recognized by Mann (1988), in which the goal of one party is to bring about a specific course of action by the other party. Yet another type is the *educational dialogue,* in which one party (the teacher) has the goal of imparting knowledge to the other party (the student). Each of these models of dialogue has a different initial situation and different rules of procedure for arriving at the goal from the initial situation. These eight types of dialogue are summarized in Table 1.0.

From the point of view of critical argumentation taken in this book, persuasion dialogue (critical discussion) is the single most significant type of dialogue. It represents an ideal, or normative, model of good dialogue because it has normative rules that, taken together, set a standard of how good persuasion dialogue should take place. However, it is important to be able to recognize other types of dialogue indicated above, because significant errors and misunderstandings may occur when there is a dialogue shift (dialectical shift) from one type of dialogue to another. If such a shift goes unnoticed, it can lead to misinterpretations, errors, and fallacies of argumentation.

1.2 COMPONENTS OF ARGUMENTATIVE DIALOGUE

Any sequence of argumentative dialogue can be broken down into four stages.[11] In the *opening stage,* the type of dialogue should be specified. At this stage, the participants should agree to engage in a specific type of dialogue, or at least indicate their willingness to take part in a certain type of dialogue. All good dialogue has procedural rules, and the rules of the dialogue should be as clear as possible to the participants as part of the opening stage of the dialogue. In some cases, these rules are explicitly stated or codified, for example, in a criminal trial. In conversation, these rules are usually matters of custom and politeness that set normal expectations of dialogue conduct (rules of Gricean[12] implicature). Nevertheless,

11 The concept of the four stages of dialogue is from van Eemeren and Grootendorst (1984).
12 Grice (1975).

Table 1.0. *Types of Dialogue*

Dialogue	Initial situation	Method	Goal
Quarrel	Emotional disquiet	Personal attack	"Hit" out at other
Debate	Forensic contest	Verbal victory	Impress audience
Persuasion (critical discussion)	Difference of opinion	Internal and external proof	Persuade other
Inquiry	Lack of proof	Knowledge-based argumentation	Establish proof
Negotiation	Difference of interests	Bargaining	Personal gain
Information-seeking	Lacking information	Questioning	Find information
Action-seeking	Need for action	Issue imperatives	Produce action
Educational	Ignorance	Teaching	Imparting knowledge

the rules can be explicitly stated, and agreed to by the participants, where it is useful and necessary, at the opening stage.

There are four kinds of dialogue rules. The *locution rules* state the kinds of speech acts or locutions that are allowed. For example, typically in persuasion dialogue, questions and assertions are permissible locutions. The *dialogue rules* specify turn taking and other guidelines for when and who is allowed or required to advance locutions. The *commitment rules* specify how each type of locution leads to commitments on the part of a participant. For example, an assertion of a proposition by a participant normally implies that this participant now has this proposition in his store of commitments. Finally, the *strategic (win–loss) rules* determine what sequence of locutions constitutes fulfillment of the goal of the dialogue.

All dialogue arises from a problem, difference of opinion, or question to be resolved that has two sides. The two sides constitute the *issue* of the dialogue. The *confrontation stage* is the stage where the issue of the dialogue must be announced, agreed upon, or clarified, so that the goal of the dialogue is clear.

The *argumentation stage* is the stage where the obligation of each party in contributing to or fulfilling the goal of the dialogue must be carried out by the appropriate methods. A participant has an obligation to make a serious effort to fulfill his own goal in the dialogue. He also has an obligation to allow the other party to fulfill his own obligation. These obligations imply certain dialogue rules. For example, they require that participants take turns in an orderly fashion to give the other party a reasonable opportunity to reply to a question or make a point.

The *closing stage* of a dialogue is the point where the goal of the dialogue has been fulfilled or where the participants agree that the dialogue can end. There are proper ways of closing a dialogue, and this has implications for the rules of conducting a good dialogue. A participant should not try to opt out illicitly just because things do not seem to be going his way. And, in general, participants must continue to carry on with a dialogue, following the rules, until the dialogue is properly closed.

These general requirements of the four stages of dialogue imply other rules that are applicable to specific problems encountered in the remaining chapters of this book. *Rules of relevance* require that a participant not wander too far off the point (the goal of dialogue), or else he can be challenged. *Rules of cooperativeness* require that a respondent answer questions cooperatively and accept commitments if they reflect his position accurately. *Rules of informativeness* require that a participant tailor his arguments to what his respondent knows or does not know. A participant should provide enough information to convince his respondent but not provide more information than is required or useful for that purpose.

Section 1.3 illustrates how these rules specifically apply to the type of dialogue called persuasion dialogue. Then Section 1.4 itemizes some negative rules or prohibitions that indicate some important types of faults or failures of persuasion dialogue. Section 1.5 gives an introductory survey of some of the most important of these failures, ones that are especially significant to watch out for in argumentation because they can be used as systematic, clever tactics of deception to cheat and trick you.

1.3 PERSUASION DIALOGUE
(CRITICAL DISCUSSION)

A persuasion dialogue can be of two basic types. In an *asymmetrical persuasion dialogue,* the type of obligation of one participant is different from that of the other. In the *symmetrical persuasion dialogue,* both participants have the same types of obligation. Example 1.1 is an instance of an asymmetrical persuasion dialogue:

Example 1.1

Karl is a committed believer in God who is trying to convince Erik that God exists. Erik is not convinced by Karl's arguments and raises many doubts. Erik is not an atheist, but calls himself an agnostic.

In this case, the obligations of Karl and Erik are of different types. Karl has taken upon himself to try to prove to Erik the positive thesis that God exists. Erik is a doubter (agnostic). He is not trying to prove the negative thesis that God does not exist. His obligation is only to raise questions that reflect his doubts about the acceptability of Karl's arguments.

By contrast, example 1.2 is a case of a symmetrical persuasion dialogue:

Example 1.2

Mary is a committed atheist who is arguing that God does not exist. Barbara is a believer in God, and she is trying to convince Mary that God does exist. Each person is trying to refute the thesis of the other.

In example 1.2, both Mary and Barbara have the same type of obligation, namely to prove her thesis. We could say that both have a positive burden of proof, whereas in example 1.1, only Karl had a positive burden of proving his thesis. Erik had only the negative burden of throwing doubts on Karl's proof.[13]

In a persuasion dialogue, the basic goal is to prove a thesis in order to resolve an issue. Hence the primary obligation in a persuasion dialogue is a *burden of proof,* meaning that the participant with an obligation to prove has the "burden" (or obligation) to carry out this task. In the symmetrical persuasion dialogue, both parties have a burden of proof.[14]

In a case like example 1.2, we also say that the obligations of the two participants are *strongly opposed,* meaning that one is obliged

---

13 See Walton (1988) for a conceptual outline of burden of proof.
14 How the concept of burden of proof is important to the theory of argument is well established in Rescher (1976).

to prove a thesis that is the opposite (negation) of the thesis the other is obliged to prove. However, in a case like example 1.1, we say that the obligations of the two participants are *weakly opposed*, meaning that one is obliged to resist, question, or not accept the attempts to prove the thesis of the other, but he is not obliged to prove the opposite of the other's thesis. In such a case, we say that the one participant has a burden of proof but the other does not. The other player has a lighter burden – it is only a burden of raising questions.

The following example is a case of a symmetrical persuasion dialogue that shows strong opposition of the participants:

Example 1.3

Bob: Tipping is good because it rewards excellence of service. If excellence is rewarded, it leads to better effort, and to better work. Therefore, tipping should be maintained as a practice.

Helen: If a person is doing a good job, he should get regular pay that reflects the worth of the work. A worker should not have to depend on the whims of his clients to get an appropriate salary. Therefore, tipping should not be maintained as a practice.

Bob's conclusion (prefaced by the word 'therefore') is the opposite of Helen's conclusion (prefaced by the same conclusion indicator word). This textual evidence indicates that the persuasion dialogue in example 1.3 is symmetrical.

One important component of persuasion dialogue is the arguer's position.[15] Let us imagine that the dialogue in example 1.3 is carried further, and that through the course of the arguments it becomes evident that each of the two participants has certain distinctive commitments.

Bob is committed to tipping as an acceptable practice because it is a free-market economy exchange. Helen is against tipping because leaving such decisions to the vicissitudes of the free-market economy is not necessarily fair or equitable, in her view. She favors government regulation to assure every working person a steady income based on the comparable worth of his job. Thus each has revealed

15 Walton (1985b).

13

a position defined by those commitments that he has incurred in his questions and replies.

Once we have followed the whole course of the argument, then, we get a picture of which propositions each arguer is committed to. According to the conception of argument modeled in Hamblin (1970), the most fundamental aspect of argument as persuasion dialogue is that each participant in the dialogue must have a set of commitments called a commitment-store. Physically speaking, a commitment-set can be visualized as a set of statements written out in a list on a blackboard. Or it could be visualized as a set of propositions recorded in the memory of a computer. The point is, in any event, that a commitment-store must be a definite set of propositions. It can be an empty set, unless the thesis of each participant must be counted as an initial, given commitment of that participant.

What Hamblin calls a commitment-set of a player we here call, collectively, the position of that participant in persuasion dialogue. Hamblin thinks of the commitment-set as being visible to all the participants. However, it does not necessarily need to be visible to all or any players at all or any times. All that is required is that it be a definite set of propositions.

The idea is that as the game of dialogue proceeds, propositions are added to or deleted from the commitment-sets of each of the players, according to the rules of the dialogue.

The goal of a persuasion dialogue sets the burden of proof. But it is important to recognize that there can be differing standards of strictness for meeting this requirement.

The most strict standard is set for the *deductively valid argument,* which requires that it be logically impossible for the conclusion to be false while the premises are true. Suppose that Helen were to argue as follows, in the dialogue on tipping:

Example 1.4

Every person who does a good job should get regular pay that reflects the value of his work.

Alice is a person who does a good job.

Therefore, Alice should get regular pay that reflects the value of her work.

This argument is deductively valid, meaning that if the premises are true, then the conclusion *must* be true. There is no weaseling out of the conclusion if you accept the premises. In other words, it is logically impossible for the conclusion to be false and the premises true. But suppose Helen had argued as follows:

Example 1.5

Most people who do a good job should get regular pay that reflects the value of their work.

Alice is a person who does a good job.

Therefore, Alice should get regular pay that reflects the value of her work.

In this case, the argument is not deductively valid. It might be that the premises are true. Yet even so, the conclusion could possibly be false. But the argument is *inductively strong* in the sense that if the premises are true, then it is probable that the conclusion is true. Clearly, inductive strength is a less strict requirement for an argument to be successful than is deductive validity.

In a third type of argument, called *plausible argument,* the requirement for success is even less strict than that of the inductively strong argument:

Example 1.6

It is widely accepted that people who do a good job should get regular pay that reflects the value of their work.

Alice is a person who does a good job.

Therefore, Alice should get regular pay that reflects the value of her work.

This type of argument is intrinsically weaker. In a plausible argument, if the premises are plausibly true, then the conclusion is as plausibly true as the least plausible premise. [16] This does not mean that it is impossible or even improbable for the conclusion to be false, given that the premises are true. It only means that the conclusion is at least as plausible as the premises. This means that if an arguer is committed to the premises, as part of his position, then he should be no less strongly committed to the conclusion. In other words, if he rejects the conclusion while he is committed to acceptance of the premises, then the burden of proof is placed upon

16 Rescher (1976, p. 15).

15

him, by argument 1.6 in this case, to show why he does not accept the conclusion as plausible.

The function of plausible argument is to shift the burden of proof. Many of the types of argument criticisms we will subsequently study are good criticisms to the extent that they successfully shift the burden of proof onto an opponent's side of the argument in persuasion dialogue.

1.4 NEGATIVE RULES OF PERSUASION DIALOGUE

The positive rules of persuasion dialogue provide a *normative model* of good persuasion dialogue, a kind of ideal dialogue against which particular cases of argumentation can be judged. These positive rules also imply *negative rules* that state prohibitions. Violating these prohibitions can result in errors, faults, and shortcomings, of various kinds, in argumentation.

Certain characteristic types of faults or errors in argumentation have traditionally been classified under the heading of *informal fallacies,* systematically deceptive strategies of argumentation based on an underlying, systematic error of reasoned dialogue. Unfortunately, however, the traditional category of informal fallacy has been stretched too widely in traditional accounts, including not only arguments that are weak or incomplete, but even ones that are basically correct and reasonable as mechanisms of argument in persuasion dialogue.

Some violations of negative rules of dialogue are better classified as *blunders* rather than fallacies because they are not systematic or clever deceptions that attempt to prove a point, but are simply errors or lapses that damage or weaken the case of their proponent rather than defeat his opponent in the dialogue. Other arguments are incomplete because they do not respond adequately to the critical questions of the participant they were designed to persuade. Such arguments are not "fallacies." They are better classified as weak or incomplete instances of argumentation.

To claim that an argument contains a fallacy is a strong form of criticism implying that the argument contains a serious logical error, and even more strongly implying that the argument is based on an underlying flaw of misconception of reasoning, and can therefore be refuted. However, we will see that many valuable criticisms of

16

argument do not completely refute the argument to make an important point of criticism. And, indeed, to interpret them so strongly would imply an unwarranted dogmatism (itself an error).

A criticism always invites a reply, but a good, well-argued criticism in dialogue also shifts the burden of proof onto the proponent of the argument criticized. However, in order for it to be a reasonable criticism, which does call for a reply, the critic has an obligation to give reasons for his criticism. We will see in coming chapters, how each type of criticism must be documented and backed up. We will see that many important kinds of faults and errors in argumentation consist of failures to answer critical questions.

Those kinds of arguments, now called informal fallacies in logic texts, are historically descended from what Aristotle called *sophistici elenchi,* meaning sophistical refutations.[17] A sophistical refutation of an argument is a refutation that plausibly appears to be a successful refutation, but is not. The term 'sophistical' refers to a certain trickery or illusion that conceals a logical incorrectness. Use of both the term *sophistici elenchi* and its descendant 'fallacies' has engendered the unfortunate misconception that all kinds of arguments coming under the traditional categories of 'fallacies' are inherently bad or worthless, that all such arguments should, by the standards of logic, be thoroughly refuted in every instance.

Now is a good time in the history of logic to reconsider the area of informal fallacies and obtain a broader perspective of the whole context of dialogue in argument criticisms in order to classify specific, important faults and failures of persuasive argumentation.

Some important negative rules of persuasion dialogue are summarized below. In Section 1.5, some major informal fallacies (to be studied in subsequent chapters) will be introduced, and it will be indicated how some of these famous fallacies are associated with violations of specific negative rules.

NEGATIVE RULES OF PERSUASION DIALOGUE

Opening stage
1. Unlicensed shifts from one type of dialogue to another are not allowed.

17 See Hamblin (1970).

Confrontation stage

1. Unlicensed attempts to change the agenda are not allowed.
2. Refusal to agree to a specific agenda of dialogue prohibits continuing to the argumentation stage.

Argumentation stage

1. Not making a serious effort to fulfill an obligation is bad strategy. Notable here are failures to meet a burden of proof or to defend a commitment when challenged.
2. Trying to shift your burden of proof to the other party, or otherwise alter the burden of proof illicitly, is not allowed.
3. Purporting to carry out an internal proof by using premises that have not been conceded by the other party is not allowed.
4. Appealing to external sources of proof without backing up your argument properly can be subject to objection.
5. Failures of relevance can include providing the wrong thesis, wandering away from the point to be proved, or answering the wrong question in a dialogue.
6. Failing to ask questions that are appropriate for a given stage of dialogue should be prohibited, along with asking questions that are inappropriate.
7. Failing to reply appropriately to questions should not be allowed, including replies that are unduly evasive.
8. Failing to define, clarify, or justify the meaning or definition of a significant term used in an argument, in accord with standards of precision appropriate to the discussion, is a violation, if the use of this term is challenged by another participant.

Closing stage

1. A participant must not try to force the premature closure of a dialogue until it is properly closed, either by mutual agreement or by fulfillment of the goal of the dialogue.

These rules are not complete, and it requires judgment to apply them to specific contexts of argumentative discourse. In general, however, for every fallacy or blunder in a context of dialogue, there is some rule for the conduct of the discussion that has been broken or tampered with.

How strictly the rules are formulated or enforced depends on the specific context of dialogue. For example, rules of relevance may be much more strictly formulated and enforced in a court of law than in a philosophical discussion.

These rules, however, give the reader the flavor of a persuasion dialogue as a coherent and regulated form of activity. The basic purpose of a persuasion dialogue (critical discussion) is to allow each participant a chance to express his opinions on an issue and to prove them if he can. Such a dialogue should be a free exchange of points of view where probing questions are freely asked and relevant answers are freely given. Each side should have a fair opportunity to express his point of view and to challenge the other's point of view.

However, there are other kinds of dialogue, like negotiation, for example, where rules may be different in certain respects from those of the persuasion dialogue. Hence dialectical shifts can influence our judgment on whether a certain speech act is "fallacious."

1.5 SOME MAJOR INFORMAL FALLACIES

Several important kinds of errors or deceptive tactics of argumentation are especially significant to learn about and have traditionally been labeled as (major) *informal fallacies*. Before proceeding to study these fallacies in depth in each chapter, the reader should be briefly introduced to them.

The *fallacy of many questions (complex questions)* occurs when a question is posed in an overly aggressive manner, presupposing commitment to prior answers to questions not yet asked. The strategy of deception is to try to trap or confuse the answerer into incurring damaging commitments that can be used to defeat him.

The classic case is the question 'Have you stopped beating your spouse?' No matter which way the respondent answers, he (or she) is in trouble; for any direct answer already presumes that the answerer has acknowledged having a spouse whom he (or she) has beaten in the past. These overly aggressive questioning tactics violate rules 2 and 6 of the argumentation stage, as will be shown in Chapter 2.

The *fallacy of ignoratio elenchi,* also often called the *fallacy of irrelevant conclusion* or the *fallacy of ignoring the issue,* occurs when an argument is directed toward proving the wrong, or an irrelevant, conclusion. Such an argument may be valid, but the problem is that it has strayed from the point (failure of relevance – see rule 5 above).

For example, an attorney prosecuting a defendant for murder in a criminal trial may argue successfully that murder is a horrible crime. However, this line of argument may be an emotionally

19

compelling, but misleading distraction if the conclusion the attorney is supposed to be proving is that this particular defendant is guilty of the crime of murder. The fallacy of irrelevance in argumentation most often is a failure of a participant in persuasion dialogue to fulfill his primary obligation to prove his thesis, which is supposed to be at issue in the dialogue. When an arguer strays too far away from his obligation to stick to the issue of contention, he can (and in many instances should) be challenged on grounds of irrelevance.

Several of the fallacies have to do with appeals to emotions like pity, fear, and enthusiasm. Emotions can be distracting in argumentation, and hence these emotional fallacies are often categorized as fallacies of relevance. But emotions can also be used to try to force premature closure of an argument, violating the negative rule for the closing stage.

The fallacy of the *argumentum ad baculum* (appeal to force) is said to be committed by an appeal to force or the threat of force (intimidation) to gain acceptance of a conclusion without giving proper or adequate argument for it. The *argumentum ad misericordiam* is the appeal to pity, and the *argumentum ad populum* is the appeal to the emotions, enthusiasms, or popular feelings of a group audience. Both of these uses of emotional appeals in argument are said to be fallacies when used to gain acceptance for a conclusion without fulfilling the obligation of supporting the conclusion by providing strong and relevant evidence to meet a burden of proof. The emotional appeal is used to disguise the lack of solid evidence for a contention when a fallacy of one of these types is perpetrated.

However, the use of emotion in argument is not intrinsically wrong or fallacious in itself. Only the misuse of an emotional appeal should be criticized as fallacious. Many examples of emotional appeals in argumentation are examined in Chapter 4. The task of argument analysis is to judge when a given emotional appeal can rightly be criticized as an irrelevant or fallacious deception or distraction in the argument.

Personal attack in argumentation is always dangerous and often leads to heightened emotions and bitter quarrels instead of reasoned discussion of an issue. The fallacy of the *argumentum ad hominem* is said to be committed when one person criticizes an argument by attacking the arguer personally instead of considering his argument on its real merits. In some cases, questions of personal conduct and character are relevant to consideration of an argument. But the *ad hominem* fallacy arises when they are not. The following two examples of uses of the *argumentum ad hominem* are quoted by Christopher Cerf and Victor Navasky in *The Experts Speak:*

Example 1.7

"The so-called theories of Einstein are merely the ravings of a mind polluted with liberal, democratic nonsense which is utterly unacceptable to German men of science."[18]

Example 1.8

"The theory of a relativistic universe is the hostile work of the agents of fascism. It is the revolting propaganda of a moribund, counter-revolutionary ideology."[19]

What is relevant in judging the scientific validity of the theory of relativity is scientific evidence. The personal, moral, or political beliefs of the discoverers or exponents of the theory are not relevant in the context of a serious, scientific investigation or corroboration of the theory. Hence the use of personal attack in examples 1.7 and 1.8 is a fallacious type of *argumentum ad hominem.*

Often the *ad hominem* fallacy arises from an illicit shift from one type of dialogue to another. In examples 1.7 and 1.8, the shift is from a scientific inquiry to a persuasion dialogue concerning political beliefs and personal convictions.

Another type of fallacy, the *argumentum ad verecundiam,* or 'appeal to modesty', is the misuse of expert opinion or authority-based sources to try to suppress someone's opinion in argument by suggesting that they dare not oppose the word of an authority on an issue. Appeal to expert opinion is, in itself, a legitimate form of argumentation, but one that can be employed wrongly, leading to violations of argumentation rule 4.

Some fallacies have to do with induction and statistical reasoning. A case in point is the infamous *post hoc, ergo propter hoc* fallacy of

---

18 Dr. Walter Gross, the Third Reich's official exponent of "Nordic Science," quoted in the *American Mercury,* March 1940, p. 339, as cited in Christopher Cerf and Victor Navasky, *The Experts Speak* (New York, Pantheon, 1984, p. 300).
19 *Astronomical Journal of the Soviet Union,* quoted in the *American Mercury,* March 1940, p. 339, cited in ibid.

wrongly basing a causal conclusion on a weak statistical correlation between two events. For example, although there may be a genuine statistical correlation between the stork population and the (human) birth rate in Northern Europe, it could be an error to conclude that there is a causal connection between these two things. Citing of statistical sources of evidence can result in violations of argumentation rule 4, studied in Chapter 8.

Other fallacies have to do with the use of natural language in argumentation. These problems arise because of the vagueness and ambiguity of terms and phrases in natural language. Vagueness and ambiguity are not inherently bad wherever they occur in argumentation. But problems and confusions can arise because of disagreements and misunderstandings about the definitions of controversial words or phrases in an argument. Chapter 9 outlines several important types of fallacies that relate to the meanings of terms in natural language. These fallacies relate to rule 8 of the argumentation stage.

Among the remaining fallacies to be pointed out, six are noteworthy here as common errors in argumentation that will be subject to analysis in subsequent chapters:

1. The fallacy of the *argumentum ad ignorantiam* (argument from ignorance) could be illustrated by the argument that ghosts must exist because nobody has ever been able to prove that ghosts do not exist. This type of argument illustrates the danger of arguing from ignorance and shows that failure to disprove a proposition does not necessarily prove it. This fallacy is discussed in Section 2.5.
2. The fallacy of equivocation arises from confusion between two different meanings of a term in the same argument when there is a contextual shift. Consider the argument 'All elephants are animals, and Henri is an elephant, and Henri is a small elephant; therefore Henri is a small animal'. The problem here is that the meaning of the relative term 'small' shifts when applied to elephants (relatively large animals), as opposed to when it is applied to animals generally. This fallacy is discussed in Section 9.3.
3. The straw man fallacy occurs when an arguer's position is misrepresented by being misquoted, exaggerated, or otherwise distorted.
4. The fallacy of arguing in a circle (also called *petitio principii,* or begging the question) occurs when the conclusion to be proved by an arguer is already presupposed by his premises. For example, suppose that Bob, an atheist, asks Leo to prove that God is benevolent, and Leo argues, 'God has all the virtues, and benevolence is a virtue; therefore, God is benevolent'. Bob could object, in this case, that Leo is assuming the very conclusion he is supposed to prove. For Bob doubts whether God

has *any* of the virtues (including benevolence), or even whether God exists at all. Hence Leo's argument begs the question it is supposed to prove. This argument is discussed in Section 2.7.

5. The slippery slope fallacy occurs when a proposal is criticized, without sufficient evidence, on the grounds that it will lead, by an inevitable sequence of closely linked consequences, to an end result that is catastrophic. For example, a proposal to permit legalized abortion in some cases might be criticized by arguing that such a step would lead to loss of respect for human life, which would eventually lead to concentration camps for the elimination of people who are not useful to the economy. This type of argument, studied in Section 9.7, proceeds by presuming that there is an inevitable sequence of steps leading down a slippery slope, once you take that first step of accepting a proposal at issue.

6. The fallacy of composition argues unreasonably from attributes of some parts of a whole or members of a collection, to attributes of the whole or collection itself. For example, it might be an error to conclude that a certain hockey team will do well and win a series because each of the players is individually excellent. The players may be good, but if they cannot cooperate, the team may do poorly. The fallacy of division is the opposite kind of questionable argumentation. For example, to argue that a certain university is noted for excellent scholarship, and conclude that, therefore, Professor Dullard, who is on the faculty at that university, must be noted for his excellent scholarship, would be an instance of this fallacy. Composition and division are treated in Section 5.7.

This list of fallacies is by no means complete, but it gives the reader an introduction to the classic types of errors of reasoning that are the main concern in informal logic.

1.6 THE CRITICAL PERSPECTIVE

Essentially, reasonable dialogue should be open and encourage the asking of probing questions on all relevant aspects of a controversial issue. The adversarial cut and thrust of pointed criticisms and forceful rebuttals is not, in itself, bad or fallacious. In fact, this adversarial interplay, which pits one argument against another is, within limits, an essential aspect of revealing and enlightening argumentation. The rules of reasonable dialogue should not be so tight that they exclude free argumentation.

Reasonable argument characteristically does have an adversarial aspect because an arguer is trying to persuade an audience or another arguer. When this adversarial aspect of the argument becomes too aggressive or personal, an argument tends to become less reasonable and more bellicose. Yet the adversarial nature of argument is not, in itself, bad or contrary to reason; for, on a controversial issue, the strength of an argument should be judged on how well it has fared in free discussion against countervailing arguments. In scientific inquiries, the test of an argument is whether it can be falsified by contrary empirical evidence. In disputation on controversial issues, where reasoned conviction is the best outcome one can hope for, the test of an argument is whether it can be refuted by contrary arguments in reasonable dialogue. Thus the adversarial aspect of reasonable dialogue is, or at least can be, an important part of what makes the dialogue reasonable.

The problem with the debate and the quarrel as models of argument is that personal victory at any cost becomes the goal, even if impartial standards of logical reasoning may have to be waived or contravened. Yet dialogue can be reasonable only to the extent that the goal of building a stronger case than the opposition is carried out within a structure that is binding on both parties. Otherwise, the argument has a strong tendency to diverge from the path of dialogue when the sequence moves toward revealing the deeper positions of the participants on the issue to be discussed. A one-sided diatribe is worthless and unrevealing.

Hence the importance of impartial criticism. An important skill is to be able to recognize those types of critical points where dialogue becomes less than reasonable or is diverted away from a better line of argument. In fact, being able to recognize these critical points in an argument, and deal with them by asking the right critical questions, are the key skills of informal logic as a discipline.

The informal fallacies listed in Section 1.5 represent the most important types of deceptive and powerful attack strategies in argumentative dialogue that can be used effectively to press forward against an opponent and prevail in the dialogue, even when the argument used for this purpose is weak or faulty. They are like the tricks and tactics used in wrestling to trip a stronger opponent and cause him to fall, or even to lose the match. But the types of tactics associated with the traditional informal fallacies are not always used illicitly (violations of rules of fair dialogue). They can, in some cases, be used fairly as well, to support legitimate objectives of reasoned dialogue. This lesson will emerge in subsequent chapters for each of these fallacies.

Moreover, in other cases, argument moves that have the same

scheme as one of those identified with a major fallacy turn out to be arguments that are not 'fallacious', but only weak, or lacking essential support. These arguments should be criticized, but they need not always be rejected as fallacious. Often, the proponent of the argument can respond to critical questioning by filling in the gaps in this argument. In this case, both participants in the argument can benefit by reasoning together.

But the fallacies are important types of argument strategies to be familiar with because they represent powerful methods of attack in argumentation that can be used for deceptive as well as legitimate purposes. In many cases, however, there is much to be said about arguments that are neither perfectly bad (fallacious) nor perfectly good.

In arguments on controversial subjects, the job of the reasonable critic is not necessarily to show that an argument he criticizes is fallacious, logically inconsistent, or based on worthless evidence that can be rejected completely. Most often, such strong refutation is simply not appropriate. More often, the job of the critic is to show that an argument is open to reasonable doubt or lacks needed support and is therefore open to questioning. This weaker form of criticism is very often enough to reserve or withdraw the commitment of the audience to whom the argument is directed. By showing gaps in an argument that can be questioned, the critic can show that the argument is open to reasonable criticism. That, in itself, may be a very valuable job, and the critic may have no more to do to have achieved a worthwhile objective. By shifting the burden of proof, a criticism may be enough to make an audience withdraw its commitment to an argument. In arguments on controversial subjects, this form of criticism occurs often enough to reasonably persuade an audience to change its point of view on an issue.

When we criticize an argument, we are often involved in its taking one side against the other. Hence the ever-present danger in argument on controversial issues that really matter to us is the loss of a proper critical perspective. This does not mean that one side of an argument is always as good as the other. It does mean that the reasonable critic must make enough of an effort to probe both sides of the argument in order to evaluate criticisms and replies in a sensitive and intelligent way. The fault of blind dogmatism, of only seeing one side of an argument as a position worth investi-

25

gation, is among the most severe impediments to reasonable dialogue. By learning the argumentation schemes and critical questions that come under the headings of the different fallacies and errors studied in subsequent chapters, the reader can learn how to criticize an opposed point of view, even while appreciating its merits. Through the application of these guidelines, arguments can be evaluated on their real merits or faults, and not just because we agree or disagree with their conclusions, or simply because they appear to be congenial with our own personal position on an issue.

2

Questions and answers in dialogue

Normally in reasonable dialogue one is obliged to try to give a direct answer to a question, if one knows the answer, and if the question is appropriate. If one does not know the direct answer, or for some reason cannot give it, then one is obliged to be as informative as possible. The reason behind this normal expectation that a direct answer will be given if available is that our usual and reasonable presumption in many contexts is that a question is a sincere request for information where the questioner expects, or at least hopes, that the answerer may have this information and be able to give it. Therefore, if the answerer does not give a direct answer, his reply may be perceived as unhelpful or evasive.

Because of these normal expectations in reasonable dialogue, the general purpose of a question is a request for information, which here refers to a set of propositions. So posing a question is a request to the answerer to supply a set of propositions.

There are several types of questions, each of which has a different format for requesting propositions.[1] A *whether-question* poses a set of alternatives and requests the answerer to select one. For example, the whether-question 'Was she wearing the grey slacks or the red dress or blue jeans?' requests the answerer to pick one proposition from the disjunction. An example of a direct answer would be 'She was wearing the red dress.' A *yes–no-question* allows only two alternatives, the affirmative or the negative answer, and is therefore a simple, two-option type of whether-question. A *why-question* asks the respondent to furnish a set of propositions that provide premises in a reasonable argument, which will enable him to infer the proposition queried.[2]

---

1 Harrah (1984, p. 716) lists eleven types of questions recognized by most theorists in the logic of questions.
2 See Aqvist (1965) and Belnap and Steel (1976) for formalized treatments of these types of questions.

A *direct answer* to a question supplies exactly the information requested. An *indirect answer* supplies only part of that information. A *reply* to a question is a response that may not be a direct or indirect answer.[3] Sometimes, a reasonable reply is to question the question itself. But as we noted above, the normal expectation is for a helpful answer.

However, this normal and reasonable expectation is not true of all questions. Some questions are not sincere requests for information. They are aggressively posed with harmful presuppositions that may discredit an answerer if he attempts to respond directly. For this reason, some questions are deliberately mischievous, and a failure to give a direct answer should not necessarily be open to criticism as evasive or irrelevant. To give a direct answer in such a case would be to fall into the questioner's trap. Therefore, some questions ought to be answered reasonably by the posing of another question.

It requires good judgment to know whether a question is reasonable in a specific context or whether a failure to give a direct answer should justifiably be criticized as an evasion or irrelevance. In this chapter, we will study several factors that should be considered in reasonably evaluating a sequence of questions and answers in dialogue.

2.1 PRESUPPOSITIONS OF QUESTIONS

A *presupposition* of a question is a proposition that is presumed to be acceptable to the respondent when the question is asked, so that the respondent becomes committed to the proposition when he gives any direct answer. In general, a question may have several presuppositions. A presupposition is itself a proposition, and this means that the asking of a question contains within it positive information in the form of a proposition. Consequently, asking questions may be a form of asserting propositions in dialogue. Therefore, asking questions can be a form of arguing and can thereby influence the subsequent course of an argument.

What is most important about presuppositions of questions, for

---

3 Harrah (1984, p. 715) notes that most theorists acknowledge the distinction between a reply and an answer.

our purposes, is that the answerer who responds directly to a question automatically becomes committed to all its presuppositions.[4] Therefore, the asking of questions can strongly affect the answerer's position, his set of commitments in a dialogue. The question itself can be argumentative.

Certain types of questions have traditionally been thought fallacious because they are packed with presuppositions that trap the answerer no matter how he responds. The most famous example is the classic spouse-beating question:

Example 2.0

Have you stopped beating your spouse?

The main objectionable feature of this trick question is that whichever way you answer, 'yes' or 'no', you become committed to having beaten your spouse at some time or other. Of course, the ordinary non-spouse-beater therefore answers the question only by being trapped into conceding a proposition that he is not really committed to. The question is a coercive trick to trap him or her into admitting something prejudicial. Hence example 2.0 is considered the classical case of the *fallacy of many questions,* sometimes also called the *fallacy of complex question.*

Questions similar to 2.0 are not hard to find. They all have the same objectionable feature:

Example 2.1

Have you always been a liar, or are you just starting now?

Example 2.2

Did you make profitable investments from the money you obtained through your unethical use of government funds?

In each case, the question contains a damaging presupposition. Whichever way the answerer replies, he concedes something incriminating. Whichever way he answers question 2.1, he commits himself to being a liar. Once having conceded this proposition, he

---

4 We will define 'presupposition' toward the end of this chapter.

is not likely to have much credibility in any further exchanges in the dialogue.

Or consider question 2.2. A subsequent context of dialogue might run as follows:

Example 2.2a

White: Did you make profitable investments from the money you obtained through your unethical use of government funds?

Black: No.

White: So you admit you made unethical use of government funds. I demand your resignation at once. Don't you know that unethical use of government funds is adequate reason for your dismissal?

Here the questioner concludes by following up his attack with another loaded question.

The basic problem, which in these cases arises from the yes–no format, is that the question does not allow a third option, or escape clause. Of course, the best way to reply to such a question may be to object to the question itself – to question the question – if that type of reply is allowed. One might reject the presupposition, or at least answer the question by questioning the presupposition. But why the first two questions above are thought to be especially fallacious is that their yes–no format calls for a simple yes or no answer. In a yes–no-question, there are only two direct answers: 'yes' or 'no'. Therefore, it is fair to say that if you fail to give a direct answer to 2.0, 2.1, or 2.2, it may not necessarily mean that you are evading the question unfairly or failing to give a relevant answer. Sometimes, the most reasonable response may not be to give a direct answer, because the question itself is not fairly framed to allow the answerer to assert his own position.

One might think that all questions that have presuppositions are fallacious. But many questions that have significant presuppositions can be reasonable and legitimate:

Example 2.3

Is the man wearing the red hat in the last row a member of the psychology class?

This question has many presuppositions. It presupposes that there is a man in the last row, that he is wearing something, that he is

30

wearing a hat, that the hat is red, and so forth. But this question may be no problem to answer, and there may be no question of its being fallacious. It is also a yes–no-question with multiple presuppositions, but in most contexts there would be no good reason to regard it as a trap question or as a fallacy of many questions.

The difference between the harmless question 2.3 and the previous three fallacious questions lies in the nature of their presuppositions. In the last case, they seem harmless or innocent. But in the case of the first three questions, most participants in argument would not want to go on record as having these presuppositions as commitments. We could call these presuppositions *unwelcome commitments* and questions that contain them *loaded questions*. Whether a question is loaded depends on the position of the answerer. If the answerer clearly would not want to be committed to a presupposition of a particular question, then the question may be described as loaded with respect to his position.

For the average answerer, in most contexts of reasonable dialogue, 2.0, 2.1, and 2.2 could fairly be described as loaded questions. Consider yourself. Would you want to or should you have to admit to spouse-beating activities? If not, then 2.0 would be a loaded question if addressed to you. Scarcely anyone would want to admit, in answer to 2.1, that he is or has been a liar. That admission would tend to discredit him in any further argument and undermine the possibility of reasonable dialogue. Finally, in answer to 2.2, anyone innocent of the allegation of unethical use of government funds would not likely want to commit himself to conceding having used such funds to make a profit. It is possible that he might wish to so commit himself, but the context suggests the profile of an average (innocent) answerer for whom such a commitment would not be welcome or appropriate. Hence 2.0, 2.1, and 2.2 would normally be regarded (with reason) as loaded questions.

2.2 COMPLEX QUESTIONS

We have seen that not all questions that have presuppositions are fallacious. Indeed, every question has some presupposition. Even a question like 'Is 2 a number?' has the presuppositions that there are numbers and that 2 is the sort of thing that can be a number. Even the most innocent question has presuppositions, but they may not be a problem or an indication that the question that contains them is in any way suspicious or fallacious.

Another lesson to observe is that there are complex questions that may not be fallacious or problematic:

Example 2.4

Is Gerta wearing a dress or slacks today?

Example 2.5

Did you pick up your shirt and put it in the laundry?

Example 2.6

Will you open the door if Kevin forgets his key?

Each of these questions is semantically complex. Example 2.4 is a disjunctive question. Example 2.5 is a conjunctive question. And example 2.6 is a conditional question.[5] However, in most contexts, none of these examples should reasonably be called a loaded or a fallacious question. In other words, there is nothing inherently wrong with a question that has complex (multiple) presuppositions.

To realize how enormously complex a question can be in an argument, it may be well to reflect on the following sample of dialogue from the Oral Question Period of the Canadian House of Commons Debates.[6] Mr. Chrétien's question is unusually complex for the Question Period, a type of dialogue in which questions are supposed to be short, and not "arguments":

Example 2.7

Hon. Jean Chrétien (Saint-Maurice): Mr. Speaker, my question is directed to the Right Hon. Prime Minister.

According to a story published in the press today, the Minister of Regional Industrial Expansion owns a company; he has a 50 per cent interest in a company that manufactures shoes, and since he is responsible for the Anti-dumping Tribunal and for setting quotas on footwear, and the president of the company said that the company was having problems because of imports, did the Right Hon. Prime Minister take the necessary precautions when appointing the Minister

5 A careful study of problems of multiple questions is given in Hintikka (1976, ch. 6).
6 *Canada: House of Commons Debates (Hansard)*, Vol. 126, November 16, 1984, p. 297.

32

of Industry, Trade and Commerce or the Minister of Regional Industrial Expansion by asking him certain pertinent questions, and did the Minister inform the Prime Minister of the potential conflict of interest that existed at the time, and if the Prime Minister was aware of the situation, how could the Member in question become the Minister of a department where he must make daily decisions that may affect the financial position of a company in which he has a 50 per cent interest?

Right Hon. Brian Mulroney (Prime Minister): I am surprised and surprised [*sic*] at the Hon. Member for asking such a question. However, I can assure him that all legal requirements were met before anyone was appointed, including the Minister in question. The Hon. Member is no doubt aware that from time to time, Canadian citizens, including Members of this House who have worked in the business world, have been faced with certain problems, and I must say I have received every assurance that all legal requirements had been met, and I am confident that the Hon. Member in question has the integrity and competence required to perform his duties as Minister.

Mr. Chrétien's question has so many presuppositions that it could be very difficult for any respondent to keep track of them. And his question is also quite aggressive. It poses an allegation of conflict of interest against a minister of the government. For all that, the question does not seem to be a basically unreasonable one for Mr. Chrétien to ask. And although Mr. Mulroney rejects the implication of the question that there may be some possibility of conflict of interest in this case, he does not appear to reject the question as inherently objectionable or inappropriate on grounds of its structure.

The rules of order for debate in the Canadian House of Commons require that a question not be a "speech" and not be of an unreasonable length. Perhaps then the speaker of the house should have intervened and barred Mr. Chrétien's long question.

However, in response to such an objection, Mr. Chrétien could possibly argue that all the matters in the question are connected together in a complex issue and that therefore, in this case, the length of the question is not unreasonable. It is known and accepted that not every restriction on questions asked in rules of debate can be applied in every case.

Thus even though Mr. Chrétien's question illustrates how remarkably complex a question can be, and that such complexity could be awkward and confusing for a respondent, it does not follow that a question should always be judged fallacious or erroneous on grounds of its complexity alone. It is the loaded nature of Mr. Chrétien's question that, combined with its multiplicity, makes it difficult for a respondent to sort out.

Thus, although there do seem to be presuppositions of the question that are not acceptable to the respondent, it would not seem right to conclude that the question is fallacious because of its complexity. Admittedly, the question is remarkably complex, but that in itself does not seem deeply objectionable, at least for the purpose of concluding that it is a fallacious question.

Although it may be true that there could be practical limits on the length of a question, it seems that a fair degree of complexity of presuppositions is tolerable. If this is so, it suggests that complexity of questions as such – within reasonable limits – is not inherently fallacious.

Moreover, to ban all complex questions from reasonable dialogue as a general policy would seem to be an extremely dubious proposal. To forbid altogether the asking of conjunctive, disjunctive, or conditional questions would be to impoverish an arguer's ability to ask many kinds of important and legitimate questions. Such an impoverishment would surely have to be balanced by a strong argument for believing that semantically complex questions are inherently misleading or fallacious. But this approach seems misdirected, for semantically complex questions seem to be fallacious only when several other factors combine to make them problematic, as in the spouse-beating question.

Complex questions can pose a problem, however, if the answerer wants to respond to each part of the question separately. A good strategy is to ask for the questions to be divided, for it may be that the answer to the one question need not foreclose an answer to the other:

Example 2.8

Do you support fair hiring practices and job quotas for racial minorities?

This question is addressed in the yes–no form, and consequently poses a problem for the answerer who may want to reply 'yes' to one part and 'no' to the other. The best strategy is to ask that the two questions be posed separately, or at any rate to answer them singly.

Another problem, however, is that dividing the question is not

34

always allowed in every context. It is a common practice in legislatures and congresses to tack a controversial bill onto a larger piece of proposed legislation that is favored by the opposition. Then the opposition can veto the controversial bill they may not like only at the cost of also rejecting the more significant piece of legislation they would like to see passed. This is essentially the same sort of problem as that posed by side effects in medical treatment. In this case it is Nature who lets you have the beneficial effects of treatment only at the cost of the negative side effects.

Fortunately, in many contexts of dialogue, it is not only permissible but quite reasonable to ask to have a question divided into smaller questions. The important thing is to be aware of this possibility and to demand it when the question reasonably requires dividing.

2.3 HAVE YOU STOPPED BEATING YOUR SPOUSE?

We have now seen that some questions are complex and some are loaded. Moreover, asking a complex question need not necessarily be fallacious. And asking a loaded question need not be, in itself, fallacious either, even though it is a good idea to be very careful in attempting to answer a loaded question. Sometimes it is better not to answer it, but to question its presupposition. Now we will see more precisely why 2.1, the spouse-beating question, can be problematic. The problem arises because it is a question that is both complex and loaded at the same time, and this combination is used in a coercive fashion against a respondent.

The spouse-beating question could be broken down into two parts by the respondent who is innocent of spouse beating, and then each part could be answered separately:

(1) No, I have never beaten my spouse in the past.
(2) No, I am not beating my spouse now.

This response by dividing would defeat the questioner's fallacious attack. And we should observe that the spouse-beating question is loaded, presuming of course that the answerer is not committed to the practice of spouse beating and does not want to acknowledge it personally.

But there is also a third aspect to the fallaciousness of the spouse-beating question. Since it is posed in the format of a yes–no-question, it is disguised as a completely harmless question. Normally, a yes–no-question is *safe,* meaning that its presupposition is trivially true. For example, the yes–no-question 'Is snow white?' has as its presupposition the trivial truth 'Snow is white or snow is not white'. Nobody could reasonably deny that presupposition, and therefore the question is harmless. It has no significant presupposition that could lead an answerer to consider it reasonably to be a loaded question. Normally, yes–no-questions are perfectly safe. However, the spouse-beating question only appears to be safe, insofar as it is posed in the format of a yes–no-question. But, in fact, either way you answer, 'yes' or 'no', you are automatically committed to an extremely prejudicial proposition (Figure 2.0). The problematic aspect is that the spouse-beating question is devised to force the answerer to accept the presupposition no matter which way the question is answered. And because the question is of the yes–no format, the answerer is directed exclusively to the two alternatives 'yes' or 'no'.

To sum up, then, the spouse-beating question is a problematic instance of a complex question because it combines three elements in one question: (1) It is a complex question, (2) it is a loaded question, and (3) it is a yes–no-question. The answerer is impaled on the horns of an unfair choice. If he has stopped, that means that he used to do it. But if he has not stopped, that means he is still doing it. Either way, he loses.[7]

The spouse-beating question is not necessarily problematic or objectionable in every context of dialogue, however. Suppose a defendant in a trial had previously admitted his or her spouse-beating activities. In that case, if the prosecuting attorney were to ask, 'Have you stopped beating your spouse?' the question could be perfectly appropriate and reasonable, and the respondent might have no objection to answering it.

Hence it is misleading to call the spouse-beating question a fallacy, or to call it the *fallacy of many questions;* for this type of question is not always erroneous, yet certainly can pose an important problem in dialogue.

The underlying problem with the spouse-beating question, when

---

7 A more detailed analysis of the various faults of the spouse-beating question may be found in Walton (1981).

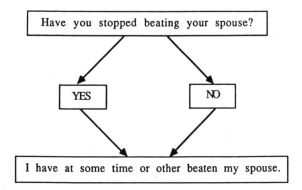

Figure 2.0. The spouse-beating question.

it is a problem, is that it does not fit into a reasonable order of questioning and answering in the context of dialogue. To see why, you must compare the context of the asking of the question to a profile of reasonable question–answer sequence for that context. Then it can be seen whether the question asked violates that reasonable order of dialogue.

The spouse-beating question, to be a reasonable question, presupposes that the respondent has already given or is committed to affirmative answers to two prior questions asked in the following order: (1) Do you have a spouse? (2) Have you ever beaten your spouse? If these two questions have not been asked and answered first, then the spouse-beating question violates the order of reasonable dialogue.

But it is not only the prior context of dialogue that is involved. The spouse-beating question also invites a subsequent attack by the questioner, once any direct answer to the question is given. Figure 2.1 shows a profile of dialogue against which the reasonableness of the spouse-beating question can be evaluated.

This profile clearly shows the strategy of the asker of the spouse-beating question. By packing the two prior questions into the spouse-beating question, the strategy is to build in affirmative answers to these questions without giving the respondent an opportunity to deny positive concessions.

A similar strategy is left open for the sequence of dialogue after the posing of the spouse-beating question. The questioner can follow up with even more incriminating questions like the bottom one in

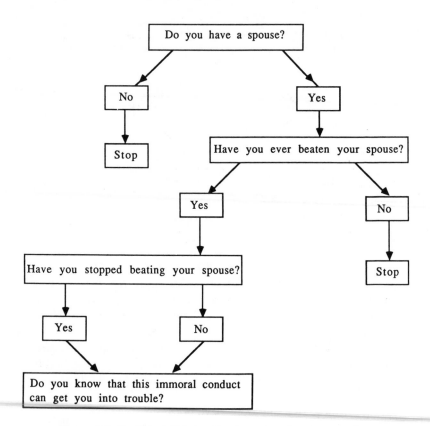

Figure 2.1. Profile of dialogue for the spouse-beating question.

Figure 2.1. Or, to cite another possible line of dialogue, he could follow up with a circumstantial personal attack by posing the following type of question: 'How can you reconcile your immoral conduct with your own personal standards of morality?' If the respondent falls into his trap, the questioner can follow up by repeating the same strategy over and over until the respondent's side of the argument is completely destroyed.

We can see then how the spouse-beating question is coercive. By not giving the respondent a fair chance to answer one question at a time, the questioner can push ahead, leaping over unanswered questions to defeat the respondent's case.

In short, the real complexity of the spouse-beating question is not just the semantic complexity of its presupposition. A pragmatic complexity pertaining to the order of a sequence of questions and answers in the context of dialogue is also involved.

The purpose of questioning in dialogue may be to extract commitments from a respondent that can later be used as concessions to persuade him. But a question should allow a respondent reasonable choice in expressing his honest opinion. The spouse-beating question attempts to force a respondent into a damaging concession and move the dialogue prematurely to closure. For this reason, it violates the requirements of good dialogue.[8]

Judging when an answer is reasonable, therefore, depends on the prior judgment of whether the question itself is reasonable. In the following example, the reply is condemned as evasive. But is this criticism justified?

Example 2.9

Q: How long are you prepared to condemn this company to continued failure by your stubborn failure to change your disastrous policies?

A: I do not accept for one moment your assumptions that my policies are disastrous or that my behavior has been stubborn.

Q: You haven't answered the question! That's typical of your evasive tactics.

The questioner's strategy here is to follow up a loaded, aggressive question by criticizing the respondent for evasiveness (irrelevance of reply). However, the respondent has replied correctly by questioning the presuppositions of the question.

Of course, normally, a respondent has an obligation to give a direct answer to a question, if that is possible and can be done without unreasonable difficulties. But in example 2.9, a direct answer would trap the respondent unfairly. Hence the "evasive" reply is reasonable.

2.4 REASONABLE DIALOGUE

When evaluating realistic samples of dialogue, one naturally tends to concentrate on criticizing the answers when looking for fallacies.

8 It may be interesting to keep the lessons of how to manage aggressive questions in mind when coming to the sportsman's rejoinder case in Section 6.2, which has the form of a question.

But even questions, though they often seem harmless enough, may commit fallacies or be open to criticism. Therefore, in evaluating dialogues, one should begin by examining the questions that were asked. First, one should ask what type of question it is. A yes–no-question is supposed to be safe, but as we have seen, many are loaded and complex in their presuppositions. Such questions are not safe.

Another type of question is the *whether-question* which poses a number of alternatives. Example 2.4 is a whether-question, or as we called it, a disjunctive question, because it poses two alternatives: Did Gerta wear a dress or slacks? One fallacy to be on guard against with whether-questions is one in which the range of reasonable alternatives is not fairly represented. This type of question is said to commit the *black and white fallacy,* in which the question poses an exclusive disjunction that is overly restrictive in representing the various reasonable possibilities that should be allowed in a direct answer. It is classically illustrated by the following question:

Example 2.10

Is a zebra black or white?

The problem with this question is that one should be allowed to answer truly that a zebra is both black and white. Yet, insofar as the question is posed or taken as an exclusive disjunction, it does not allow for the answer 'Both'. In other words, the presupposition of the question is that a zebra is either black or white but not both. Presuming that this presupposition is false, the question may rightly be regarded as objectionable because it does not permit an answerer to respond correctly or at least directly in a way he feels is reasonable.

Examples of this type of question are not hard to find:

Example 2.11

Are you a pacifist or a warmonger?

Example 2.12

[Book title] *The Abolitionists: Reformers or Fanatics?*

These disjunctive questions can be objected to when they are too restrictive and therefore do not permit a respondent reasonable

40

latitude in giving a direct answer. Once again, the best answer may be to rebut the presupposition by posing another question as your reply. Though normally it may be reasonable to require a direct answer, with questions like these such a requirement is overly restrictive.

But, in principle, there is nothing wrong with asking a disjunctive (either–or) type of complex question. So what exactly is wrong with either–or-questions when they are objectionable? The basic problem with objectionable disjunctive questions is the same one characteristic of the spouse-beating question. Such a question, when it is objectionable, violates the reasonable order of question asking and answering in dialogue. Consider the following question:

Example 2.13

Should we allow the government to take total control of medicine or must we allow physicians to be completely free of government regulation? EITHER/OR

The problem here is the presumption by the questioner that a reasonable respondent must accept one or the other of the posed alternatives. However, this presumption is highly implausible and would need to be established by a prior question, or sequence of questions and answers, before the question in example 2.13 could be established as reasonable.

In some cases of very aggressive use of disjunctive questions, the strategy is even more transparent.

Example 2.14

Is snow black, or are you one of those crazy people who think it's white?

Here, the questioner has tried to preempt the expected answer by portraying it within the question as an option that has already been ruled out as "crazy." The reasonable order of questioning would be to first inquire whether snow is black, and if the answer is 'Snow is white' then to criticize that answer.

Another type of question is the *why-question,* which may demand an explanation for something, or a reason for accepting some proposition. One important kind of why-question in reasonable dialogue

41

is the request for grounds for accepting a proposition that is subject to question or controversy:

Example 2.15

Why is pacifism morally wrong?

Quite often the context of this sort of why-question is a dispute in which the answerer has adopted or is committed to a certain position. The question can be a challenge for the answerer to provide premises that imply the proposition queried, where that proposition is a significant part of the answerer's position. In example 2.15, the context of the disputation could be that the answerer is defending a position that is opposed to pacificism, and the questioner is challenging him to supply grounds for his acceptance of the proposition that pacificism is morally wrong.

The problem with why-questions is to know how direct an answer must be to qualify as relevant. A direct answer to a why-question like 2.15 may be defined as a set of propositions that implies the presupposition of the question by valid arguments according to the rules of valid argument appropriate to the dialogue. However, sometimes an answerer in a controversial dispute needs room to argue. He may not be able to prove the queried proposition directly, but may need to obtain the concession of other propositions from the questioner as additional premises in order to work toward proving his conclusion. But how much room to argue should a questioner reasonably allow to the answerer of a why-question? Once again, judgment is needed to evaluate whether an answer is relevant, if it seems to be heading in the right direction. One must not be too quick to condemn an answer as irrelevant if it does not immediately give the required proof in one step.

To sum up, then, there are several kinds of questions, including yes–no-questions, whether-questions, and why-questions. The first step in the analysis of any dialogue is to identify the type of question involved. The second step is to identify and state the presuppositions of the question. The third step is to ask whether the presupposition of the question is complex. The fourth step is to evaluate whether the presupposition of the question is loaded. If the answer to both of the last two questions is 'yes', then the fifth step is to ask whether the question is an instance of the fallacy of many questions. Having evaluated the question, it is now appropriate to turn to an evaluation of the answer.

The sixth step in the analysis of dialogue is to evaluate whether the answer is a direct answer. If not, then the seventh step is to ask whether the answer is reasonably relevant. However, this seventh step must always be judged relative to the appropriateness and reasonableness of the question. If the question is fallacious or overly aggressive, then the fact that a direct answer was not given may be no good grounds for criticizing the answer as irrelevant or evasive. Whether the answer is to be judged as relevant must be evaluated on the basis of the fairness of the question in the context of the objectives and rules of reasonable procedure of the dialogue.

In the analysis of any argument, questions or answers to questions (assertions) should never be evaluated in isolation from each other. In other words, every argument is really a dialogue and should be evaluated as such. Every argument has two sides.

2.5 ARGUMENTS FROM IGNORANCE

It is the obligation of a respondent in dialogue to give an informative and relevant direct answer to a reasonable question if he can. But if an answerer truly does not know whether the proposition queried is true or false, he should have the option of jreplying 'I don't know' or 'No commitment one way or the other'. In other words, the ignorant answerer should be able to admit his ignorance; for as Socrates reminded us, the beginning of wisdom is to admit your ignorance if, in fact, you really do not know the answer to a question. Hence any reasonable game of dialogue that does not allow an answerer the 'No commitment' option, in replying to questions, would not be tolerant of wisdom.

The idea that an answerer should concede that he does not know the answer, if he really does not, is reflected in a traditional fallacy called the *ad ignorantiam* fallacy:

Example 2.16

Elliot: How do you know that ghosts don't exist?
Zelda: Well, nobody has ever proved that ghosts do exist, have they?

Here, Elliot asks Zelda to give justification for her commitment to the proposition that ghosts do not exist. Zelda answers by shifting

43

the burden of proof back onto Elliot to prove that ghosts do exist. However, this reply is said to commit the fallacy of arguing from ignorance *(argumentum ad ignorantiam):* Just because a proposition has never been proved true does not mean that it is false.[9]

For example, Fermat's last theorem in mathematics has never been proved true. (Fermat wrote the theorem in his notes one night, but then omitted to put in the proof.) However, it is a separate question whether it can be shown that Fermat's last theorem is unprovable. It might be unprovable, but then again it might just be very difficult to prove, or not very obvious. Thus the question of whether a proposition has been proved is separate from the question of whether it *can* be proved. It might be the case that it has not been proved because it cannot be proved. But then again it might not. That may remain to be shown. You cannot argue from ignorance.

The *ad ignorantiam* argument can be defined as an argument of one of the following two forms:

(I1) Proposition A is not known to be true; therefore, A is false.

(I2) Proposition A is not known to be false; therefore, A is true.

As an instance of (I2), we might cite the following example:

Example 2.17

Some philosophers have tried to disprove the existence of God, but they have always failed.

Therefore, we can conclude with certainty that God exists.

The problem with example 2.17 is similar to the previous examples of arguing from ignorance. It might be that nobody has ever disproved the existence of God, but it does not follow that it is impossible to prove it. That is a separate question that remains to be shown. Hence both (I1) and (I2) are rightly regarded as forms of argument that are not generally valid. To presume that they must be valid in every instance could therefore be an erroneous argument from ignorance.

The next point we must recognize, however, is that arguments

---

9 See Woods and Walton (1978).

having the form of *ad ignorantiam* are not always unreasonable. Consider the following case:

Example 2.18

Mr. X has never been found guilty of breaches of security, or of any connections with the KGB, even though the Security Service has checked his record.

Therefore, Mr. X is not a KGB spy.

This argument has the form of an *ad ignorantiam* inference. But is it a fallacy? Well, if the Security Service has checked Mr. X out very thoroughly, and there is absolutely no grounds for doubting Mr. X, and he has an excellent record of service and loyalty, then there is at least some basis for the plausible presumption that Mr. X is not a KGB spy. Of course, we probably never know such a thing for sure. So to assert conclusively that, "beyond doubt," Mr. X cannot be a KGB spy could easily be an overly strong conclusion to draw and could therefore be an unjustified argument from ignorance. Nonetheless, if the search was very thorough, it could be reasonable to draw the plausible conclusion that Mr. X is not a spy, until we find evidence to suggest otherwise. Hence the *ad ignorantiam* argument is not always fallacious, and it is misleading to call it a fallacy.

What this case suggests is that the *ad ignorantiam* argument is a plausible, if weak, form of reasoning, depending on the context. Here the context is how thorough the Security Service search was.

If the conclusion of the argument is phrased in strong terms – for example, using the term 'definitely' or 'conclusively' – then that is a sign that the argument could be fallacious. If the conclusion is phrased as a plausible presumption, however, and the context of dialogue supports it, then these are signs that the argument from ignorance may be reasonable (nonfallacious).

For example, we saw that if a mathematical proposition has never been proven, then it would be a fallacious *ad ignorantiam* argument to conclude that it cannot be proven, for proving that it has not been proven yet and proving that it cannot be proven are two different things. However, if many clever mathematicians have tried to prove the propositions by all of the most powerful methods and never succeeded, then that may be plausible grounds for concluding that the best way to proceed is to presume that the proposition is false. The suggested course of action would then be to concentrate on trying to prove that it is false, rather than to carry on trying to prove that it is true.

In short, then, as a weak (plausible) form of argument, an *ad ignorantiam* argument can sometimes be nonfallacious. It depends on the context. But the argument from ignorance can become weak or erroneous when it is taken as a stronger form of argument than the evidence warrants.

In effect, this means that arguing from ignorance may not always be fallacious in reasonable dialogue. Although, as we saw before, (I1) and (I2) are not generally valid forms of argument, in some cases arguments having those forms can be reasonable. Consider (I2) for example. Sometimes, even though a proposition is not known to be false, it may be reasonable to presume that it is true:

Example 2.19

I do not know that this rifle is unloaded. Therefore, it is reasonable to presume that it is loaded.

In this case, the argument from ignorance could be reasonable. Even though I may have no good evidence to indicate whether, in fact, the rifle is loaded, it may be reasonable to conclude that I should commit myself to the proposition that it is loaded, at least until I find out one way or the other. That is, sometimes it is reasonable to presume commitment, even though you do not know the answer to a question.

The reason for the reasonableness of example 2.19 has to do with the normal context of the argument. In normal circumstances, safety when handling dangerous weapons is a high priority. Therefore, the burden of proof is always to assume that the weapon may be loaded. In this context, if you have not checked the firing chamber, it is best to assume that there may be a round in it. We make this presumption because the possibility of accidentally discharging a loaded rifle is very dangerous. Hence our standards of safety must be very high.

However, notice that in another context, if I do not know whether the rifle is loaded, it may be better to operate on the presumption that it is not loaded. If a soldier is under attack by a dangerous, hostile enemy, then he may be well advised to make sure that his rifle is loaded. If he cannot be sure, it may be best for him to presume

46

that it is not loaded and check to make sure. In this context, example 2.19 would not be a plausible argument.

The burden of proof varies from one context of dialogue to another. So it is the context of dialogue that can make an *ad ignorantiam* argument plausible or implausible in a given case. But it is important to recognize that when an argument from ignorance is reasonable, it is a weak form of argument that depends on the context of dialogue. To treat it as a strong or deductively valid form of argument that leads to a conclusion beyond doubt is a presumption that can easily lead to error and confusion.

With arguments from ignorance, care is needed to take each case individually, because sometimes these arguments are not unreasonable. Certainly (I1) and (I2) could be fallacious in many cases if they are taken to be deductively valid arguments of the following form, taking (I2) as the example: Proposition A is not known to be false; therefore, it must follow that A is known to be true. But if (I2) is taken in a weaker form, it can be reasonable in some cases: Proposition A is not known to be false; therefore, it is reasonable to commit myself to the presumption that A is true.

Whether an *ad ignorantiam* argument is reasonable often depends on the burden of proof as indicated by the context of dialogue. For example, the criminal law presumes that a person is not guilty if he has not been shown to be guilty. This is an *ad ignorantiam* form of argument, but it can be reasonable in the context of the rules of argument in criminal law. In criminal law, there is a burden of proof on the prosecution to prove that the defendant is guilty *beyond reasonable doubt*. This is a very high burden of proof because it is extremely difficult to prove anything beyond all reasonable doubt. The reason the standard is set so high is to safeguard against the possibility that an innocent person could be ruled guilty in a criminal trial. This outcome is thought to be more significant than the possibility that some guilty persons could go free. Hence the burden of proof is asymmetrical.

Similarly with example 2.19, in which there is a serious potential danger to be guarded against, the burden of proof may be adjusted to minimize the possibility of realizing that outcome. It is in such cases that the *ad ignorantiam* form of argument can be plausible.

In reasonable dialogue there is very often a reasonable presumption of burden of proof. If I am heavily committed to one side of

47

a dispute and my position indicates a strong presumption that I accept a certain proposition, then it is fair for my questioner to presuppose that proposition in his questions, to ask me directly about my acceptance of that proposition, and to expect a direct answer. My position obliges me to defend and acknowledge propositions that I have accepted and should reasonably accept as part of that position.

This means that in reasonable dialogue, if I am asked 'Why A?' where A is in fact a thesis I have advocated, I may not be allowed to shift the burden of proof back to my questioner with the *ad ignorantiam* reply 'Why not-A?' In other words, if asked 'Why do you accept A?' I should not always be allowed to bounce the ball back to your court and reply 'Why don't you accept A?' Before making that move in reply, I may be reasonably required first to give some reason or argument for positively accepting A. Otherwise, the argument could go back and forth forever with no real dialogue or constructive interaction taking place at all. For example, the believer and the atheist could ask back and forth forever, 'Why don't you believe in the existence of God?' *versus* 'Why do you believe in the existence of God?' This procedure would not advance the argument at all. To get anywhere, each side must assume a reasonable burden of proof. In dialogue, this means that each side must sincerely try to justify his adopted position, and to incur commitment when queried, if his position truly requires that commitment. Just as questions can be loaded, in some cases *ad ignorantiam* arguments can also be "stacked" against the respondent:

Example 2.20

No person who is reasonably intelligent and well-informed could doubt that there has never been any serious and well-established evidence for extrasensory perception. Therefore extrasensory perception does not exist.

The premise of example 2.20 is loaded with the presupposition that anyone who could accept the evidence for ESP would be an un-intelligent or ill-informed person; for anyone who might not be committed to the premise would, according to the premise, have to fall into one or more of these categories. This creates pressure against anyone who might question the premise, for by conceding that he falls into one of these categories, he might weaken his own credibility to continue on with the argument.

The best way for the respondent to argument 2.20 to proceed is to ask what putative evidence has been alleged for ESP and why has it been shown to be so dubious. And of course it should also be pointed out that arriving too hastily at the conclusion to reject ESP on the basis of ignorance could be a dogmatic and premature dismissal of an argument.

In short, one must always try to avoid the error of making overly firm conclusions too readily on the basis of ignorance. That is called dogmatic reasoning, and it is the worst mistake in reasonable dialogue. One must always be aware that there could be reasonable arguments on the other side of an issue as well as on one's own side. On the other hand, in moral and political controversies, for example, one may often have to make commitments even without knowing for sure that one is completely justified in accepting a proposition. Consequently, it is often reasonable to make commitments based on what seems plausible according to the best arguments you have, as you see the issue. Without a willingness to incur commitments, even with due caution, no argument on a controversial issue would ever get anywhere. Sometimes you must try your best to address a question honestly and sincerely, even if you do not know the answer, if the question is reasonable and relevant to an issue on which you have taken a stand in dialogue.

2.6 REPLYING TO A QUESTION WITH A QUESTION

If a questioner asks a loaded question, the burden of proof ought to be on him to prove the presuppositions of the question. However, argument is often like a game of tennis in the respect that failure to return the ball strongly enough at the next move may result in a loss of the exchange, or even a loss of the game; for when a question is posed aggressively, it often does shift the burden of proof onto the respondent to justify his position. If he fails to do this strongly enough, the accusations in the question may appear to be conceded and confirmed.

What the respondent ought to do in such a case is to require that the questioner give evidence for the assumptions made in the question or, if he cannot, to retract them. This approach makes it clear that the burden of proof should be on the questioner to support his allegations.

Richard Whately (1846, p. 114) warned that if the victim of an unsupported accusation takes upon himself the burden of trying to prove his innocence, instead of defying the questioner to prove his charge, he may appear to concede his own guilt: It is a case of "Qui s'excuse, s'accuse." Whately (1846, p. 113) compared it to the case of a body of troops, strong enough to hold a fort, who sally forth into the open field and are defeated. In other words, if you have the presumption on your side, to concentrate on trying to defend your own case could be a serious error, for you might be overlooking one of your strongest arguments – the burden of proof. In short, sometimes the policy of questioning the question is both reasonable and strategically sound in dialogue.

Generally speaking, the strategy of aggressive questioning is to pack so much weighted information into the presupposition of a loaded question that the answerer would be severely implicated and condemned by any attempt to give a straight answer. But if he fails to give a straight answer, 'yes' or 'no', then the questioner can accuse him of being evasive and failing to answer the question. No matter which way the answerer proceeds, he could be in trouble. If he answers the question directly, he becomes committed to some proposition that can then be used against him. If he attempts to divide up the question and separately address its presuppositions, he may appear to be failing to answer the question honestly. Such a loaded question is trickily aggressive – its purpose is to deflect the burden of proof onto the answerer and, if possible, aggressively attack the answerer's position by the mere act of asking a "harmless" question.

Generally, the best strategy for the answerer of such a question is to try to deflect the burden of argument back onto the questioner while trying not to appear too evasive. But then, of course, the best strategy for the questioner is to accuse the answerer of being irrelevant, or of failing to answer the question. In either case, whether a question or reply is to be judged as reasonable may depend very much on a prior evaluation of the burden of proof.

Although in many cases it is sensible to reply to a question by questioning the question itself, such a strategy can become an abuse of reasonable dialogue in some cases, if carried too far; for, in general, there is an obligation to answer a question, if possible. However, there may be many good reasons for not answering a question, including the following. The question may be unduly aggressive or argumentative. The question may lack clarity and be misleading or ambiguous. The question may repeat a previous question. The respondent may not know the answer or, for various legitimate reasons, may not be able to give it, even if he knows it. If the question is addressed to the respondent as an expert, it may be outside his field of expertise. Thus if a respondent gives any one of these or other good reasons for not answering a question, his obligation to answer it can be removed, or excused, by the questioner.

The burden on a respondent, then, is either to answer a question or give some justifiable reason for not answering it. It follows that not every reply to a question with another question is a reasonable or nonobjectionable reply.

In some cases using a question to reply to a question can be an evasive attempt to shift the burden of proof back onto the questioner. The context of the following dialogue arose through the practice of using for-profit hospitals to treat teenagers with drug or alcohol dependence problems. It was alleged that some of these teenagers were not being properly supervised, and a controversy arose about whether any proper treatment was being given in these institutions:

Example 2.21

Parent: Why weren't you looking after my child properly?

Hospital director: How can we look after thirty-six when you can't take care of one?

In this case, the hospital director was evading answering the question by shifting the burden of proof back onto the parent with another question. The strategy in this case was to avoid answering the question while at the same time appearing to give a reasonable reply. But is the reply reasonable?

The question appears to be a reasonable one to ask in the given context of dialogue. However, as a means of diverting the questioner and audience from the real issue, the reply is an effective tactic because of its emotional impact on the parent; for the parent is probably deeply disturbed about the problems he or she has had with the teenager and may feel partly responsible or guilty. Hence it would be difficult for the parent not to be distracted by this clever reply.

51

However, in this case, the use of the question to reply to the question is an objectionable tactic used to try to shift the burden of proof and avoid the obligation to answer the question.

In the next chapter, the topic of the relevance of answers to questions will be taken up. Because there is generally an obligation to answer a question, a reply that is irrelevant or evasive can, in many cases, be criticized as an objectionable move in reasonable dialogue. So to avoid answering a question is not always an acceptable type of response.

When is the tactic of replying to a question with a question allowable in reasonable dialogue? The most general answer relates to where the burden of proof in dialogue lies. If the context of dialogue and the respondent's commitments and assertions make it clear that he is obliged to justify or explain a specific proposition, then there is a burden on the respondent to answer a question that asks for such justification or explanation. If he fails to answer the question without giving a good reason, his reply may be judged irrelevant or unduly evasive. But if the question is unduly aggressive, or is packed with presuppositions that the respondent does not accept, this could be an excellent and fully justifiable reason for questioning the question.

Questions of burden of proof are decided by looking at the context of dialogue and determining, in accord with the outline of dialogue given in Chapter 1, what the issue really is and what each participant in the argument should be trying to prove.

2.7 BEGGING THE QUESTION

In a persuasion dialogue, the goal of each participant is to prove his conclusion from premises that are accepted as commitments by the other participant. However, if a premise has not already been explicitly accepted by a respondent, it must at least be a proposition that he could possibly accept, consistent with his own obligation to prove his conclusion. Otherwise, the argument using this premise as a basis could not be useful for the purpose of persuading the respondent to accept its conclusion. This type of inadequate or useless attempt at proof is a violation, error, or shortcoming in a persuasion dialogue, because such an argument stands no chance of fulfilling its proponent's obligation to prove his conclusion in the discussion.

The following example is a case in point. Suppose that Bob and Leo are engaged in a critical discussion, and Bob is a skeptic who doubts the existence of God. Leo is a religious believer who has taken on the burden of proving to Bob that God exists. At some point in the dialogue, Bob asks Leo to prove that God is benevolent. Leo advances the following argument in reply:

Example 2.22

God has all the virtues.

Benevolence is a virtue.

Therefore, God is benevolent.

What would Bob's likely response be? The answer is that, since Bob is a committed skeptic, he has every right to object that Leo's argument begs the question. Bob might reply: 'Well, of course, if you accept both premises of your argument, Leo, then you have to accept the conclusion of this valid argument. But since I don't accept the conclusion, how can you reasonably expect me to accept the first premise? Consistent with my point of view as a skeptic about the whole enterprise of religion, I not only doubt whether it is correct to say that God has any of the virtues, I even doubt that God exists as an entity that can have virtues'. Given Bob's obligation to question the existence of God, he can hardly accept statements like 'God has all the virtues' without virtually conceding the whole issue by making his own position inconsistent.

In this sort of situation, Leo's argument could be criticized as begging the question, for Leo's argument only "begs for" Bob's acceptance of the proposition (question) to be proved, instead of doing the proper job of proving it by deduction from premises that Leo has a chance of proving in his persuasion dialogue with Bob. An argument that begs the question is also often said to commit the fallacy of arguing in a circle. In this case, there appears to be no way that Leo could prove the premise 'God has all the virtues' without already presupposing that 'God is benevolent' as a prior assumption (given that it is accepted that benevolence is a virtue). We could say then that Leo's argument "chases its own tail" or goes in a circle.

Circular sequences of questions and answers are not always fallacious instances of begging the question in contexts of dialogue.

53

Suppose I ask you, 'Why does Bruno like Betty?' and you reply, 'Because Betty likes Bruno'. This sequence is circular, but it need not be a fallacious explanation of human behavior. It could be that both Betty and Bruno are the kind of people who respond to affection. They like others because other people like them. Thus their behavior as a mutual admiration society is an instance of a circular feedback process between Betty and Bruno. But explaining this behavior by pointing out its circular structure is not fallacious or an erroneous case of begging the question.

Begging the question is a fault in persuasion dialogue because a circular argument is useless for the purpose of persuading someone to accept a conclusion on the basis of premises that they are, or can become, committed to. An argument that begs the question is doomed from the outset as a persuasive proof.

An argument that begs the question does not count as a useful move to facilitate an inquiry either. In an inquiry, the premises must be better established or known than the conclusion to be proved. Otherwise, the inquiry makes no progress. If I ask you to prove that three is a prime number, and you reply, 'Three is a prime number; therefore, three is a prime number', your 'proof' is deductively valid. But it is of no use in proving that three is a prime number. To do that, you have to start from premises that are better established than the proposition queried. Otherwise, your argument goes nowhere.

2.8 QUESTION–ANSWER RULES IN DIALOGUE

We have examined several different types of questions, each of which has a different type of direct answer. The direct answer to a yes–no-question is 'yes' or 'no'. The direct answer to a why-question is to produce a set of propositions that implies the proposition queried. The direct answer to a whether-question is to produce a proposition that represents one of the alternatives posed by the question. But no matter what type of question you are confronted with, the important thing to remember is that every question has presuppositions. In effect, then, answering questions does incur commitment, because presuppositions are propositions. And if you answer a question directly, you then become committed to these propositions. And this means that, by answering a question, you make positive assertions, whether you realize it or not.

Despite the fact that there are different types of questions, the concept of a *presupposition of a question* may be generally defined as follows. A presupposition of a question is a proposition that one becomes committed to automatically, simply by giving any direct answer to the question. Although, as we have seen, questions have many presuppositions, generally there is one important or main presupposition to any question. Or, in the case of complex questions, there may be two or more main presuppositions. For example, the spouse-beating question presupposes that the answerer has a spouse and that the answerer has beaten this spouse at some time in the past.

Generally speaking, the important presupposition of most questions is fairly clear. In a yes–no-question, the important presupposition is normally that either the yes-answer is true or that the no-answer is true. For example, the important presupposition of 'Is snow white?' is the disjunction: Either snow is white or snow is not white. In a why-question, the important presupposition is that the proposition queried is true. For example, the important presupposition of 'Why is chlorine heavier than air?' is the proposition that chlorine is heavier than air. In a whether-question, the important presupposition is that at least one of the alternatives is true.

However, great care and judgment are needed in determining the important presuppositions of some tricky or objectionable questions. For example, the spouse-beating question seems like a harmless yes–no-question. But it is not. In fact, its important presupposition is that the answerer has engaged in the past practice of spouse beating.

Now, at any rate, we understand why questions are not harmless and why questions can in fact be arguments in some cases. Normally, we would say that a logical error is a wrong argument of some sort, where an argument is defined as a positive claim made by a set of propositions advanced. But questions are not propositions. So how can questions exhibit faults of logic? The answer is that questions have presuppositions and, therefore, can advance a set of propositions in the following way. A question calls for or requires an answer, but when the answerer gives a direct reply, as requested, he automatically becomes committed to certain propositions. And that is why questions can influence the course of an argument most decisively.

But when exactly does a question become objectionable? We have seen that questioning becomes especially dangerous and objection-

55

able when it becomes too aggressive. We saw in example 2.9 how a highly aggressive question can be a form of attack in political debate. The problem with answering this type of overly aggressive question is that if the answerer gives a direct answer, as directed by the question, he is clearly undone and discredited. Obviously, he would be naive and ill-advised to reply that he is now prepared to condemn his company to continued failure for the next ten days because of his stubborn failure to change his disastrous policies. Yet that would be a direct answer of the sort the question requires. So this type of question violates a reasonable order of questioning and answering in dialogue, and does not give the respondent a fair chance to express a direct reply.

Now notice that, on the other hand, an aggressive question requires a direct answer and that, if the answerer does not give a direct answer, then the questioner can accuse him of being evasive (committing an error of irrelevance). In example 2.9 we saw that the questioner can accuse an answerer of not having answered the question, when the answerer has tried only to rebut an unwelcome presupposition of the question. In political debate, such an accusation could easily make the answerer look guilty and evasive. So the problem is that the answerer must answer. But what fair and reasonable rules of dialogue should regulate when and how an answerer must answer?

If a person does not know the answer to a question, and he is forced to answer the question 'yes' or 'no', then the rule of dialogue that requires this direct answer, in effect, commits a form of *ad ignorantiam* fallacy. In effect, that is, the answerer is unwisely forced to argue from his own ignorance. Therefore, in reasonable dialogue we do not want to have question-answering rules and conventions that are so strict that the *ad ignorantiam* error is built right into the rules. Such a conception of dialogue would not represent reasonable dialogue, unless the participants were omniscient.

Now a question becomes especially objectionable when it is overly aggressive. But when is this the case? A question is overly aggressive when it attempts to force the answerer, by an unreasonable sequence of questions, in dialogue, to accept unwillingly propositions that are presuppositions of the question and that are unwelcome to the answerer. By *unwelcome,* we mean propositions that the answerer is not committed to, propositions that he should not become committed to because they are prejudicial to his side of the argument.

Hence a question is objectionable if it attempts to preempt the answerer's acceptance of the unwelcome proposition by presupposing that the answerer already accepts it.

This is the problem with begging the question. It is an attempt to push an argument on a respondent where a premise (or premises) could be accepted by that respondent only at the cost of prejudicing or destroying his own point of view in the issue of the dialogue.

But there is a dilemma in trying to deal fairly with these aggressive types of tactics in a persuasion dialogue; for if we were always to allow an answerer the 'No commitment' option to any question, then the answerer could always frivolously play the skeptic, if he wished, and say 'No commitment' in answer to every question. Then the dialogue could go nowhere, and a truculent participant in dialogue could prevent his companion in dialogue from proving anything or getting anywhere in his questioning. An answerer could be as evasive as he wished, with no penalty. And that would not be conducive to reasonable dialogue either.

The solution to this dilemma is to require that, in reasonable dialogue, an answerer's answer cooperatively reflect what he honestly and truly thinks, if he has a definite opinion or commitment on the question. If he has no firm commitment on the matter, he should reply 'No commitment'. But if he is truly committed to a proposition, then his answer should reflect that commitment. This way of regulating question–answer procedures is the best way to ensure the progress of reasonable dialogue on an issue. Such rules are matters of politeness and helpful collaboration, which are essential to the progress and success of a critical discussion.

For example, if I were to ask you the question 'Why is three an even number?' you would rightly feel that the question is objectionable. Why? Well, if you are an intelligent arguer, the proposition that three is an even number will not be acceptable to you. You would not, and should not, accept that proposition as a commitment. However, if you give a direct answer to the question, you are automatically forced to accept that commitment, like it or not, because the question is too aggressive. Your best reply is to reject the presupposition instead of directly answering the question. You should reply, 'Three is not an even number'.

If the question was 'Why is three an odd number?' then you would, or should, have no similar objection to it. If you accept that three is an odd number, then the question is not a problem for you. It is no longer overly aggressive or objectionable.

In short, then, when a question is overly aggressive, the answerer must attack the question itself. He must question the question's presuppositions. In some cases, he must firmly reject an important presupposition of a question if it is very damaging to his own side of the argument. When the question is overly aggressive, the answerer must be somewhat aggressive too, though in a reasonable way. The answerer must bounce the ball back into the questioner's court and shift the burden of proof back onto the questioner to justify the presuppositions alleged by the question.

To say that a question is fallacious is to say that it is objectionable to the answerer because it is constructed to force him to accept a proposition that he should not.[10] This problem is compounded if the question is also semantically complex. A semantically complex question is one that contains a connective, 'and', 'or', or 'if–then' in its presupposition. Once again, the answerer must question the question by requesting that the propositions in the presupposition be separated into units that he can reasonably deal with.

To say that a question is objectionable is to say that it is open to reasonable criticism or objection by the answerer. Reasonable dialogue requires that the answerer sometimes be allowed to query or criticize a question, for example, when the question is overly aggressive.

The problems and errors of question asking encountered in this chapter show that, in reasonable dialogue, an answerer should not always be forced to give a direct answer to every question. The argument from ignorance has the same lesson. Sometimes the best answer to a question is 'No commitment' or 'I don't know'. On the other hand, an answerer should not be allowed to duck every question, or he would never have to make any commitments, and reasonable dialogue would not be well served.

The solution to this problem is to be sought by requiring that each party in reasonable dialogue have the burden of proving his own thesis and defending his own position on the issue. If questioned to prove, clarify, or defend a proposition that he is clearly committed

10 Ruth Manor concludes that a question that is an act of presupposing a proposition not previously accepted by an answerer can be wrong in dialogue when it denies the answerer the chance to react to the presupposition by questioning it. See Manor (1981, p. 13).

to, an answerer should directly respond. If the question presupposes propositions that he may not be committed to, an answerer should have a right to question the question.

In general, the basic rule of burden of proof in reasonable dialogue is: He who asserts must prove.[11] Someone who has previously asserted a proposition as part of his position should be accounted as answerable to that proposition unless he retracts it or removes his commitment to it subsequently. Once I am committed to a proposition A, I should not be freely allowed to say 'No reply' if I am asked again about it. I may not know, in fact, whether A is true, but if I am committed to A, then I should be guided by that commitment in subsequent dialogue.

If a question is loaded, it makes an assertion, at least for the respondent who must answer it. Therefore, a burden of proof justifying his presupposition can reasonably be placed on the one who asks a loaded question. And therefore it is reasonable for the respondent of such a question to challenge it by asking the questioner to meet the burden of proof inherent in his question.

11 See Walton (1987).

3

Criticisms of irrelevance

One of the most common kinds of criticism made in argument is the reply 'That's beside the point!' or 'That's irrelevant'. However, 'relevance' is such a broad term that the criticism of being irrelevant could refer to many kinds of failures or shortcomings in an argument. The study of relevance in argument begins by clarifying and classifying these alleged failures that can prompt the criticism that a breach of relevance has been committed in argument.

The primary basis of allegations of irrelevance stems from an important basic feature of all reasonable dialogue. Every argument presupposes a context of dialogue in which there is an issue, or perhaps several issues, being discussed. An *issue* means that there is a proposition or question of controversy under discussion. Typically, an issue in dialogue suggests that there are two sides to the discussion. In other words, there is a certain specific proposition being discussed, and one participant in the dialogue is committed to that proposition's being true while the other participant is committed to its being false. Of course, dialogues are not always this clear or simple, but when they are of this form, they may be called *disputes* (or *disputations*). A dispute is a dialogue in which one side affirms a certain proposition and the other side affirms the opposite (negation) of that proposition.

This means that a characteristic of reasonable dialogue is that each participant in an argument should have a particular proposition assigned to him or designated by him that represents his *thesis,* or conclusion to be proved. The two theses of the two participants in the argument define the issue of the argument. And the issue is the primary factor in enabling us to evaluate fairly claims concerning what is or is not relevant to the issue of a particular argument.

Of course, one main problem in the practical job of evaluating realistic argumentation is that arguers may not even be clear on what they are arguing about. Allegations of irrelevance cannot be settled fairly if the issue of the argument was never stated or understood in the first place.

Sometimes an argument is ostensibly about one issue but really about another. A husband and wife may be arguing about who should take the garbage out this morning. But the real issue may be that one of them came home late the night before with no explanation.

So arguers should be clear on what they are arguing about, or at least be able to clarify it. Only then can allegations of irrelevance be reasonably adjudicated and settled.

3.1 ALLEGATIONS OF IRRELEVANCE

The traditional fallacy of *ignoratio elenchi* (ignoring the issue, sometimes also called irrelevant conclusion) is said to be committed when an argument fails to prove the conclusion (thesis) it is supposed to prove and, instead, is directed toward proving some irrelevant conclusion. The following is a traditional case:

Example 3.0

A particular proposal for housing legislation is under consideration. A senator rises to speak in favor of the bill. However, his whole argument is directed to the conclusion that all the people should have decent housing.

The reason this example is said to be a case of the fallacious *ignoratio elenchi* is that the senator should be proving that this particular bill is worth voting for because it will improve the housing situation. However, instead he argues for the proposition that all people should have decent housing, a proposition that is not the real issue of the dispute and one that virtually any party to the dispute would agree to anyway. Thus his argument misses the point and may therefore be criticized as irrelevant.

From one point of view, the criticism of irrelevance here amounts to the claim that the senator's argument is not valid. In other words, the senator has really argued as follows:

[Premise]	All people should have decent housing.
[Conclusion]	This particular proposal will improve the housing situation.

61

The proposition marked 'conclusion' is the proposition that the senator should prove, according to the procedures for dialogue of this legislative assembly. But the information the senator actually puts forward, marked 'premise', is not sufficient to establish the required conclusion by valid argument. From this point of view, the charge of irrelevance basically amounts to the criticism that the senator's argument is simply not valid, when directed to its proper conclusion. From another point of view, one could say that the mistake is that the senator got his own argument wrong. He misidentified his own conclusion. Or perhaps better, he attempted to mislead his audience into taking a proposition for the conclusion that is, in reality, not the correct conclusion to be argued for.

Another interesting observation about example 3.0 is that the senator is being criticized not so much for what he did, as for what he did not do. Probably all of us accept the premise 'All people should have decent housing'. However, what remains to be shown is how the proposal at issue will provide decent housing in the present circumstances. Because the senator's argument failed to establish that missing premise, it is a very weak argument indeed.

Notice, however, that the senator's argument could possibly be improved if he could go on to show why the proposal at issue could provide decent housing in the present circumstances. Then the premise 'All people should have decent housing' would not be irrelevant, because it would be an essential part of a valid argument for the right conclusion. In other words, though the senator's argument (example 3.0) is open to criticism or questioning for what it lacks, it is not necessarily a fallacious argument if by 'fallacious' we mean illogical or so hopelessly bad that it cannot be repaired by continuing with it. For example, the senator's argument might be even worse, or more irrelevant, if his only premise was something like 'All people deserve dignity and freedom'. This premise does not seem to have anything at all to do with the proper conclusion he is supposed to prove. At least the former premise was more closely connected to that conclusion, even if it did not prove it. So although irrelevance should rightly be open to criticism in reasonable dialogue, to call irrelevance a fallacy in every case is an exaggeration.

The force of the criticism that the senator's argument is an *ignoratio elenchi* depends on the presumption that the senator has finished his argument, and that is all he has to say on the subject. It might be that, if he were to say more, he would show why his premise is connected to the conclusion and, therefore, why his argument is relevant. The question of how final the criticism of irrelevance should be taken, therefore, depends on whether the dialogue can be continued. In the present case, perhaps it could not be. But in many cases, it can be. And therefore it is often wiser to treat the *ignoratio elenchi* allegation as a criticism that could be replied to, rather than as a fallacy or conclusive refutation that wholly destroys the worth of the argument against which it is directed.

The point here is that, in the midst of dialogue, it may be hard to see where another participant's argument is headed. If so, you can always ask, 'Is that proposition relevant?' And in some cases the arguer may reasonably reply, 'Yes, it will turn out to be relevant once I get to that point in my argument. Hang on for a bit and I'll show you why'. This reply is sometimes a reasonable one, especially if the required chain of argumentation is long and complex. Hence one has to be careful that a serious criticism of irrelevance may not be premature. Sometimes a criticism of irrelevance is best treated more as a request for more information.

The term *ignoratio elenchi* was taken by Aristotle to mean 'ignorance of refutation'. The origin of this term derives from the Greek tradition that contestive argument is like a game of dialogue in which each participant has a thesis or conclusion to be proved. But the argument is contestive, that is, a dispute, if the thesis of the one participant in the dialogue is opposed to the thesis of the other. Therefore, the point of the game is for each player to refute the thesis of the other. Any argument that seems to refute the thesis of the other, but really does not, could be seen as a case of ignorance of refutation. In other words, the arguer only thought his argument refuted his opponent's thesis, but in reality he was ignorant of the fact that it did not refute that thesis.

To go back to example 3.0 as an illustration, the following proposition is the issue to be contested:

(S1) This bill will improve the housing situation.

(S2) This bill will not improve the housing situation.

The senator's argument is supposed to refute (S2) by establishing his own conclusion to be proved, (S1). However, the whole problem was that his given premise failed to prove (S1). So Aristotle would say his argument is an *ignoratio elenchi* because it fails to refute (S2).

It merely refutes the proposition 'Not all people should have decent housing' at best. And that is not the proposition to be refuted in this particular game of dialogue. In other words, there is only ignorance of refutation instead of genuine refutation of the thesis at issue.

Aristotle's conception of *ignoratio elenchi* represents the basic idea of the criticism of irrelevance in reasonable dialogue. However, his conception is a very broad one. The basic purpose of all argument in reasonable dialogue is to prove one's conclusion or thesis that is set as the proposition to be established by the argument. And any argument that fails in this objective could therefore be fairly said to be open to criticism or improvement. So virtually any of the traditional fallacies or shortcomings of arguments could potentially fall under the classification of *ignoratio elenchi*. In fact, we will see that many of the appeals to emotion are said to be fallacies, in large part, because they are weak arguments of the *ignoratio elenchi* type. For example, the abusive and circumstantial *ad hominem* fallacies could mostly be classified as arguments that are open to criticism because they fail to prove or refute successfully the conclusions they are supposed to in reasonable dialogue.

In short, the criticism of irrelevance is a broad category of criticism in evaluating arguments, and several more specific criticisms of particular kinds of irrelevance can usefully be identified. We now turn to these categories. But the basic fallacy of irrelevance is simply the misidentification of the proper conclusion to be proved in reasonable dialogue.

3.2 GLOBAL IRRELEVANCE

A reasonable dialogue is a sequence of questions and answers where each participant has a thesis or conclusion to be proved. Over the whole sequence of the dialogue, a proposition may be said to be *globally irrelevant* if it occurs at some stage of the dialogue but fails to be relevant to the ultimate conclusion to be proved by the party who advanced that proposition in the dialogue. As we have seen, one main problem with adjudicating allegations of global irrelevance is that, in some arguments, the participants have not made it clear exactly what each of their ultimate conclusions is supposed to be.

In some contexts, however, the objective of the dialogue does make it clear what the thesis of each arguer is supposed to be. For example, in a criminal trial in a court of law, the prosecuting attorney is supposed to prove that the defendant is guilty of an alleged offense. The defense attorney is supposed to refute the prosecuting attorney's argument by showing that it does not prove that the defendant is guilty. In other words, the burden is on the prosecution to prove guilt, beyond reasonable doubt. The defense has only to show that there can be reasonable doubt. That is, the defense has only to show that the opposing argument is weak, or at any rate not strong enough to convict the defendant.

This type of argument is not exactly a classical dispute, where one arguer has to prove one proposition and the other has to prove the opposite proposition. But it is like a dispute, because the conclusions of the two parties are opposed to each other. Yet the defense attorney does not have to prove positively that his client did not commit the crime. He has only to prove the weaker conclusion that the prosecutor's arguments do not show that the defendant committed the alleged crime. Here, the conclusions to be proved are asymmetrical. The defense attorney does not need to *strongly refute* the prosecuting attorney's thesis, that is, to show that it is false. He needs only to *weakly refute* the prosecuting attorney's thesis, that is, to show that it is subject to reasonable doubt.[1]

In short, the criminal trial is not a *symmetrical dispute,* in which one arguer has to prove a proposition A and the other arguer has to prove the negation, not-A. It is a kind of asymmetrical dispute in which the burden of proof is stronger on one side than on the other. In fact, the burden of proof is (positively) on the one side only. The other side needs only to defend by weakly refuting the first side's argument. Let us call this kind of asymmetrical dispute a *weakly opposed dispute* or *asymmetrical dispute.* In a weakly opposed dispute, one party must positively prove his thesis, the other need only show that the first party's proof does not succeed. He is not required to show that the first party's thesis is false but only that it is open to doubt or reasonable challenge. The criminal trial is an

---

1 It is very important not to confuse weak and strong refutation. In fact, the following form of this confusion is exactly the *ad ignorantiam* fallacy: An arguer purports to have strongly refuted a proposition at issue when in fact he has given evidence to support, at best, a weak refutation of the proposition. In other words, just because a proposition is subject to reasonable doubt, it does not necessarily follow that the proposition is shown to be false. To so argue is the *ad ignorantiam* fallacy.

asymmetrical dispute, but many civil cases in law are symmetrical disputes in which the burden of proof is evenly weighted.

Whether a trial is an asymmetrical dispute or a symmetrical dispute, then, the thesis to be proved by each attorney is clearly defined at the outset by the procedural rules of dialogue for that particular type of case. If an attorney's argument seems to wander, the other attorney or the judge can question the relevance of a line of argument to the thesis to be proved by that attorney. Such a question is a criticism of global irrelevance. The judge may query, 'Can you show the court why this line of argument is relevant to your case?'

Example 3.1

The prosecuting attorney in a criminal trial is supposed to prove that the defendant is guilty of murder. However, the prosecuting attorney argues at length that murder is a horrible crime. He holds up the victim's bloody shirt for the jury to see. He expostulates at length on the horror of this crime and all crimes of murder.

As the prosecuting attorney's argument along this line goes on and on, the court may begin to wonder if he is ever going to get around to arguing that this particular defendant is guilty of the admittedly horrible crime of murder. As it becomes reasonable to question whether such an argument is forthcoming, it becomes appropriate to question the relevance of the attorney's line of argument so far. If the attorney finishes his argument without really coming around to the question of the guilt of this particular defendant, then he may fairly be accused of committing a classical *ignoratio elenchi,* for he has failed to prove what he was supposed to prove by his argument. In short, the reasonable suspicion may be that he has tried to convince the jury that the issue of the trial is whether murder is a horrible crime. But of course that conclusion is not a basis for conviction. So a criticism of *ignoratio elenchi* has a sharply defined edge in law because the thesis to be proved by each participant in the dialogue is defined by the procedural rules of the law.

What is worth noticing here, however, is that, until the case is finally concluded, an allegation of global irrelevance is not a conclusive refutation of an argument. Suppose that the prosecuting attorney spends a lot of time arguing that murder is a horrible crime. But then suppose that the attorney also shows evidence that the defendant exhibited traumatic behavior just after the time the crime was alleged to have taken place. He might be about to argue that this unusual behavior is consistent with someone committing a horrible crime. If so, the premise 'Murder is a horrible crime' might play a legitimate role in his global network of argumentation as he builds a case for his conclusion that the defendant is guilty of murder.

So one has to be careful here. An allegation of global irrelevance cannot be finally or conclusively decided as justifiable or not until the dialogue is terminated. Otherwise, it is best treated as a challenge, or weak refutation at best, and not as a clearly established fallacy.

In reasonable dialogue, criticisms of irrelevance should be treated as fundamentally global in nature, but very often such criticisms are meant to be taken in a local way. We have already seen, for example, that failure to give a direct answer to a question is often labeled as a kind of irrelevance. However, the irrelevance here is primarily local, for the reply may be criticized because it is not thought to be a direct enough answer to one particular question at some point in a dialogue. So one important type of criticism of relevance is that of question-answering relevance.

3.3 QUESTION–ANSWER RELEVANCE

In some cases, a criticism of irrelevance relates to a specific question–answer pairing during a sequence of dialogue. The criticism 'That's irrelevant' in such a case means that the respondent's reply was not an answer to the specific question asked. This type of criticism is not one of global relevance. Rather it is a local irrelevance concerning the relation between a reply and a specific question asked at some point in the sequence of dialogue. Also, this type of criticism is not one that, strictly speaking, concerns a relationship between assertions or propositions.[2] Instead, the relationship is one between a question and a reply to that question. We could call this type of relevance *question–answer* relevance, because the failure occurs when the reply does not answer the question. Or, at any rate, the reply is not a direct enough answer to the question to satisfy the critic who cites it as irrelevant.

2 Epstein (1979, p. 156). See Sperber and Wilson (1986) on some other kinds of relevance.

In the following example, a reporter asks a specific question, and a university dean gives an answer that appears to be relevant:

Example 3.2

Reporter: I am concerned about affirmative action programs and would like to ask how many of the proposed faculty cuts at the university are women's positions.

Dean: Only one position in the women's studies department will be cut. But that is balanced by the new proposal for the women's chair, which will mean adding a new position to women's studies.

Reporter: My question wasn't about women's studies. There are a number of faculties that are cutting positions, including arts, science, and engineering. I want to know how many of those faculty members who are women will be cut.

Note that, in this case, the problematic question and reply were topically related – both were about women faculty members whose positions were being cut. And they were globally related on the same general issue. Yet even so, the reporter's criticism that the respondent did not answer her question could and would be described as a criticism that the reply was not relevant to her question. As she put it, her question was not *about* women's studies. And so, we might say, the reply about women's studies was not strictly relevant, meaning that it did not address the specific question asked.

There is an unfortunate tendency in ordinary conversation, and even in logic textbooks, to use 'irrelevance' as a kind of catch-all criticism for any sort of failure of argument or weak argument. An instance of this sort in a logic text is cited below.

The following dialogue was cited as an instance of diversion from the point at issue by L. Susan Stebbing (1939, p. 196), where it was quoted from the British *Press Reports*. Sir Charles Craven was the director of Vickers-Armstrong Ltd., an armaments firm:

Example 3.3

When Sir Charles Craven was being questioned by Sir Philip Gibbs yesterday, he said Messrs. Vickers' trade was not particularly dangerous.

Sir Philip: You do not think that your wares are any more dangerous or obnoxious than boxes of chocolates or sugar candy? – No, or novels.

Sir Philip: You don't think it is more dangerous to export these fancy goods to foreign countries than, say, children's crackers?

Sir Charles: Well, I nearly lost an eye with a Christmas cracker, but never with a gun.

According to Stebbing's evaluation of this case, Sir Charles's reply to Sir Philip's second question is an irrelevant response because the issue of the dialogue is supposed to be armaments:

> It is difficult to believe that these replies were intended to be serious. There is an obvious diversion from the point under the guise of a contemptuous joke. At least, I think it must have been meant for a joke, although it is certainly a poor one. (1939, p. 196)

Stebbing goes on to object that armaments, unlike firecrackers, are made "solely for the purpose of killing and wounding people and destroying buildings." Her objection is that it is armaments that are being discussed, not firecrackers.

Stebbing is certainly justified in criticizing Sir Charles's reply as weak, unconvincing, and even morally reprehensible. But is she justified in criticizing it as *irrelevant*? To answer this question, note that it was Sir Philip, in his question, not Sir Charles, in his reply, who first introduced the topic of firecrackers into the dialogue. Therefore, if the topic of firecrackers is irrelevant, it is Sir Philip's question that is irrelevant, not Sir Charles's reply. Sir Charles's reference to the topic of firecrackers, in his reply, is locally relevant to the subject matter of Sir Philip's question that preceded it.

This particular example reveals two special features of relevance in dialogue. First, it suggests that a question can be relevant or irrelevant. This is interesting because, usually, we encounter criticisms of irrelevance, at the local level especially, where a reply to a question is said to be evasive or irrelevant. But can questions themselves be irrelevant? It seems possible that they can be. For example, if you and I are discussing the sale of a building near the university, and I unexpectedly inject the question 'When was Albert Einstein born?' into the dialogue, you may well ask me why my question is relevant. Or in some cases, you might even criticize my question as irrelevant to the discussion. Therefore, it seems that questions, as well as answers, can be criticized as irrelevant to a discussion.

Second, example 3.3 illustrates how there can be a conflict in some cases between relevance at the local level and relevance at the global level. Stebbing criticized Sir Charles's reply on the grounds that the topic of the discussion is armaments, not firecrackers. However, even granting that this claim is true at the global level, it nevertheless remains that Sir Charles's reply on the subject of firecrackers and armaments is relevant, at the local level, to Sir Philip's question.

So there seems to be a conflict in the evaluation of this case. Which is more important – relevance at the global level or relevance at the local level? Stebbing seems to think the former more important, but this contention does not seem very plausible, for the following principle seems generally reasonable: If a questioner introduces a new subject matter into a discussion via a question, then the respondent should be allowed to incorporate that subject matter into his reply as well, without necessarily being reasonably criticized for irrelevance.

Another case will illustrate a kind of reply where a question is criticized as irrelevant. Curiously, in this case, the respondent is trying to avoid answering the question. His evasive reply, however, adopts the highly aggressive tactic of trying to claim that the question is irrelevant.

The following discussion was an interview by Barbara Frum on the CBC television program *The Journal,* on September 26, 1986. The subject of the interview was the declaration of a No Crime Day by the city of Detroit, a city that had been plagued by a high crime rate and, in particular, a high murder rate. The persons being interviewed were the mayor of Detroit and an athlete who had proposed the idea of the No Crime Day, a public appeal to keep the city of Detroit free of violent crime for one day. A reconstruction of the interview is given in example 3.4:

Example 3.4

Mrs. Frum: The number of people murdered in Detroit so far this year is more than three hundred. More people were murdered last month in Detroit than during this year in Toronto so far. Do you feel that this represents a failure or problem, from your point of view as mayor?

Mayor: You are asking me questions about the high murder rate in Detroit. That is not the question. Other cities like New York also have high rates. The topic is No Crime Day. This murder rate question is not relevant.

Mrs. Frum: Well, yes, it really is relevant. [She then goes on to ask a question of the other person.]

70

The first thing to notice about this case is that the mayor's reply is simply false. Mrs. Frum is quite justified in replying that the question of the murder rate in Detroit is relevant to the topic of No Crime Day; for murder is certainly a type of crime, and a very important one to be sure.

The mayor may see the topic of the murder rate as "irrelevant" because it poses a political liability for his standing as mayor. But Mrs. Frum certainly sees it as part of the topic. Of course, we do not know whether Mrs. Frum and the mayor agreed to any fixed agenda or topic prior to the interview. But even if they did agree that No Crime Day was to be the subject of the interview, murder is clearly related to crime, and to No Crime Day as a topic.

In an interesting way, this case is the opposite side of the same problem noted in example 3.5, the case of the discussion on the closing hours of the library. There, Harry is trying to maintain that tuition fees are relevant to the topic, whereas their relevance is too marginal to the discussion to sustain his case. In the case above, by contrast, the mayor is claiming that the murder rate is not relevant, whereas in fact the two topics at issue are so closely related that his disclaimer cannot be sustained.

3.4 SETTING AN AGENDA FOR A DISCUSSION

One way of keeping the issues of a controversy within manageable proportions is to restrict the set of admissible topics to what is directly relevant to a specific issue. In the following example, a meeting of the library committee has been scheduled, and the only item on the agenda is the issue of whether library hours should be extended on Sundays. The library is open for eight hours on Sundays, and the Student Association has made a proposal to extend the Sunday library hours to ten. During the meeting, the following exchange takes place:

Example 3.5

Harry: Not only should the library remain open longer so that students can have a place to study, but student tuition fees should be lowered as well.

Pam: Hold on, Harry. The topic of this meeting is the proposal for the extension of library hours. What does the topic of tuition fees have to do with it? I don't see the relevance of that issue.

71

Harry: Well, if students didn't have to pay so much tuition, they could afford better lodging, and therefore better facilities to study at home. I mean it's all connected because many factors are responsible for not providing students with adequate facilities for studying. Therefore my point is relevant.

But is Harry's point relevant? No doubt it can be related to the issue of extended library hours, which was specified as the topic to be discussed at this meeting. But the issue of changing tuition fees was not on the agenda, although it may well be an issue of other meetings held in the university thoughout the year. So, although Harry has responded to Pam's criticism by establishing a connection between the issues, we need to ask whether the connection is a legitimate one, of a sort to require the meeting to include the discussion of tuition fees.

If a group of students and faculty were having an informal discussion, it might be quite reasonable to include arguments on tuition fees with those on library hours. In some ways, the two issues could be connected. But if a meeting is called on the topic of a specific proposal to extend library hours, the issue is purposely defined very narrowly, and it may be appropriate to restrict discussion to issues directly relevant to the proposal at hand. Thus, although Harry has made a connection between the two topics, it is not strong enough to reply adequately to Pam's objection that the topic of fee decreases is not relevant.

Not all discussions have a specific agenda devised to set their boundaries. But where irrelevance can be a serious problem, an agenda can be useful. An *agenda* may be defined as a specific set of issues (propositions) to be discussed, often in a specific order.

What is or is not reasonably relevant to a discussion, however, may be highly controversial in some cases. To rule on such criticisms of irrelevance fairly, we have to look carefully at the agenda set for discussion, if one has been set by the participants, and ask how specific the issue under discussion is supposed to be. If the issue is a specific proposal, other controversial issues may reasonably be excluded from the discussion if they are only tangentially relevant and cannot therefore be adequately dealt with in the context of another issue that must be resolved.

Hence a criticism of irrelevance is a procedural point of order in a regulated dialogue that challenges the relevance of an argument to the question at issue. Where the issue is clearly delimited at the outset by the participants in the discussion, such a point of order can and should be reasonably restrictive.

How strictly relevance of arguments should be controlled by a chairman or moderator of a discussion, however, varies with the context of dialogue, and specific agreements made or accepted by the participants. In a stockholders' meeting to decide whether to declare a dividend, for example, any discussion not directly related to the agenda may be cut off peremptorily. The urgency of the decision may require strict standards of relevance, and the stockholders may want these standards enforced. Thus the question of tolerance of irrelevance in a discussion may be a question of judgment relative to the goals of the discussion and the narrowness of the agenda.

There is an inherent practical problem in ruling on questions of relevance in a specific context of dialogue. This is essentially because it may be impossible for a moderator or other participants in a discussion to see where a particular arguer may be leading us. This, of course, is because an argument in dialogue is made up of a series of links at the local levels that are uncompleted as a chain until the argument has been concluded. In midstream, it may be difficult to see where an argument may be leading us. In retrospect, once the argument is completed, it may be much easier to judge relevance. But a moderator or referee of a discussion may have to try to judge relevance during the actual debate. Therefore, in the midst of discussion, judgments of relevance may have to be based on reasoned trust, a willingness to cooperate, or on the reassurance of a speaker that his line of argument will turn out to be relevant.

However, even in the midst of a discussion, a move in dialogue can be judged irrelevant if it is not an appropriate response to the previous move by the other participant. Thus if you ask me a question, and I respond with another question that does not reply to, or even address, the first question, my response may rightly be judged as irrelevant.

Many of the problems of irrelevance studied so far pertain to the argumentation stage of a dialogue, but irrelevance can also be a problem even at the confrontation stage of a discussion.

A practical problem is that participants in a discussion may actually have differing preconceptions of what the issue of a case should be. In a case described by Moore (1986, p. 173), a social service organization planned to build a health clinic for low-income patients in a residential neighborhood. The group of neighbors opposed the location of the project in their neighborhood. They defined the issue of the discussion as whether or not the clinic should be located in their area. But according to Moore (1986, p. 173), the issue for the social service organization was how the project of setting up the clinic could be carried out: "They want to discuss *how* a building can be leased and what resistance they will encounter in locating their facility." If each group in this case were asked to define the issue of the dispute, one group would give a quite different answer than the other.

In this case, the discussion appears to be a dispute, but in fact each party is prepared to discuss a different issue. Hence if they were to begin to engage in the process of argument, in fact they would be arguing at cross-purposes.

In this case, the thesis of the one party is partially opposed to the thesis of the other; for if the building cannot be located in the neighborhood, then of course the project of building the clinic there cannot be carried out. So there certainly is some opposition, and some room for dispute.

However, there can be a serious problem nonetheless; for if each party defines the issue differently, then it may be difficult or impossible for the dialogue to lead to any resolution of the controversy. Arguments supporting one side of the alleged issue may be rightly perceived by the other side to be irrelevant to the issue as they define it. Lacking any basic agreement on global relevance, both parties may well be led into sequences of questions and replies that lead only to objections and criticisms of irrelevance that cannot possibly be resolved to the satisfaction of both sides. So, in fact, this kind of misunderstanding about the issue of a dispute can undermine reasoned dialogue and lead to a failure of resolution of the controversy.

Thus there are many very real practical difficulties in ruling on relevance in a dispute. The agenda may only seem to be defined, but the disputants may in fact misunderstand how the issue is defined. Or the participants may even strenuously disagree on how the issue should be defined. In union–management disputes for example, negotiations may be deadlocked because the disputing parties cannot even agree on what should be on the agenda. Here, difficulties of setting standards to define relevance can be extreme, even before the main stages of entering into argumentation.

But even if the issue has been clearly defined, and all participants have agreed to the agenda, practical difficulties of preventing very aggressive arguers from going off track into emotional appeals, personal attacks, and other digressions may require a skilled moderator with sensitive judgment. To define relevance is one thing; to interpret it fairly in a discussion is something else.

3.5 VARIETIES OF CRITICISMS OF IRRELEVANCE

One type of argument that exhibits a questionable failure of relevance is an attack in which an opponent's conclusion in a dispute is distorted or exaggerated in order to make it appear unreasonable:

Example 3.6

The environmentalists keep insisting that the problem of acid rain is serious and threatening. They think that if we solve this problem our country will be a heaven on earth.

The criticism that might reasonably be advanced here is to query whether the environmentalists cited are really advocating the thesis that solving the problem of acid rain will create a heaven on earth. It is quite possible that they are not and, if questioned, would strongly object to having that thesis attributed to them as their conclusion. A common strategy for making someone's argument look bad is to exaggerate his conclusion in order to make it seem implausible, and impossible to prove.

Example 3.6 represents a classical case of *ignoratio elenchi*. The basic error is to identify a proposition as the arguer's conclusion that is, in fact, different from his real conclusion or thesis to be proved. But this case is a special type of *ignoratio elenchi* that works because the proposition selected is a similar, but exaggerated form of the correct proposition. So the general fallacy of *ignoratio elenchi* can, in practical terms, take different forms.

Sometimes the conclusion of an argument is gotten wrong because it is overlooked that the conclusion is complex, and a simpler proposition is substituted instead:

Example 3.7

Alfred and Boris are arguing about gun control on a panel discussion. Alfred is an expert on gun control in Alabama. As his part in the discussion, he has agreed to give evidence to support his contention that, if gun control is not introduced in Alabama, there will be much greater incidence of violent crime. However, during the course of his argument, Alfred stresses that the majority of people in Alabama have been strongly against gun control by stricter licensing laws for firearms. Alfred concludes that gun control will not be introduced in Alabama.

If this example is a fair description of Alfred's argument, then it is open to a criticism of *ignoratio elenchi,* for Alfred was supposed to prove the conditional proposition: If gun control is not introduced in Alabama, there will be much greater incidence of violent crime. Instead, Alfred has directed his argument to proving the antecedent of that conditional as his conclusion. But proving that the antecedent is true does not prove that the whole conditional is true. In short, his argument is not valid when directed to its proper conclusion. It is a classical *ignoratio elenchi.* This type of argument that confuses simple and complex propositions is a common form of fallacy of irrelevant conclusion.

Sometimes the premises of an argument, rather than the conclusion, can be criticized as irrelevant. In such a case the conclusion may be fairly clear and some of the premises relevant, but then the arguer gets "off the track" and brings in irrelevant premises. On one occasion, Senator Paul Martin rose to defend his hometown of Windsor, Ontario, against a passage in Arthur Hailey's novel about the U.S. auto industry, *Wheels.* Hailey had written about "grimy Windsor" just across the border from Detroit, "matching in ugliness the worst of its U.S. senior partner." Martin's response reads as follows:

Example 3.8

When I read this I was incensed. . . . Those of us who live there know that [Windsor] is not a grimy city. It is a city that has one of the best flower parks in Canada. It is a city of fine schools, hard-working and tolerant people.

To begin with, Senator Martin's argument makes a reasonable point. The fact that Windsor has a flower park does serve as reasonable evidence to rebut the thesis that Windsor is an ugly city. But at that point, as Johnson and Blair (1983, p. 87) point out, Martin has changed the subject: "Fine schools and hard-working, tolerant people are no doubt an asset, but they have nothing to do with whether a city is fair or ugly." Accordingly, Johnson and Blair criticize Senator Martin's argument as a *red herring*, or irrelevant shift in argument.

The novelty here is that some of the premises in the argument, rather than the conclusion, are perceived as irrelevant. The first premise about the flower park is relevant to the conclusion that Windsor is not an ugly city. But the next premises, citing the fine schools and the hard-working citizens, are not relevant. So the problem is not that Senator Martin has selected the wrong conclusion. Rather, he has gone "off the track" and started bringing in irrelevant premises.

However, we can see that this example does follow the pattern of the *ignoratio elenchi* failure of relevance if we realize that the premises and the conclusion of a reasonable argument must be connected to each other. So you could say that, by introducing premises that are irrelevant to the proper conclusion, an arguer is, in effect, shifting to a different conclusion. Senator Martin was sticking to the proper conclusion when he talked about the flower parks. But when he went on to introduce the premises concerning hard-working and tolerant citizens, he was, in effect, giving an argument that, if reasonable, could only prove some other conclusion, that is, that Windsor is a city that has nice, upstanding citizens. So whether you focus on the premises or the conclusion, the problem is the same. The right sort of relationship between the given premises and the proper conclusion is lacking.

While *ignoratio elenchi* is the fallacy of getting the wrong conclusion or thesis in reasonable argument, sometimes the problem stems from specific premises used or needed in getting to that conclusion. But the basic problem of *ignoratio elenchi* is that the relation required between the premises and conclusion in reasonable argument is lacking. Therefore, we say that the arguer has strayed off the thread of argument and committed a red herring move which opens his argument to a criticism of irrelevance.

3.6 SUMMARY

In every reasonable dialogue, each participant should theoretically have a clearly designated thesis or conclusion that he is obliged to prove in the argument. This means that he is under a burden of proof to establish this particular conclusion. Hence if there is justifiable reason to think he may be straying off the course of fulfilling this burden of proof, his argument is open to a charge of *ignoratio elenchi* (irrelevance).

This irrelevance may be global or local. Global relevance concerns the overall direction and trend of a participant's arguments as they move toward establishing his thesis in a long and possibly complex chain or network of linked arguments. Once the dialogue is concluded, it is much easier to make judgments of global relevance. Local relevance concerns the relationships of particular propositions that occur at single stages of an argument. Local relevance may pertain to the relationship between a question and an answer in dialogue. Or it may pertain to the relationship between a pair of propositions in an argument.

Within both local and global relevance, there are two basic ways a premise may be said to be relevant to a conclusion. First, there is subject-matter relatedness. Here we need to ask whether the premise is connected to the conclusion by sharing some common subject matters. Second, there is *probative relevance,* which plays some part in proving or disproving the thesis at issue. Here we need to ask whether the premise plays some role in counting towards or against the conclusion at issue.[3]

There are two separate types of relevance to check for. A premise could be subject-matter-related to a conclusion without playing any part in proving or disproving the conclusion in the argument. For example 'Bob has red hair' and 'Bob is guilty of aiding a criminal' are subject-matter-related because both share the topic 'Bob'. But it may be that 'Bob has red hair' does not play any part in proving or disproving the contention that Bob is guilty of aiding a criminal, in the argument under discussion. On the other hand, the proposition 'Bob was seen selling weapons to Harry, a known criminal' may be relevant to the proposition 'Bob is guilty of aiding a criminal' in both types of relevance in an argument.

We can sum up by generalizing that there are four types of relevance to be considered:

---

3 According to Govier (1985, p. 101), a statement A is relevant to a statement B "if A either counts towards establishing B as true, or counts against establishing B as true." According to Wright and Tohinaka (1984, p. 197), first you should ask whether a premise "has a bearing on the topic by dealing with a related matter" and, second, "[d]oes the premise lend some support to the conclusion?"

Global relevance	Local relevance
Subject–matter relevance	Probative relevance

The proving-or-disproving (probative) kind of relevance was also called *pertinence* in the Middle Ages. According to the medieval logician William of Sherwood (see Walton, 1982, p. 63), a *pertinent* statement is one that either follows from what precedes or is logically repugnant to what precedes. What William presumably meant is that relevance should be judged in relation to the previous statements that an arguer is committed to in the course of dialogue. This would be a partly global conception of relevance.[4] And what makes a proposition probatively relevant is its relationship, either of following logically from or of being inconsistent with this previous set of commitments. At any rate, the notion of proving-or-disproving relevance was recognized in the older traditions of logic.

In addition to the general categories of relevance and irrelevance, the examples we have studied suggest several specific ways in which the *ignoratio elenchi* can be committed in practice. We have distinguished several kinds of criticisms of irrelevance that can be brought against an argument:

1. Drawing the wrong conclusion from one's own argument is the basic type of *ignoratio elenchi* fallacy.
2. Sometimes *ignoratio elenchi* means a failure to refute one's opponent's thesis in a dispute. In a dispute, there are two arguers, and the thesis of one is the opposite of the other. One variant of the *ignoratio elenchi* (called misconception of refutation by Aristotle) occurs when the argument of one disputant fails to refute or provide reasonable evidence against the thesis of the other disputant.
3. A type of *ignoratio elenchi* we did not mention occurs when the whole issue is changed by introducing a distracting parallel that may not be relevant. Suppose in a criminal trial that the defense attorney proposes that the real issue is discrimination, because the defendant belongs to an ethnic minority. Care may be needed if that is not the real issue at all, for, if the jury gets so excited over the issue of discrimination as a generally interesting topic, they may lose sight of the real issue.
4. One extreme form of irrelevance is the failure of subject-matter overlap.

4 The conception is partly global because a proposition has to be locally related only to the previous propositions in the argument, not the propositions that may occur in subsequent dialogue.

If some of the propositions introduced in an argument are so irrelevant that they do not even share common subject matters with the proposition to be established, then the relevance of these propositions may reasonably be challenged.

5. One type of *ignoratio elenchi* occurs when an arguer exaggerates the conclusion his opponent is supposed to prove.
6. Sometimes the conclusion of an argument is gotten wrong because the fact that the conclusion is a complex proposition is overlooked. For example, a conditional proposition may be incorrectly treated as a simple proposition.
7. Sometimes the focus of a charge of irrelevance falls more onto the premises than onto the conclusion. In this case, the arguer may build a good case up to a point and then introduce additional premises that go "off the track."

Each of these seven types of criticisms of irrelevance has the common, root idea that every reasonable dialogue should be about an issue or controversy. That is, each arguer must have a side, a thesis, or a conclusion to be proved in the argument. When he tends to stray away from this task, his argument can become open to a charge of irrelevance.

It is most important to remember, however, that charges of irrelevance can sometimes be successfully replied to by someone who defends his argument. Until a dialogue is concluded, an arguer may be able to vindicate his argument as relevant, once he has filled in more steps. Therefore, most often, irrelevance is best treated as a criticism that can, in some instances, be replied to, rather than as a fallacy or knock-down refutation of an argument. Thus a criticism of irrelevance that occurs in the middle of an ongoing argument is often best treated as a procedural point of order requesting an arguer to show why his contention is relevant to the issue under dispute. Such a request, if reasonable, must be replied to if the arguer wants to avoid the failure of his argument in reasonable dialogue on grounds of irrelevance.

Relevance in argumentation presupposes that an agenda has been set before the actual stage of engaging in the dispute itself. Practically speaking, however, this precondition may not be met, or interpreted correctly or unanimously by all parties to the dispute at the confrontation stage. Another practical problem is that even if the agenda is set and relevance is theoretically well defined, an opportunity may yet remain to consider whether a point is relevant enough to merit extended time for discussion. Ruling in a particular case may require the good judgment of a mediator who can sensitively interpret the goals of the dialogue, the urgency of the debate, the relative importance of the main concerns that should be aired in the debate, and the standards of strictness of relevance best suited to the context of dialogue.

Many of the fallacies studied in the subsequent chapters are specific failures of relevance in argumentation that are powerful tricks for distracting an opponent.

4

Appeals to emotion

Argumentation that takes place in the conversational marketplace of everyday, persuasive appeals is heavily interlaced with emotional overtones and suggestions. As an example, successful advertising seems for the most part to consist of well-orchestrated appeals to emotions. And it is quite plausible to suggest that many political debates and controversies are decided as much on the basis of emotional appeals and loyalties as on purely dispassionate reasoning.

Personal attack is often so successful as an argument tactic because of its hot appeal to personal emotions, as Chapter 6 will indicate. However, in this chapter we turn to several other types of argument that have traditionally been regarded as problematic or fallacious because they use the pull of certain basic emotions. We will be concerned mainly with the emotions of pity, fear, and group solidarity.

Popular rhetoric is argument designed to persuade a target audience or readership. The objective is to build a personal bond with this audience, to establish a personal link between the arguer and the recipient of his message. The successful building of this emotional relationship invites the person to whom the argument is directed to trust the person who addresses him, to give him loyalty, and to suspend the queries and criticisms characteristic of argument and reasonable dialogue. Personal rhetoric is therefore directed more to the instincts than to calculative reason. The emotional appeal targets the person's unthinking reactions, and so attempts to bypass the critical questioning and logical assessment normally characteristic of reasonable dialogue. Too often, such appeals are tactics that violate the first of the negative rules of persuasion dialogue in Chapter 1. That is, they are attempts to successfully avoid any serious effort at fulfilling the obligation to meet a burden of proof in argument.

Traditionally, appeals to emotion in argument have been distrusted and even labeled categorically as logical fallacies. There is a common tendency to contrast "impartial reason" with "the passions" and to distrust the latter in reasoned argument. And this tendency is often affirmed in logic texts where appeals to emotion have been treated as inherently illogical and subject to strong censure.[1]

However, some decisions to act on an emotional reaction, like fear, can turn out to be sound and justified conclusions that have survival value. Moreover, many arguments on controversial issues, for example in politics and religion, may quite rightly be based on passionate conviction. Especially when morals and values are involved, to ignore our "decent instincts" may be to overlook some of the best reasons for adopting a certain position. And it is a given of democratic politics in free countries that political loyalty based on instincts or appeal to deep, emotional wellsprings of conviction may be a legitimate and important part of election speeches and political dialogue. Lincoln's speeches were deeply emotional, but that should not lead us to conclude that they were inherently fallacious or illogical. Far from it. Because they do appeal to our deep instincts on what is right, their arguments are judged more compelling and important.

Hence it is not always easy to sort out when emotional appeals in argument should be properly subject to criticism on logical grounds. Practical decisions to act are often rightly made on the basis of personal experience, which may manifest itself in emotions or a "gut feeling" about the best way to proceed. There is nothing wrong with this, and in many cases practical skill and experience may be the best guides. A technical expert who gives you advice on how to solve a problem, based on his instinctive feeling about the best course of action, may be giving you the best advice (external proof) you could get.

But one problem with emotional appeals is that they tend to be inherently weak (plausible) arguments. And if stronger and more objective arguments are also available, the problem is not to overlook them and be seduced by the more attractive pull of personal emotions and interests. Hence emotional appeals can induce a failure to ask the right questions, or mask a failure to back up an argument properly (negative rules 6 and 4 in Section 1.4). Appeals to emotions are powerful distractions that can be used to cover any of the failures described by the negative rules of persuasion dialogue in Chapter 1.

---

1 See Hamblin (1970) and Walton (1987).

4.1 ARGUMENTUM AD POPULUM

The *ad populum* (to the people) fallacy is traditionally characterized as the use of appeal to mass enthusiasms or popular sentiments in order to win assent for the conclusion of an argument not supported by good evidence. One can easily appreciate the effectiveness of this sort of strategy in argument. Most of us like to think that our views are in line with popular trends, and any feeling that we are left out of the accepted styles or leading opinions of the day would not be welcome. Any arguer who is in the business of public persuasion would not get very far if he were ignorant of the popular beliefs and accepted views of his target audience.

One type of example of persuasive argument often cited as a case of *ad populum* appeal is the commercial advertisement:

Example 4.0

A television commercial for life insurance portrays a scene of a happy, handsome family having a picnic on a river bank. They are fishing in the river and generally having a good time together. The commercial message is a series of slogans about happy family life, including phrases like "peace of mind today" and "security for the future." The insurance company is described as a place where the family and the insurance agent can "work things out together." No mention is made of the types of policies available, the interest rates paid on these policies, or other specifics for anyone interested in shopping for the best insurance coverage at reasonable rates.

The reason commercial messages of this sort are often cited as instances of the *ad populum* fallacy is not hard to appreciate. Clearly the scene portrayed in the commercial is carefully produced to appeal winningly to popular sentiment. The insurance agent is portrayed as a fatherly man whom one would be inclined to trust, and so forth. But in its exclusive preoccupation with this appeal, the commercial message has failed to give us any useful information about the relative merits of the policies of the agent's company. The folksy appeal of the commercial hits the heartstrings of its target audience but does not give us any information about the relevant aspects of insurance policies that should play a role in a reasonable person's decision to take out a form of coverage from this company.

What seems most fallacious or open to criticism about this sort of commercial message is what it lacks. The appeal to sentiment need not necessarily, in itself, be a bad thing. But the fact that it is a substitute for genuinely useful information makes the appeal to sentiment open to criticism. Our criticism may then be that the appeal to sentiment in the portrayal of the happy family scene is actually irrelevant, or only marginally relevant, to the real issue that the commercial message should address. Is the insurance coverage by this company a good buy that offers advantages over the competition? The whole commercial seems to be a systematic evasion of the issue. In other words, the *ad populum* fallacy here seems to be a failure of relevance (negative argumentation rule 5 of Section 1.4).

If the insurance company were addressed with this criticism, how do you think it might reply? It might respond that it is in the business of selling insurance, and to do that it must be competitive. It must draw attention to its product. The company evidently has come to the conclusion that the best way to do this is to present a commercial that has popular appeal. Perhaps it might say that, if the commercial simply gave the facts and figures about interest rates and coverage benefits, the public would be bored, and the company's competitors would do better business by presenting more lively commercials. After all, the time to discuss facts, figures, and rates, the company might say, is when you talk personally with your insurance agent. Hence, it might argue, in a commercial message on television, the popular appeal type of approach is not irrelevant and not fallacious.

What is one to say to this type of reply? First, one should acknowledge that the reply is based on two sound points about allegations of emotional fallacies.

The first point is that there is nothing wrong per se with an appeal to popular sentiment.[2] Sometimes we do decide to trust people based on our instincts, and that is not necessarily bad in every case, even though it is wise to be careful about whom you trust. No business in a mass market can be successful unless its products are popular. There is nothing wrong in trying to appeal to a popular audience or constituency, and in fact it can sometimes be commendable and reasonable. So we should concede that the insurance company is not necessarily being fallacious by competitively drawing popular attention to its product.

The second point is that, if the insurance company is only trying to direct attention to its product and the company, it may not even

2 See the discussion of this point in Walton (1987).

be trying to present an objective argument – premises and conclusion containing information about its policies and so forth – in its commercial message. Instead of fulfilling a burden of proof, perhaps all the commercial is really trying to say is, "Trust us. We are a large, reliable company with values that you share. Next time you are shopping for insurance, consider us." Notice that, if this is the message, it is not even clear that it is an argument designed to persuade the viewer of the benefits of this company's insurance policies. Instead, it is a subjective appeal to the customer to accept this insurance company as trustworthy and reliable. If this is right, then it is not so clear that the insurance company's appeal to emotion is irrelevant. It depends on what the purpose of the commercial is, or should be, as a type of argumentation.

The problem here is that the insurance company's message seemed to be fallacious because the appeal to popular sentiment is an irrelevant argument. But if the company's replies to this objection are acceptable, perhaps it was not trying to argue for the benefits of its policies at all. In short, if there is no burden of objective proof, there may be no fallacy of irrelevance. Or at any rate, it may be not so easy or straightforward to pin down exactly what the alleged fallacy consists of, and the replies open to the defender of a popular appeal like example 4.0 may contain some reasonable points.

Nevertheless, the bottom line is that many of us may justifiably feel that there has been an evasion in this type of popular appeal. True, the insurance company message may have to include emotional, popular appeals in order to be competitive, but surely it should also include some relevant facts about the insurance of this company for the intelligent consumer. Instead of appealing to the lowest common denominator, the message should contain useful information. Anyone who feels that the value of this company's insurance to the consumer is the real issue has the basis of a criticism of irrelevance. Even if the fallacy is not just the use of an emotional appeal in itself, still, one might reply, the fallacy could be the evasion of a burden of proof where there should be objective argument given about the value of this company's product.

In short, then, the issue comes down to the question of whether there ought to be a reasonable burden of proof on the insurance company to supply information in its commercials over and above the emotional appeals. If so, then an *ad populum* criticism is justified.

If not, then this criticism could be defended against with some justification.

So far, what can be open to criticism in an *ad populum* argument is the use of popular emotional appeal to disguise a failure to address the real issue of an argument. But such criticisms must be evaluated with care, because there can still be opportunity at the confrontation stage of an argument to determine what the real issue is. What is the proper agenda of a television commercial? Is it to persuade the viewer to buy a product on its merits, or is it only a vehicle to draw attention to the product, to give "brand name recognition"? The viewer who uncritically accepts the commercial message for something it is not could be failing to ask the right questions and ignoring better sources of evidence that would enable him to arrive at an informed decision. This failure may not be so much a fallacy as simply a blunder.

4.2 THE ARGUMENT FROM POPULARITY

One of the most common types of argument cited as an instance of the *ad populum* fallacy is the political speech of the "cracker barrel" or "down home" type. For example, suppose a political candidate who has a Ph.D. in economics is addressing a group of local farmers in a rural riding. The politician has a "hobby farm" to supplement his income as a consultant and university professor. Part of his speech runs as follows:

Example 4.1

The other day when I was out working in the fields, seeing the sun glinting on the wheat, I reflected on how hard it has become for the farm producer to make a living. We farmers are the food suppliers of the nation, and we've got to stand solidly on the side of freedom against the collectivists and other parasites that are ripping us off with higher taxes and restrictive marketing regulations. We good citizens, the producers who work the land to feed the nation, must stand together to fight for our rights and the interests of the middle majority of productive contributors to our standard of living in this great country.

It is easy to spot the phony aspect of this argument, and no doubt its intended audience would perceive it as well. The speaker is not really a full-time working farmer, but he tries to pose as one in order to appeal to a sympathetic feeling of group solidarity in his audience. What, then, is the fallacy?

Well, of course, one criticism is that the speaker is just not a real farmer, so his appeal is based on a false posture, a kind of hypocrisy or lie. We feel that he may be talking down to his audience because of his phony posture and heavy-handed attempts to enlist sympathy. However, these faults are not necessarily fallacies, or even incorrect arguments. It may be simply that the man's attempt at persuasive rhetoric is clumsy and unconvincing. It is not that an appeal to group solidarity is intrinsically wrong or fallacious; it is just that this man's attempt at it is bad. What may be wrong is not so much fallacious argument as simply bad speechmaking, which is not necessarily a failure of logic but a failure to communicate with this audience.

Of course, the argument could be a failure of relevance. But perhaps there was no set thesis or conclusion for the speech, so that is not the problem.

What could be wrong, alternatively, is that the speaker has tried too hard to zero in on the position of this audience by appealing to their pride and interests exclusively and transparently, even to the point of trying to pass himself off, somewhat weakly, as a member of the audience. Just as the *ad hominem* argument, as we saw, appealed to the personal position of the opposing party, so the *ad populum* argument targets the position of the specific group to whom it is directed in persuasion. Instead of advancing objective premises that any reasonable person should accept, the *ad populum* argument uses premises that may be weak but that have strong rhetorical appeal to the sentiments of group solidarity of an audience. Surely such a selectively subjective appeal is open to the charge of being fallacious.

But is it? We will see in Chapter 6 that the *ad hominem* argument, despite its being directed to a particular arguer's position, is not always fallacious. The same could be said here.

In a democratic country, any stance or argument taken by a politician will be successful in the political forum of debate only if it positively appeals to a broad majority of constituents. Hence popular appeal to a majority, or to a particular audience of constituents, is not an absolutely wrong objective in a politician's argument. We saw that in persuasion dialogue (critical discussion), arguments are properly directed to the opponent's position. In political debate, if a politician wants to convince an audience of his stance on an issue, he had better use propositions as premises that this audience is committed to, or can be convinced to accept. In democratic countries, political debate is essentially an adversarial arena, and the successful politician must carefully address his argument to the audience he wants to convince to support his position. There is nothing wrong with this partisan element of democratic political argumentation in itself. It becomes fallacious, or at least open to criticism, only when it is subject to particular abuses or excesses. So what are the errors connected with the *ad populum* appeal?

One argument that is implicit in the *ad populum* appeal is that, broadly speaking, popular belief does not establish the truth of a matter. In other words, the following two inference forms are not, in general, deductively valid:

(P1) Everybody accepts that A is true.

Therefore, A is true.

(P2) Nobody accepts that A is true.

Therefore, A is false.

We could call (P1) and (P2) the basic forms of the *argument from popularity*. Then an argument could be criticized as a weak argument from popularity if it treats either of (P1) or (P2) as being deductively valid or as being a stronger argument than the evidence merits. In other words, if all the arguer has to offer as premises for his conclusion that A is true (or false) is the evidence that many people accept A as true (or that nobody accepts A as true), then his argument is likely to be a weak one. Certainly it is not, in general, deductively valid. So if he treats the argument as a strong one, or even as a valid one, he commits a significant misjudgment, and his argument should be open to reasonable criticism.

However, we must be careful here. Although (P1) and (P2) are not deductively valid forms of argument, they can represent weaker forms of argument that can reasonably shift the burden of proof in dialogue. If I propose to argue for a proposition that virtually everyone rejects as false or wildly implausible, then the burden of proof that should be imposed against me should be much stronger than if I propose to argue for a conclusion that virtually everyone accepts as highly plausible, or even certainly true.

Similarly, (P1) and (P2) are weak arguments in some cases that nevertheless have some plausibility value in directing a person to-

89

ward a particular line of action when objective knowledge of the facts is lacking, yet a practical decision must be made. For example, if I am late for my train and do not know where the train platform is located, I may be guided by seeing everybody else in the area heading toward a tunnel. Suppose I ask someone to direct me to the platform and he replies, 'Everyone is heading for the platform. They are all going through that tunnel'. Now this person could be wrong, or he could be misleading me. But unless I have reason to think that this is so, it is reasonable to act on the presumption that he is probably (or plausibly) right and giving me good advice. Hence (P1) and (P2) are weak, but sometimes reasonable types of argumentation. So *ad populum* arguments are not inherently wrong, but because they are weak can easily go wrong in various ways.

Thus the traditional *ad populum* fallacy is most often a combination of two main kinds of errors in argument. One is the fault of irrelevance. The other is the misuse of the argument from popularity, a weak argument that may be overestimated, or taken as more compelling than it should be. The two errors are often combined, because a weak argument may divert our attention from more relevant considerations or mask the fact that these other arguments are lacking and have not been considered.

4.3 PROBLEMS WITH APPEALS TO POPULARITY

Operating on the basis of a consensus of what the majority wants, or what the majority does, is a common way of deciding how to act. There is nothing inherently wrong with it as a kind of argument to decide how to act personally. But there are often specific problems with how this type of argument from popularity may be used to try to persuade someone to act in a similar fashion.

Politicians often try to persuade people to follow their policies because, they claim, that is what the majority of citizens now want. But do they? Polls may be appealed to, but public opinion can be fickle and change fast. It may be better political wisdom to look deeper and explore the reasons for a particular policy, or even to stick to an unpopular conclusion, for what is now popular has a way of becoming unpopular when circumstances change.

Often, arguments from popularity contain an appeal to what is currently accepted as a custom or standard of behavior in a group the arguer wants to identify with or cite as an authoritative source of norms. But too often there is an element of "peer pressure" implicit in these arguments. Consider example 4.2:

Example 4.2

Mother: I thought you would say 'Thank you' for all the work I put into planning your birthday party.

Daughter: Mom, people just don't talk that way any more these days.

No doubt the daughter feels that she has had the last word on the issue. But if her claim is true that the people she associates with do not have the sensitivity or good manners to say 'Thanks' when thanks are due, it may simply be a reflection of their lack of good values or immaturity. So identification with the group should not be the final word. The question remains whether the group values or standards can be justified.

If some practice is accepted as a custom or standard by a dominant or popular group, it may take a strong argument to go against this establishment of cited precedents. But there are always exceptions to customs, and there may be opposing groups who have a different custom. Often, the argument comes down to whose group is more "progressive" or trendy, that is, in line with currently accepted views. But claims of whose group is more dominant at any particular time may be hard to support with real evidence. And even if evidence is given, there remains the question of whether the group practice cited can be justified as a good or reasonable standard of behavior.

In some cases the argument from popularity is mixed with a kind of weak appeal to authority. The argument is that everybody who is knowledgeable, civilized, enlightened, etc., is doing it; therefore, you should be doing it too:

Example 4.3

If we vote to return the death penalty in Canada, we, along with a few states, will be the only jurisdictions in the Western world with a death penalty. Not one country in Europe has a death penalty. New Zealand doesn't have it. Australia doesn't have it. It is on the books in Belgium, but there hasn't been an execution in that country since 1945. It is abolished in all other Western countries. We will be joining countries like Africa and Turkey that are not models of democratic civilization or human rights.[3]

By arguing that all civilized countries ban capital punishment and suggesting that countries with capital punishment may be less civilized, this argument uses the bandwagon strategy to try to create a presumption against capital punishment. However, even if the arguer's statistics are right that most Western countries do not have capital punishment, it may be questioned whether these countries are the only countries that are models of democratic civilization and human rights. But even if this argument were to be conceded, the possibility exists that these countries might change their policies if strong arguments for capital punishment in the present context of law enforcement were brought forward by its leading advocates. If these countries do not have capital punishment, then they must have reasons for this policy, or at any rate, arguments can be given either for or against these policies. The important thing, then, is to examine the arguments rather than simply assume that these countries must be right because they are "models of democratic civilization." Thus this appeal to popularity is a weak argument at best.

Yet another type of problem with popular appeal can occur when a speaker tries to subvert or shut down reasonable dialogue by closing the audience's reception to any possible contrary viewpoint. This can occur when an arguer tries to appeal to bonds to unite himself with his audience in a common cause and exclude outsiders from the mutual interest group. The outsiders are portrayed as potential enemies whom we must not listen to or allow into consideration. It is as though the argument gives the message that what is important is group solidarity, so that any possibly contrary point of view in dialogue must be excluded at the outset, or given no attention.

An example of this type of popular appeal rhetoric is provided by Bailey (1983, p. 134), who quotes a speech of Walter Reuther in 1957 on the topic of racketeering in trade unions:

3 This example is based on an argument the author heard in a televised interview with a politician on the CBC program *This Week in Parliament*, February 28, 1987.

Example 4.4

I think we can all agree that the overwhelming majority of the leadership of the American movement is composed of decent, honest, dedicated people who have made a great contribution involving great personal sacrifice, helping to build a decent American labor movement. . . . We happen to believe that leadership in the American movement is a sacred trust. We happen to believe that this is no place for people who want to use the labor movement to make a fast buck.

A reasonable observation about this speech is that it attempts to put its conclusion beyond question by portraying it as a fact with which everyone must agree. In effect, then, the listener is left no room for further argument. The *ad populum* message cuts off reasonable dialogue. The "we" who accept the movement are included. The "people who want to . . . make a fast buck" are excluded. In other words, either you join the labor movement position or you are an offending outsider who is immoral and against the movement. Those are your choices. As Bailey (1983, p. 135) comments, this type of *ad populum* tactic is the "rhetoric of belonging." If you do not belong, then your word is worthless, and your point of view is of no account.

What is objectionable in this type of *ad populum* appeal is not only that the argument is weak in the way the previous types of *ad populum* arguments we noted are, but also that there is an attempt to thwart or seal off the argument and reasonable dialogue, and dogmatically enforce one's own position. The tactic open to criticism here is the unreasonable exclusion of further argument. It is a problem of premature closure of dialogue that violates the rule for the closing stage, the last of the negative rules of persuasion dialogue given in Section 1.4.

4.4 THREATENING APPEALS TO FORCE

The *ad baculum* fallacy is traditionally said to be the resort to force or the threat of force to make someone accept the conclusion of an argument. *Ad baculum* literally means (to the stick or club). The examples often given for this type of fallacy cite the use of "strong-arm methods" and "goon squads":

93

Example 4.5

According to R. Grunberger, author of *A Social History of the Third Reich*, published in Britain, the Nazis used to send the following notice to German readers who let their subscriptions lapse: "Our paper certainly deserves the support of every German. We shall continue to forward copies of it to you, and hope that you will not want to expose yourself to unfortunate consequences in the case of cancellation." (*Parade*, May 9, 1971)[4]

One can easily see why this sort of threat or appeal to force is contrary to the aims and methods of reasonable dialogue. In reasonable dialogue, an arguer should have the freedom to decide for himself whether to accept a conclusion based on the argument for or against it. The threat of force no longer leaves these options open to reason, and tries to close off the possibilities of free dialogue.

On the other hand, an appeal to force can, in some instances, be not altogether unreasonable. For example, there are laws in some countries that impose severe penalties for convictions of drunken driving. Although such laws do seem to constitute an appeal to force or to the threat of forceful intervention, it could be argued that they are not unreasonable. It could be argued that such laws are both fair and necessary, and that appeal to them in arguing against drunken driving in public service messages is not fallacious. Certainly, it is not clear why reminding the public of these laws in order to discourage drunken driving should be regarded as a fallacious argument.

Let us go back to example 4.5. What is fallacious about that argument that is not fallacious in the drunken driving case? One suggestion is that the argument in example 4.5 describes an ugly, menacing threat that would terrorize its recipient, unlike the other case, in which it is only a warning, not a threat that is conveyed. But what is the difference between a threat and a warning? If the penalty for drunken driving is a two-year sentence in jail or on a work detail, that may be extremely threatening if directed to most of us. Generally, whether something is a threat or a warning may depend on how it is taken, and that seems variable and hard to predict in many cases. Granted, warning someone of danger or dangerous

---

4 Example 4.5 first came to the author's attention in Irving M. Copi, *Introduction to Logic*, where it was cited as an instance of the *ad baculum* fallacy.

consequences may not be fallacious at all, but in both cases above there does seem to be a threat or use of force, as well as a warning.

Perhaps we are inclined to see a significant difference between the two cases because we think that the one penalty is reasonable whereas the other is not. Most of us probably think that a good case can be made for having severe penalties for drunken driving. But we feel that everyone should have the freedom to make up his own mind about what newspaper to read. Using the threat of force to compel someone to read a particular newspaper is just not fair or reasonable.

However, this distinction is a matter of opinion. In some countries, for example in the USSR, readers are not given a choice. *Pravda* is the official news source, and foreign papers are forcefully excluded by law. Does this mean that an *ad baculum* argument could be fallacious in the United States but nonfallacious in the USSR? Such a conclusion is not acceptable. The distinction between an argument that is fallacious and one that is not must rest on more than just opinions about what is reasonable or what laws are fair. So it is not easy to tell exactly what is the significant difference between these two cases of appeal to force. What makes one possibly legitimate while the other is not?

Perhaps the key difference is that we feel that the penalty for drunken driving is, or can be, based on reasonable arguments that could, at least to some extent, be challenged or backed up by reasonable dialogue. However, the context of example 4.5 suggests that, if one were to try to reason with the Nazi newspaper vendors, one would expect to get beaten up, or perhaps put in a concentration camp. But in the other case, even though a law against drunken driving is enforced, if one were to question its fairness one could expect to be given reasons why this law is reasonable. In short, then, the Nazi notice is essentially a nonrational type of intimidation because no argument as to why one should reasonably subscribe to this newspaper is given, and no challenge or questioning of any such argument would be tolerated, at least, so one may reasonably presume from the context of example 4.5. Hence the problem here is similar to the type of *ad populum* argument we considered (example 4.4) in which the illicit tactic was the attempt to close off reasonable dialogue prematurely. In the drunken driving case, the law also is forceful but at least leaves open the reasonable consideration of the basis for or reasoning behind this law. You may have to follow the law, but you are allowed to question or discuss its reasonableness without fear of force.

These two examples indicate that appeals to force must be examined carefully, for not all are fallacious. And one must be prepared to state clearly why a particular appeal to force is to be criticized as an instance of an *ad baculum* error or fault in argument.

We saw that the *ad baculum* fallacy has been described as the threat of force. But one must be careful, in some cases, to distinguish between a threat and a warning. Suppose Lois is a newspaper reporter investigating a possible case of criminal conspiracy. A person she is interviewing makes the following remarks:

Example 4.6

I would be very careful if I were you. Pursuing this story further could be very dangerous. Recently someone else who was investigating these same people was run over by a bulldozer after his family had been threatened.

Now, if these remarks are taken as a threat, it could be quite reasonable to propose that they might constitute an instance of an erroneous *ad baculum* argument. But much depends on who the speaker is, what the reporter knows about him, and the tone of voice he uses to convey these remarks. It could be that the speaker is sincerely concerned about the safety of the reporter and is trying, perhaps even at risk to himself, to warn her of the danger in her present course of action. If so, his remarks could best be interpreted as a warning, and not as a threat at all. Perhaps they were not meant as a threat and should not reasonably be so taken. If that is the right interpretation, then a criticism that the speaker has committed an *ad baculum* fallacy would be unwarranted and incorrect. Here, it depends on what type of speech event is involved in the dialogue to determine whether the speech act is that of a threat or a warning.

Commonly, there may be a fairly reasonable presumption that an argument contains a threat but little unequivocal evidence of a threat that can be clearly documented. Most threats are veiled because a frank threat could result in legal or other recriminations. Thus, even when it is reasonably clear that a threat has been made, citing irrefutable evidence of this may be problematic or even impossible:

Example 4.7

Oral Roberts, the fundamentalist preacher cited a deadline from God that he must raise eight million dollars in one year, by March 31, or die. Reverend Roberts retired to his Prayer Tower to fast and pray for the money. The evangelist said on his national television program that his life would end at the end of March if the money was not raised by then: "I'm going to be in and out of the Prayer Tower until victory comes or God calls me home."[5]

Now does this plea for funds contain a threat or not? Most of us would be inclined to interpret Reverend Roberts's statements as containing a kind of threat. But no doubt he might deny that this was so, claiming that the outcome was in God's hands.

On the other hand, Reverend Roberts's speech takes the classic form of a threatening argument: 'Either do this or something bad will happen'. But is this his argument? The question of whether he has committed an *ad baculum* fallacy rests on this question of interpretation of his speech act.

4.5 FURTHER *AD BACULUM* PROBLEMS

One problem the *ad baculum* appeal shares with other emotional appeals is that it may not be clear that a decision arrived at on the basis of emotion or instinct is really an argument. The suspicion may be that the decision was based on fear, self-interest, self-preservation, or instinct rather than on evidence at all.

Animal behavior is often described in terms of instincts. In many cases, it also seems natural to describe behavior as a kind of reasoning process ascribed to the animal in which one emotion overcomes another:

Example 4.8

A bird being photographed by a naturalist alights at the mouth of its burrow in the bed of a creek with a minnow to feed its chicks. Afraid of the photographer's camera light, the mother bird backs away, and flies off. Returning several minutes later, it approaches a chick and gives it the fish. The commentator describes the situation by saying that the mother bird's maternal instinct overcame its fear of the camera light.

5 Associated Press Report, "Roberts Ransom Assured," *Winnipeg Free Press*, March 22, 1987, p. 1.

Could the bird be engaging in a kind of practical (goal-driven) reasoning based on its instincts and perceptions of a situation? If so, then many an emotional appeal may be based on a kind of argument or reasoning, rather than being a replacement of reason by emotion. Much depends on what we are prepared to call "reasoning" in this type of situation.

In the same way, the prisoner who "confesses" under threats or the fear of force may not be illogical or have thrown argument to the winds and embraced emotions. He may simply be responding to a different kind of argument or basing his decision on a kind of practical reasoning that puts survival over telling the truth, at least for the moment. So there are questions here about the *ad baculum* appeal as a kind of argument.[6] It may involve a kind of argument or reasoning that we are not familiar with in traditional logic and that is difficult to interpret because of its emotional and instinctive nature. But whether it is reasoning or not, it is a powerful tactic used in argument and a common way of arriving at a course of action.

The lesson is that the *ad baculum* appeal is used as a tactic in argument to influence unduly an opponent in dialogue. When this type of tactic is used, it is not always necessary to determine whether it is itself a special kind of reasoning. What is important is to try to see how it is being used as a strategy of argumentation that may violate one or more of the negative rules of persuasion dialogue.

The types of problems that can be identified with *ad baculum* appeals are often similar to the varieties of *ad populum* problems. Sometimes the threat of force is used as an emotional distraction that is irrelevant to the real issue. Therefore, in approaching discourse having an *ad baculum* appeal, it is important to try to identify the conclusion that is supposed to be proved. And therefore identifying the argument containing the *ad baculum* appeal can be important.

We may have a case in which there is a threat, but the threat may not necessarily be used as an argument, or part of an argument, to persuade somebody to do something or to influence him with regard to a conclusion at issue. The person who admittedly made the threat may argue – in some cases with reason – that there was no connection between the threat and the conclusion at issue:

6 See also Walton (1987).

Example 4.9

Ed Brutus, gangland figure, is accused of using threats to force Shakey Trembler, owner of a chain of pizza outlets, to make him a partner in the pizza business. Mr. Brutus acknowledges that he had threatened to use physical violence against Mr. Trembler. However, he argues that his threat was a response to Mr. Trembler's failure to pay back a loan.

Could Mr. Brutus have a reasonable argument to defend himself against a charge of using threats to force Mr. Trembler illegally to enter into a business contract with him? Each case must be decided on its own merits, but here we should allow that it is possible that Mr. Brutus's threat was not intended to force Mr. Trembler to make him a partner.

What this shows is that, just because a threat has been made, it does not necessarily follow that an *ad baculum* fallacy can be declared or claimed to have been committed in relation to a specific argument or case. There may be a threat, but the threat may not be related in the right way to the conclusion advanced by an arguer for us to claim with justification that an *ad baculum* fallacy has been committed. If an allegation of *ad baculum* fallacy has been made, but there is a failure of relevance between the threat issued by an arguer and the conclusion of his argument in a case, then the *ad baculum* allegation itself is a failure of rule 5 of the negative rules of persuasion dialogue listed in Section 1.4. Other violations of these rules could also be involved in differing cases of the *ad baculum* fallacy.

Intimidation has been used as a tactic not only to divert an argument, but even to try to prevent the argument from getting started or to prevent the procedure of dialogue from getting underway:[7]

Example 4.10

The trial of the terrorist group Direct Action was delayed in the French courts because of jury intimidation. The defendant threatened the jury with the "rigors of proletarian justice," on the first day of his trial, by asking, "I would like to know how long security measures will continue to be applied to the jurors?" Direct Action claimed responsibility for many recent terrorist attacks in France, and police suspected that the recent murder of a French auto executive was intended to

7 Fred Coleman, "A Threat of Proletarian Justice," *Newsweek*, December 22, 1986, p. 38.

99

frighten this jury. Evidently, the intimidation tactics were successful, for the trial had to be indefinitely delayed because so many jurors failed to appear in court.

In this case, the question asked by the defendant does not explicitly state that the jurors will be harmed. Semantically speaking, his question is about security measures. However, quite clearly the jury members would take this question as a serious threat. And indeed, they would have good reason to take it that way in view of what is known or suspected about the activities of the Direct Action group.

In this case, the question can be seen as a breach of procedures of reasonable dialogue, because the defendant has used it as a tactic to convey an emotional message that will have the effect of subverting or closing off the process of dialogue to be undertaken. Here, when the defendant asks his threatening question, it may not be clear that he is in fact arguing, nor may it be clear exactly what his statement amounts to because the threat is implied rather than explicitly articulated. Even so, it is clear that he is blocking off the dialogue by his move, which is a move inimical to reasoned dialogue. Therefore, from the point of view of dialogue as due process in the legal system, the threat offered in the question should be regarded as objectionable and open to criticism, as it relates to the argument to be undertaken in the trial.

The conclusion of the dispute should come from the dialogue, which should guide the jury in arriving at a verdict from the evidence presented in the trial. The *ad baculum* maneuver, in this instance, short-circuits that process of dialogue and thereby prevents the conclusion from being arrived at on the basis of the evidence available. Instead, the issue remains undecided for fear of the jury's safety.

When it is difficult or impossible to pin down a precise set of premises in an *ad baculum* appeal, the emotional petition may not be made up of propositions at all, but other units of speech. For example, a warning may be a proposition, that is, a unit of speech that is, in principle, true or false. But a threat may not be true or false, or meant to be. A warning is a prediction that something will or might happen, and may be true or not. But a threat is not true or false. Threats are evaluated differently, as being convincing or hollow, effective or weak. But they are not, strictly speaking, true or false in the same way that propositions are. So a speaker's remarks that convey threats may not be propositions at all. Hence they may not be an argument, but only part of an accompanying argument. In evaluating *ad baculum* criticisms, one must be careful to examine the justification of an allegation that an appeal to force should be interpreted as a threat. But then, even if there is good evidence of a threat of force, the second step of analysis is to identify a specific failure or fault in the argument if the threat is to be taken as a fallacy. A threat of force may be rude, vicious, illegal, or immoral, but that does not necessarily mean it is a fallacy or subject to criticism as an erroneous, or failed, argument.

The *ad baculum* criticism is appropriate where there is a faulty argument, a violation of some procedure of reasonable dialogue, or at least a criticizable failure to engage in reasonable dialogue. A threat, therefore, is not necessarily a fallacy. Because some speech or action should be condemned, it does not necessarily follow that it should be criticized as illogical, fallacious, bad, or a failure of reasonable argument.

4.6 APPEALS TO PITY

Another type of appeal to emotion is the *ad misericordiam*, or appeal to pity. What can be fallacious about this appeal is the same error that we found in relation to the two previous types of emotional appeals – that it can be used as a distraction from relevant evidence that should be brought forward to support a conclusion. In this respect, the *ad misericordiam* fallacy is just another variant of the *ignoratio elenchi* fallacy except that the special distraction utilized as the *modus operandi* of the irrelevant appeal is the emotion of pity.

Typical examples of the traditional *ad misericordiam* fallacy are the following. In the first, example 4.11, a defense attorney pleads on behalf of his client accused of murder. In example 4.12, a student pleads for a professor to accept her late essay without penalty:

Example 4.11

My client comes from a poor, hard-working family in the poorest part of town. As you can see, he is only a young man, and his physical disabilities and traumatic emotional scars have made life a cruel struggle out there in the jungle of the crime-ridden streets. He is a victim himself, an individual who has been crushed by forces beyond his control.

Example 4.12

I know that this essay is six weeks overdue and the final exam is over, but I have many personal problems. I have a part-time job that I need to scrape together enough money to stay in school, and I have been having emotional problems. The person I have been living with has just left me, and my dog just died. Also, my grandmother is very sick. Even so, I would have handed this essay in earlier, but my typewriter was broken and I could not afford to fix it. Also, I only need this one course to graduate, but if I fail it I can't stay in this country any longer to complete my degree because I have already booked my flight home.

In example 4.11, what should be questioned is whether the attorney is trying to get the jury to forget about the issue of the guilt or innocence of his client on the charge of murder for the robbery-killing of a senior citizen by arousing pity for the defendant's special circumstances. If so, the fallacy is a classical *ignoratio elenchi* that is also an *ad misericordiam* fallacy because the emotion appealed to is that of pity.

Another point about 4.11 is that, since the crime was a vicious one, we may feel that the appeal to pity is inappropriate. But if the crime had been less serious, many of us might feel that the appeal to pity may not be completely irrelevant. As Hamblin (1970, p. 43) has pointed out, more than simple assent to a proposition may be involved when the dialogue is a lawsuit or political speech: "A proposition is presented primarily as a guide to action and, where action is concerned, it is not so clear that pity and other emotions are irrelevant." In example 4.11, we are certainly right to be on our guard lest the powerful appeal to pity distract us from the real issue of whether the defendant is guilty or innocent of the crime he is charged with. But having decided that argument, it could be that his pitiable circumstances are relevant to a decision of whether he should be eligible for leniency in sentencing. On this issue, the appeal to pity might not be irrelevant in every case.

In example 4.12, the professor must decide whether to accept the late essay. It is an ethical decision that must be made on the following grounds: If the student has a note from a physician certifying a medical reason for the delay, or if there is documentable evidence of some other legitimate reason, for example, a death in the immediate family or a traffic accident, then the professor should make, or allow for, special arrangements. However, unless he is satisfied that there is a good reason for making this case an exception, the cost of his accepting the essay may be to discriminate against the other students in the class who dutifully handed the essay in on time, even though some of them may have had special hardships as well. If the professor accepts this one essay on very weak grounds of pity for this one individual, the word will soon circulate that anyone who has a story of some hardship can expect to be able to hand in his essay late: "After all, you let this other person hand in his essay late, and my case is similar to his." This pressure to be consistent in treating similar cases alike is a common type of argument, and we will go on to study it in depth in Chapter 9.

Example 4.12, then, seems to be similar in some respects to example 4.11. The professor should take special circumstances into account in arriving at a decision, but the appeal to pity should not distract from the primary issue – a certain date for the essay had been announced, and the burden of proof is on the student to show why her case should be treated as a legitimate exception. However, it is the professor's job to grade the student on this course, and he should not exempt the student from a reasonable penalty for lateness or give the student a grade she has not academically earned because of her alleged problem with flight bookings. This alleged problem could be verified, and perhaps some action could be recommended to help with the problem, if there is one. What this example shows is that good judgment may be needed to decide the relevance of an appeal to pity in a particular case. Though pity may be relevant in arriving at a decision on a course of action in a particular case, one must be careful to see whether the appeal to pity may not be good grounds for accepting the conclusion of an appellant's argument.

4.7 OVERT, PICTORIAL APPEALS TO PITY

Many charitable pleas for aid or assistance use overt appeals to pity. Example 4.13 below is a full-page advertisement[8] asking readers to send in money for the relief of famine victims in Ethiopia. Much of the space on the page is taken up by a photograph of a pathetically starved, crying child, squatting on a dirty, torn blanket. The appeal to pity virtually leaps out from the photograph of the miserable

8 *Newsweek,* March 4, 1985, p. 75.

child. The text starts with large headlines, reading ETHIOPIA: THE MOST DEVASTATING HUMAN CRISIS OF OUR TIME, and then continues as follows:

Example 4.13

THERE **IS** SOMETHING

YOU CAN DO ABOUT

THIS TRAGEDY . . .

You've seen the news reports . . .

• Thousands of people a day are starving to death!

• More than 6 million people are threatened by starvation.

• More than 100,000 could die from hunger and its related diseases in the next 60 days.

THE TIME FOR ACTION IS NOW!

HERE'S WHAT YOU CAN DO TO HELP!

Your gift of $15 is all it takes to feed a hungry child for a month! Just $30 can feed two children for a month. And $75 will provide emergency food for an entire family of five for a month!

The page concludes with a coupon to send in with your donation.

Example 4.13 is a direct appeal to the emotion of pity, and yet the emotional appeal in this case seems appropriate and justifiable. There is plenty of very good evidence that there is a famine in Ethiopia and that many thousands of innocent people are dying from starvation. We should, indeed, have a sympathetic response to this terrible situation, and it should include pity. Moreover, this emotional, humanitarian response should serve as a basis for action. Scarcely anyone would be inclined to deny all this. In other words, the appeal to pity in this case is not fallacious.

The lesson of this is that we must be very careful not to fall into the trap of concluding hastily that any appeal to pity is an *ad misericordiam* fallacy. Pity is a reasonable, legitimate, humane response in some situations, and the emotion of pity can be a sound and intelligent basis for taking action.

Nevertheless, even in the case of example 4.13 or similar cases, we should be careful to specify exactly what the conclusion of the argument is. We may all agree that the situation in Ethiopia is pitiable and calls for action. But another issue is precisely what form of action should be called for. Getting aid to people in distress is often very difficult, given all the bureaucratic regulations involved in international shipping and the transport problems in countries with few roads or vehicles. Whether the particular agency sponsoring this advertisement for aid is one to get that aid to the famine victims is an issue that should also be considered by anyone who wants to help the famine victims. In this ad, several television celebrities are pictured as "friends" of the agency in question who urge you to "join in this humanitarian effort." If you, as a potential donor, think that the sponsorship of these celebrities is a relatively weak argument for accepting the conclusion that this agency will or can deliver the required aid through your funding, then you may have some further reasonable questions to ask. If you feel that this issue has not been given proportionate attention, or backed up strongly enough by the argument of the advertisement, then you may still have a reasonable basis for an *ad misericordiam* criticism of the advertisement.

4.8 SUMMARY

Although there is a distrust of emotion that has often been remarked upon by philosophers, and continues to be strongly felt, it should be clear that there is nothing fallacious per se about an appeal to emotion. The emotion of fear may have survival value. The emotion of pity can prompt a compassionate response to help someone who is suffering. It is because we are so powerfully moved by our feelings, however, that they can be accorded undue weight in arguments, in which specific errors may take place.

The Roman philosopher Seneca felt that reason could be trusted because it considers only the question at issue, whereas the emotions may be moved by "trifling things that lie outside the case."[9] The basic shortcoming one should look for in any appeal to emotion in argument is that of irrelevance. One must determine what the case or issue of a particular argument is, or should be, and then evaluate the relevance of the emotional appeal to that issue.

Two types of questionable *ad populum* arguments occur (1) when speech acts expressing an irrelevant appeal to popular sentiment are offered instead of relevant premises or (2) when the appeal to popular sentiment could be considered relevant, but weak, and only mas-

9 Seneca, *De ira* I, XVII.5–VIII.2.

querades as a serious effort to fulfill an obligation to prove. Another type of *ad populum* argument that is often open to criticism is the fallacy of popularity, which may take the following two forms of argument as valid as or stronger than they really are:

(P1) Everybody accepts that A is true.

Therefore, A is true.

(P2) Nobody accepts that A is true.

Therefore, A is false.

Both (P1) and (P2) are weak, but sometimes reasonable forms of argument. For example, if a proposition is widely accepted and you have no evidence against it, then if you have to make a decision, it could be more reasonable to presume that it is true than to presume that it is false. But such a presumption is only a matter of plausibility, of not objective proof. If (P1) and (P2) are overrated, an erroneous *ad populum* appeal may have been put forward as a tactic for covering a failure to give adequate proof of what is on the agenda.

Another aspect of what has gone wrong in many *ad populum* arguments is that the speaker has concentrated too exclusively on the commitments of the particular audience he has addressed. Typically, the *ad populum* argument attempts to forge a common bond between the speaker and his audience. It is as if the speaker is saying, 'I am really one of you. We all belong to the same group.' The problem with this type of argument is that there may be no serious attempt to give sufficient proof. The speaker, by reaffirming the audience's commitment, may be generating a cosy climate of emotional solidarity. But we need to ask in such a case whether the speaker is really arguing for the particular conclusion he is supposed to prove. If not, is his affirmation of the audience's commitment even relevant to the conclusion he is supposed to be proving? It could be that he is only trying to plead for the audience to accept that conclusion on purely emotional grounds.

Another type of *ad populum* fallacy can occur when a speaker tries to shut off reasonable dialogue by dividing the world into "us" and "them." The fallacy here is the attempt to exclude or prematurely close off reasonable argument. The *ad baculum* fallacy may take this form as well. The threat of force may be used to suggest that any further reasonable argument will be pointless, or even dangerous. However, one must be careful here to remember that not all appeals to force are fallacious arguments, and sometimes it may be hard to

106

distinguish clearly between a threat and a warning as types of speech acts.

An appeal to pity can be the basis of a legitimate excuse or claim for leniency. So in evaluating such appeals, one must be careful to decide what the real issue is. The appeal to pity should not distract from the primary issue, but it may be legitimate to take it into account in deciding on a course of action in a particular case. Here, as in the case of any emotional appeal, one must try to determine what the real issue of the argument is and evaluate the relevance of the appeal to that issue.

The same kind of approach is needed in relation to arguments containing a threat of force or an appeal to the emotion of fear. In such a case, we must resist the tendency to automatically pronounce the argument a case of the *ad baculum* fallacy. Though it is true that we generally condemn the use of force, and even true that the threat of force may be rightly condemned in a particular case, it by no means follows that anyone who uses the threat of force has committed a logical fallacy. A speaker's utterance may be rude, immoral, illegal, or even brutal without being a fallacious argument or a violation of the rules of argumentation appropriate in a particular case. However, the use of emotional appeals to force may be a critical sign of a weak or irrelevant argument, or even an attempt to subvert reasonable dialogue. Thus any such appeal must be carefully examined by the usual steps of analysis: What is the conclusion that the speaker should be proving? And does the appeal to force come down to a specific set of propositions that might be premises? If so, are the premises relevant to the conclusion? If not, is the argument weak, or even entirely lacking premises? Is the appeal to force being used to convince or persuade the person to whom the argument is directed to accept that conclusion? These are the questions to be asked in approaching a particular case.

The types of emotional appeal we have examined are, to a significant extent, often basically failures of relevance, as studied in Chapter 3. But each of these types of emotional appeal has certain characteristics that make it worth individual study as a type of move in argument to be cautious about. When dialogue has become very emotional and comes too close to the personal level, it is generally a bad sign. The objectives of the argument may be closer to the personal quarrel than to those of reasonable dialogue. The problem may be a dialectical shift from one context to another.

5

Valid arguments

The basic building blocks of arguments are propositions. Propositions, in contrast to questions, commands, challenges, and other moves made in arguments, are units of language that are true or false. Locating the propositions asserted in an argument can be the first positive step in identifying and evaluating the argument. In practice, real arguments are most often macrostructures made of many smaller arguments, or subarguments. Often the best way to get a handle on a large and complex network of argumentation is to identify and clearly state one or more of these subarguments.

For this purpose, it is necessary to understand the concept of valid argument. With this ideal in mind, it can be much easier to organize an argument and to interpret it fairly prior to considering evaluation. And, of course, being able to identify valid arguments is also a useful skill when it comes to evaluating arguments as reasonable or unreasonable.

In this chapter, we will see how, once an argument is identified, the form of the argument can be revealed. Certain forms of argument are valid, while others are invalid. Some characteristic forms of argument are very common in reasoning. To learn to identify these forms is a valuable tool in the business of evaluating arguments reasonably.

Another important concept related to validity is that of inconsistency. To allege that someone has adopted a stance in argument that is logically inconsistent can be a serious and damaging type of criticism. So understanding the logical basis of inconsistency is another valuable tool.

5.1 DEDUCTIVE VALIDITY

Many arguments we are confronted with in realistic contexts of disputation are lengthy, confusing, and incomplete and seem to wander in an unclear direction. Most often, before we can begin to evaluate the argument properly as good or bad, we have a formidable job of trying to determine just what the argument is.

Even though an argument, as a whole, may be very confusing, there are sometimes certain key junctures where a definite conclusion appears to have been reached. A good indicator of such a juncture may be a conclusion indicator like 'therefore', 'hence', 'since', 'accordingly', or 'because'. When this juncture is indicated, we can single out one proposition in an argument as a *conclusion,* a proposition maintained or argued for by the person advancing the argument. A conclusion is argued for on the basis of other propositions also maintained by the arguer, called *premises.* When we find a set of premises and a conclusion in an argument, it means that the arguer has taken a certain stance or position at that point and may be open to criticism. Before advancing any criticism, however, the first requirement is to identify the specific propositions that are the premises and the conclusion.

Suppose that in the middle of an argument on politics, the following sequence of statements is advanced:

Example 5.0

If inflation is receding, the government's economic policies are sound.
Inflation is receding.
Therefore, the government's economic policies are sound.

This part of the argument is made up of three propositions. The first two are premises and the third one is a conclusion. Once we have located this juncture in the argument, we can at least pin something down. These two premises support the conclusion. They give reasons why anyone to whom the argument is directed should accept the conclusion, if he accepts the premises. Of course, he may not accept these premises. And there may be other propositions elsewhere in the argument that give reasons to support these premises. But even so, by identifying the two premises and conclusion, we have identified an argument that may be part of a larger argument.

Another thing to notice is that example 5.0 has a general form or structure that is very common in argumentation. Let A stand for the proposition 'Inflation is receding' and B stand for the proposition 'The government's economic policies are sound'. Then the structure of example 5.0 is revealed as a particular form of argument:

(MP)   If A, then B.
    A.
    Therefore, B.

This form of argument is so common that it has a traditional name, *modus ponens,* or MP. Is it a valid form of argument? The answer depends on how we interpret the conditional (if . . . then) in the first premise. We could interpret the conditional as meaning that it is not true that A is true and B is not true. Under this interpretation, MP is a valid form of argument, for if it is not true that A is true and B is false and if, as the second premise says, A is in fact true, then it must follow that it is not true that B is not true. It follows, by deleting the double negative, that B must be true.

We see then that MP is a valid form of argument, and therefore example 5.0 is a deductively valid argument. What do we mean by *deductively valid argument* here? We mean that, in a deductively valid argument, it is logically impossible for all the premises to be true and the conclusion to be false. In other words, if the premises are true, the conclusion *must* be true, meaning that the conclusion follows from the premise by deductive validity of the argument.

Recognizing that certain forms of argument are deductively valid is a highly valuable tool in the analysis of argumentation. We can use this knowledge to build up sequences of valid arguments; for if each step in the sequence, that is, each individual argument, is deductively valid, then the whole sequence will never take us from true premises to a false conclusion. But even before going on to study how to evaluate arguments, it will be useful to see how knowledge of the form of an argument can be used to identify the argument that is being advanced.

5.2 IDENTIFYING ARGUMENTS

In example 5.0, the conclusion draws our attention to the fact that the arguer has reached a definite stage in his reasoning. The conclusion 'The government's economic policies are sound' is a proposition that the arguer has thought important enough to single out and back up with premises. Discovering this kind of juncture in

110

an argument is a way to identify and locate a key part of the argument that can then be used to help us to reconstruct other parts of it.

In the argument 5.0, the indicator word 'so' enabled us to determine which proposition is being designated by the arguer as his conclusion. But what if there were no indicator word given? Consider the following collection of propositions that might occur as part of an argument:

Example 5.1

Air safety should be given high priority.

If we must try to prevent disastrous accidents, then air safety should be given a high priority.

We must try to prevent disastrous accidents.

When confronted with these propositions, how should we interpret them as an argument? Which proposition is the conclusion? And which propositions are meant to be premises?

To begin with, it seems likely that the arguer would be linking the middle proposition (the conditional) with one of the other propositions in order to deduce the conclusion. Consider what the argument would look like otherwise:

Example 5.2

We must try to prevent disastrous accidents.

Air safety should be given a high priority.

Therefore, if we must try to prevent disastrous accidents, then air safety should be given a high priority.

Do you think that this is a plausible candidate for the argument? It seems not, for even if both premises are true, there is no apparent way to link them together that would justify the conclusion.[1] Could it be that both premises are true, and yet that there might be other

---

1 It might be interesting to note that argument 5.2 would have a valid form of argument according to some formal theories of logical inference. That is because, in these theories, no account is taken of the connections between propositions, over and above their individual truth values. In this chapter, the subject of relevance will be taken to include a consideration of such connections between pairs of propositions in arguments.

ways to prevent disastrous accidents, in addition to giving high priority to air safety? If so, the premises of example 5.2 may still leave open the link required to say that the conclusion must be true.

For all we can determine, example 5.2 could be like the following argument: 'Roses are red; Einstein was a genius; therefore, if roses are red, Einstein was a genius'. This argument does not appear to be valid. But even if it is valid, depending on what we mean by 'if . . . then', it seems to involve a failure of relevance in the conditional conclusion. So let us rule out example 5.2 as a possible candidate and consider the remaining possibilities.

Both remaining possibilities involve letting the conditional proposition be a premise. But there are two possible arguments of this configuration:

Example 5.3

If we must try to prevent disastrous accidents, then air safety should be given a high priority.

We must try to prevent disastrous accidents.

Therefore, air safety should be given a high priority.

Example 5.4

If we must try to prevent disastrous accidents, then air safety should be given a high priority.

Air safety should be given a high priority.

Therefore, we must try to prevent disastrous accidents.

Which one of these possible interpretations of example 5.1 would most plausibly represent the best conclusion?

Of course, the only foolproof way to determine which choice of conclusion was meant would be to ask the proponent of the argument what he really meant to conclude. But suppose he is not available to answer the question. If, as critics, we must make a choice, the best way is to interpret the argument helpfully so that it seems to make the most sense. In that light, let us turn to a comparative examination of examples 5.3 and 5.4.

Consider example 5.4 first. If we let A stand for 'We must try to prevent disastrous accidents' and B stand for 'Air safety should be given a high priority', then example 5.4 has the following form:

112

If *A*, then *B*.

B.

Therefore, *A*.

This way of interpreting the argument certainly does not result in a valid argument. If we grant the premises, it does not follow that we have to grant the conclusion, any more than it does in the following parallel argument:

Example 5.5

If I graduate, I have paid my tuition.

I have paid my tuition.

Therefore, I will graduate.

In example 5.5, the premises might well be granted as true. But it does not follow that the conclusion must be true. There may be requirements other than paying one's tuition in order to graduate. In other words, even if both premises are true, it does not necessarily follow that the conclusion must be true. And therefore example 5.5 is not a valid argument. Even if both premises are true, it may turn out that the conclusion is false.

This leaves us with example 5.3. We can see immediately that it is a valid argument, because it has the form of argument previously designated as MP.

Our problem was to find the conclusion in example 5.1. The problem was that there was no indicator word like 'therefore' or 'so' to show which of the three propositions was meant to be the conclusion. Yet, even in the absence of an indicator word, we could arrive at a plausible reconstruction of example 5.1 as an argument. Once we eliminated example 5.2 as a plausible reconstruction on grounds of the absence of a relevant connection, the two possibilities represented by examples 5.3 and 5.4 remained.

Why did example 5.3 seem to be the plausible and natural choice? The best explanation is that this interpretation is the one that made the resulting argument valid. This does not mean that this selection was the only possible choice, but that it represents the most plausible interpretation of how the arguer might have meant his argument to be taken.

The problem here is occasioned by the fact that people are some-

113

times unclear about what their conclusion is in an argument. But even if an arguer does not explicitly indicate which proposition is meant to be the conclusion of his argument, there may still be some evidence available enabling us to pick the most plausible candidate for the conclusion among the available choices. We can do this by making the assumption that the arguer in question is a constructive participant in reasonable dialogue and is trying his best to come forward with strong arguments for his side of the issue.

The reason that 5.3 is the most plausible interpretation of example 5.1 is to be sought in the *principle of charity*. When there is doubt or question, other things being equal, the fairest and most reasonable interpretation is to prefer a designation of the conclusion that makes the argument valid (and plausible) to one that makes it invalid (or implausible). It is the principle of charity that explains and justifies our inclination to interpret the first proposition in example 5.1 as the conclusion; for 5.3 is the only interpretation that is clearly valid and plausible as an argument.

To sum up, knowing when an argument is valid can be very helpful in identifying arguments. In the next section, the concept of a valid argument is elaborated.

5.3 VALIDITY AS A SEMANTIC CONCEPT

An *argument* is an interaction between two or more participants that involves a claim by each participant that his contention can be justified. Arguments may involve complex and lengthy sequences of steps, questions, answers, and objections. At any stage of an argument, however, we should be able to identify its semantic core. The *semantic core* is a set of propositions made up of one or more conclusions and some sets of premises.

A *semantic* concept is one that has to do with truth and falsehood. A proposition is said to be a semantic concept because it may be defined as a unit of language that is either true or false. We may not know, in a particular case, whether a proposition is, in fact, true or false. But a proposition is the sort of thing that, in principle, has the property of being true or false. For example, the proposition 'There is life on another planet in our galaxy' is, in principle, true or false, even if we may not know, at present, whether it is true or false. That is enough for us to identify it as a proposition.

The semantic core of an argument is normally surrounded by

pragmatic structures. In the practical analysis of arguments, one often finds that there are missing premises, not clearly stated as propositions by the arguer. Filling in these missing or problematic premises is one part of the pragmatics of arguments. An argument is said to be an *enthymeme* if there are premises needed to make the argument valid that are only tacitly, but not explicitly, stated or advanced as part of the argument. It may be a difficult job to judge fairly and reasonably whether such enthymematic premises were truly meant to be asserted by the arguer. For example, if someone argued, 'All men are mortal; therefore, Socrates is mortal', it would, in most contexts, be reasonable to presume that it may have included the premise, 'Socrates is a man', needed to make the argument valid. But if someone argued, 'All men are mortal; therefore, Elizabeth Anscombe is mortal', would it be reasonable to presume that the proposition 'Elizabeth Anscombe is a man" is an enthymematic premise? In most contexts, probably not, although adding that proposition would make the argument valid. More plausible, in light of the context, is that the proposition 'And all women are mortal' should be included as a premise, thereby changing (or extending) the argument.

Determining enthymematic premises is a pragmatic task of argument analysis. Whether a proposition can reasonably be said to be an enthymematic premise in someone's argument depends to a significant extent on that arguer's position, the set of commitments he has previously adopted in the context of the dialogue or dispute.

In short, we often need to distinguish carefully between the semantic and pragmatic aspects of an argument. The semantic aspect has to do with the truth and falsity of the propositions. The pragmatic aspect has to do with what the arguer may reasonably be taken to be committed to in the context of dialogue. The concept of a valid argument is a semantic notion.

The basic property of a valid argument is that it never takes you from true premises to a false conclusion. In other words, a valid argument must be *truth-preserving*, meaning that if the premises are true then the conclusion must be true as well. Validity is one of the most fundamental semantic concepts in the study of argument.

The defining characteristic of a valid argument is that it is absolutely airtight – there are no loopholes. If the premises are true, then it is absolutely guaranteed that the conclusion must be true. Consider the following argument:

115

Example 5.6

If Bob goes west, he will arrive at Steinbach.

If Bob goes east, he will arrive at Carman.

Either Bob goes east or Bob goes west.

Therefore, Bob will arrive at Steinbach, or he will arrive at Carman.

This argument is deductively valid, meaning that, if the premises are true, then the conclusion must be true as well. This is not necessarily to claim that the premises are true, or even that the conclusion is true. It is only to claim that if the premises are true, then the conclusion must be true too. In other words, validity is a conditional concept. It is the relationship between the truth or falsity of the premises of an argument and that of the conclusion.

It may well happen, for example, that there is an argument that is valid but has false premises. Consider the following argument:

Example 5.7

If Plato was born in Chicago, then Aristotle was born in Toronto.

Plato was born in Chicago.

Therefore, Aristotle was born in Toronto.

This argument is valid, meaning that, if the premises are true, then so is the conclusion. But the premises are not true, as a matter of fact. And neither is the conclusion, for that matter.

In summary, then, a valid argument always takes you from true premises to a true conclusion. But the fact that the argument is valid is no guarantee that the premises are, in fact, true. To say that an argument is valid is to say something positive about it. But it is not to say that the argument is as good as it could possibly be in all respects.

Another thing to remember is that not all good arguments have to be valid arguments. Inductive arguments can be good or reasonable, but they are not valid – they do not guarantee the truth of a conclusion, but only yield probability. So validity is not the only thing to be worried about when analyzing arguments. But it is very important as a tool for evaluating arguments.

In the practical job of evaluating real argumentation, the first question to be asked is, 'What are the propositions that make up

116

this argument?' Hence identifying the semantic core of an argument is of critical importance for practical logic.

5.4 VALID FORMS OF ARGUMENT

If you want to build up some arguments to support your contention or to mount arguments to criticize somebody else's contention, there are certain basic building blocks that are useful to know about. These building blocks are structures or forms of argument that are always valid, which means that, if a part of your argument has this structure, then it will never take you from true premises to a false conclusion. A valid argument is "fail-safe," meaning that, if the premises are true, the conclusion has to be true too, simply in virtue of the structure of the argument. The notion of structure will turn out to be important in understanding the nature of valid arguments. An example is the following argument:

Example 5.8

If jobholders feel that the workplace rewards extra effort, then they do good work for its own sake.

In fact, jobholders do not do good work for its own sake.

Therefore, jobholders do not feel that the workplace rewards extra effort.

This argument is valid, meaning that, if the premises are true, then the conclusion must also be true. Now the premises above may or may not be true. Whether they are is a question of the sociology of industrial management, one may suppose. But if they are true, then logic tells us that the conclusion must be true too. Why is this so?

The answer is that this particular argument has a form of structure that guarantees its validity. Let A stand for the proposition 'Jobholders feel that the workplace rewards extra effort' and B stand for 'Jobholders do good work for its own sake'. Then the argument above may be said to have the following structure:

Example 5.9

If A, then B.

Not B.

Therefore, not A.

117

This structure is a valid form of argument, meaning that, whatever pair of propositions you put in for *A* and *B*, the resulting argument is always valid. You can be sure of it. Consider the following argument:

Example 5.10

If Captain Kirk is a Vulcan, he has pointed ears.

Captain Kirk does not have pointed ears.

Therefore, Captain Kirk is not a Vulcan.

This argument clearly has the same form as the jobholders argument. But in this case, the letter *A* stands for 'Captain Kirk is a Vulcan' and the letter *B* stands for 'Captain Kirk has pointed ears'. Since both arguments have the same (valid) structure, both are valid arguments.[2]

In constructing or evaluating arguments, it is most useful to know what some of the basic valid forms of arguments are. Some of them follow, along with their customary names:

Modus ponens (MP)	*Modus tollens* (MT)
If *A*, then *B*.	If *A*, then *B*.
A.	Not *B*.
Therefore, *B*.	Therefore, not *A*.

Hypothetical syllogism (HS)	*Disjunctive syllogism* (DS)
If *A*, then B.	Either *A* or *B*.
If *B*, then *C*.	Not *A*.
Therefore, if *A*, then *C*.	Therefore, *B*.

How can we prove that each of these forms of argument is valid? To do this we need to show that if both premises are true, in each

---

2 The only caution here is that you have to be uniform in your use of propositional letters *A*, *B*, *C*, and so forth, to stand for propositions in an argument. For example, once you have used the letter *A* to stand for the proposition 'Captain Kirk is a Vulcan' in the first premise of example 5.10, then you must use *A* again to stand for the same proposition when it appears in the conclusion of 5.10. In other words, your substitution of propositions for propositional letters in representing the form of an argument must be *uniform*. You must not switch horses in midstream, as it were. This principle of uniform substitution is generally stated in Section 5.9.

case, the conclusion has to be true too. Let us consider each form of argument.

Consider DS first. What does the proposition 'Either *A* or *B*' mean? Under what conditions is this form of proposition true or false? Well, one basic fact about a disjunctive proposition 'Either *A* or *B*' is that it is true if at least one of the disjuncts is true. In other words, if you have a disjunction like 'Either Bob has the measles or chicken pox', then you know that at least one of the following propositions is true:

Example 5.11

Bob has measles.

Bob has chicken pox.

One could be false, but both cannot be if the disjunction 'Either Bob has measles or chicken pox' is really true. So at least one must be true.

In general, then, if 'Either *A* or *B*' is true, then at least one of the pair, *A* or *B*, must be true. But suppose *A* is not true. Then *B* must be true. Why? Well, at least one must be true, according to the first premise of DS. But if, according to the second premise, *A* is not true, then *B* must be true. *B* cannot be false, if both premises are true. So in general, any argument having the form of DS must always be valid. If its premises are true, then its conclusion must be true too.

In effect, then, DS is a valid form of argument because of the meaning of 'either . . . or'. In any disjunction, at least one of the disjuncts must be true. If both were false, it could not be a true disjunction.

Much the same proofs for the validity of the remaining three forms of argument can be given. If a conditional proposition 'If *A* then *B*' is true, then it has to be false that *A* is true and *B* is false. For example, let us suppose that the following conditional proposition is true: 'If Karl drops the egg he is holding, it will break'. Now whatever else we might want to say about the truth or falsehood of this conditional, we must at least say that, if the whole conditional is true, then it has to be false that Karl drops the egg but it does not break. Why? Well, because that is what we mean when we say that, if Karl drops the egg, it will break. We are denying that we can consistently say both that Karl drops the egg and

119

that it fails to break. So *modus ponens* is valid and has to be always valid as a form of argument, simply in virtue of the meaning of the conditional as a logical connection between the propositions. By similar reasoning, it can be proved that MT and HS are valid forms of argument as well. The actual proofs that each of these forms of argument is, indeed, valid, according to the way we have defined 'valid argument' is not as important for the present as your satisfaction and assurance that they are valid; for once you are so satisfied, then you can use them to build up arguments, confident that the basic parts are valid. These forms of argument, then, are basic building blocks for constructing longer arguments. In each case, if you know the premises are true, you can be assured that the conclusion must follow logically, by valid argument.

Proving the validity of HS can be done by looking at its premises and remembering that MP has already been proved valid. Now assume that *A* is true. By MP and the first premise, *B* must be true. But if *B* is true, then by the second premise and MP, *C* must be true. Hence, if *A* is true, *C* must be true too. Therefore, the conclusion of HS follows validly from its premises.

In proving the validity of several valid forms of argument, we have made certain assumptions about the semantics of disjunctions and conditionals. It is now useful to summarize these assumptions. First, we define a *disjunctive proposition* as one that presents two or more alternatives in the form 'Either *A* or *B* or . . .' In the simplest case, there are just two alternatives, *A* and *B*. The rule for disjunction we presumed earlier can be summarized as follows:

Rule for disjunction: If the disjunction 'Either *A* or *B*' is true, then at least one of the pair, *A* or *B*, must be true.

This rule implies that if both *A* and *B* are false, then the whole disjunction 'Either *A* or *B*' must be false.

We also relied on an assumption about conditionals. Let us define a *conditional proposition* as one that presents one proposition as true on the assumption that another proposition is true. A conditional has the form 'If *A*, then *B*'. The part that makes the assumption is called the *antecedent*. The part that is presented as true on the assumption made in the antecedent is called the *consequent*. The rule for conditionals reads as follows:

Rule for conditional: If a conditional 'If *A*, then *B*' is true, then it is false that the antecedent (*A*) is true while the consequent (*B*) is false.

This rule means that, for a conditional to be true, it must not have a true antecedent and a false consequent. In this respect, there is a certain parallel between a true conditional and a valid argument, because a valid argument never takes you from true premises to a false conclusion.

Indeed, the *rule for conditional* characterizes a type of conditional appropriate only for a context of deductive logic. A conditional appropriate for inductive contexts of reasoning would have a different rule. For example, the inductive conditional 'If Karl drops this egg, it will probably break' could still be true, even if there is an instance when Karl dropped the egg, but it did not break; for the conditional could still be true if there were many other instances when Karl dropped similar eggs, and all or most of them broke.

But in the context of deductive reasoning, a conditional is treated as parallel, at least in one respect to the concept of a valid argument. Any exception to the rule stated by the conditional makes it false.

However, just because this parallel exists, we must not conclude that a true conditional and a valid argument are the same thing. Truth and falsehood are properties of propositions. Validity and invalidity are properties of arguments. So it makes no sense at all to speak of a "valid proposition" or a "true argument," or any more sense than it would to speak of a "valid pair of socks."

Now that we are able to recognize and are familiar with some of the common forms of valid argument, we are in a better position to orient ourselves in sorting out a complex and confusing network of real argumentation. If some parts of it are valid arguments, we can at least identify these parts. If other parts would be valid except for missing premises, we are in a somewhat better position to tackle the job of querying what the arguer may be including or leaving out.

5.5 INVALID ARGUMENTS

A valid form of argument is one in which no argument having that form can have true premises and a false conclusion. So the concept of validity has a certain generality – we can say of every argument that has a valid form that, if the premises are true, the conclusion must be true. The validity of an argument form guarantees the validity of every one of the countless arguments having that form.

For example, any argument that has the form of *modus ponens* must be valid, no matter what particular subject matter it has.

With invalid arguments, however, the form of the argument does not have the same guarantee of generality. This asymmetry between validity and invalidity arises because it is possible for a particular argument to have more than one form. Consider the following argument:

Example 5.12

If computers can reason, they can ask questions.

Computers can reason.

Therefore, computers can ask questions.

This argument has the form *modus ponens,* so it must be a valid argument. So construed, the argument has the form 'If *A,* then *B; A;* therefore, *B*'. However, *modus ponens* is not the only form that this argument has. It also has this less specific form: '*A; B;* therefore, *C*'. Instead of representing the first premise as a conditional, we could also represent it as a simple proposition, *A*. Of course, representing it as a conditional would be more specific. But if we did represent it in this less specific form, it would break no rule of logic we have, so far, required. And that form of argument is invalid. Even if both *A* and *B* are true, it is quite possible that *C* could be false, for all logic tells us.

So we have to be careful here. Even if we know an argument has an invalid form, it need not automatically follow that the argument must be invalid. To be assured of that, we would also have to know that the form presented is the most specific form of the given argument. Despite this reservation, the criticism that an argument is invalid can be legitimate. However, it is not a decisive refutation of an argument using formal logic unless the critic can show that the specific form of the argument has been represented.

An argument that is deductively invalid is not necessarily bad or incorrect. Even if it is deductively invalid as presented, it could still be correct by inductive standards. Or it could simply be incomplete. To criticize an argument as deductively invalid is simply to point out that, in the form given, it does not meet the standard of deductive validity. Whether the arguer meant it to meet that standard, or should be so required, are other questions.

Despite these limitations, the finding of deductive invalidity can be important in evaluating an argument. If an argument is shown to be invalid as presented, it may mean that it could be improved by additional premises or by further qualifying the nature or limits of the argument in various ways.

Now let us contrast our four valid forms of argument with some examples that are not valid:

Example 5.13

If *A*, then *B*.

B.

Therefore, *A*.

Example 5.14

If *A*, then *B*.

Not *A*.

Therefore, not *B*.

Example 5.15

If *A*, then *B*.

If *C*, then *B*.

If *A*, then *C*.

Example 5.16

Either *A* or *B*.

A.

Therefore, *B*.

To see that these forms of argument are not valid, it may suffice to look at some examples. In each case, it is possible for both premises to be true and the conclusion false:

Example 5.17

If it rains, the car will get wet at that time.

The car is wet now.

Therefore, it is raining now.

123

Example 5.18

If I drop this egg, it will break.

I do not drop this egg.

Therefore, it will not break.

Example 5.19

If I move my knight, John will take my knight.

If I move my queen, John will take my knight.

Therefore, if I move my knight, then I move my queen.

Example 5.20

Either Turku is in Finland or it is in Norway.

Turku is in Finland.

Therefore, Turku is in Norway.

Consider the last argument. Assume both premises are true. Does the conclusion now have to be true? Not at all. In fact, the premises imply that the conclusion is false, if we interpret the disjunction in the first premise as an exclusive one. That is we might assume that the first premise means that Turku is in either one of the countries, Finland or Norway, but not both. Then once we determine that Turku is in Finland, as stated by the second premise, it follows that Turku cannot be in Norway. So interpreted, the premises not only fail to imply the conclusion, they actually conflict with it by implying the opposite. No matter whether we interpret the first premise as an exclusive disjunction or not, the argument fails to be valid.

The key to evaluating whether an argument is valid is to determine the form of the argument. The common argument forms we have encountered are valid or invalid in virtue of the propositional connectives that occur in them. The rules for the connectives very often enable us to determine whether a particular form of argument is valid.

5.6 INCONSISTENCY

Inconsistency is a very important concept in logic and the analysis of arguments. If an arguer is found to be inconsistent, then that is a very strong form of criticism or condemnation of his position. An *inconsistent set of propositions* is one in which a contradiction can

124

be deduced by valid arguments. A *contradiction* is a conjunction of a proposition and its negation. For example, consider the following set of propositions:

Example 5.21

If courage is a virtue, then courage is an excellence of conduct.
Courage is a virtue.
Courage is not an excellence of conduct.

What would we say of someone who maintained all three of these propositions in his argument? We would say that the position he has adopted is inconsistent. Why? By *modus ponens,* the first two propositions imply 'Courage is an excellence of conduct'. But that proposition is the negation of the third proposition 'Courage is not an excellence of conduct'. We can see, therefore, that the three propositions imply a contradiction. Hence these three propositions are collectively inconsistent.

But what is so wrong with contradictions? you may ask. The answer is that a contradiction can never be a true proposition. Why not? The answer has to do with the concepts of negation and conjunction.

The negation of a proposition is usually indicated by the 'not' particle. For example 'Paris is not in France' is the negation of the proposition 'Paris is in France'. If a proposition is true, its negation must be false, If a proposition is false, its negation must be true. We can summarize this information in the following rule for negation:

Rule for negation: If the negation 'not-A' is true, then A must be false; if the negation 'not-A' is false, then A must be true.

In other words, the negation of a proposition always has the opposite truth value of that proposition.

The conjunction of two or more propositions is often indicated by the word 'and' in English. For example, if I say 'Paris is in France and Cologne is in Germany' then I assert a conjunction of two propositions. For the conjunction to be true, it is required that both of its propositions be true. Hence the rule for conjunction:

Rule for conjunction: For the conjunction 'A and B' to be true, both A and B must be true.

This rule for conjunction means that if either one of the propositions in a conjunction is false, then the whole conjunctive proposition must be false.

Now we understand conjunction and negation; we can see why a contradiction must be false. A contradiction is a proposition of the form '*A* and not-*A*'. If *A* is true, then not-*A* must be false, by the rule for negation. But also by the negation rule, if not-*A* is true, then *A* must be false. Any way you look at it, at least one of the pair, *A* or not-*A*, must be false. Hence the conjunction '*A* and not-*A*' can never be true. To sum up, then, a contradiction must always be false.

The fact that a contradiction must always be false shows what is open to criticism about an inconsistent set of propositions maintained by an arguer. If an inconsistent set of propositions implies a contradiction, and a contradiction must always be false, then the inconsistent set of propositions can never be all true. At least some of the propositions contained within it have to be false. This means that a position that is inconsistent should be open to criticism or revision. An inconsistent set of propositions may contain some true propositions, but at least one must be false, even if we do not know which one it is.

Inconsistency can be very difficult to deal with. Psychologists know that, when laboratory animals are subjected to inconsistent treatment, they can start to exhibit frustration and loss of interest in activity. Children who receive inconsistent demands or messages from parents can experience behavior problems as a result.

An interesting example studied in Jones (1983) is the case of the double-bind situation. A young schizophrenic patient was visited by his mother in hospital. Bateson (1956, p. 188) described the patient's reaction to the visit as follows:

Example 5.22

He was glad to see her and impulsively put his arm around her shoulders, whereupon she stiffened. He withdrew his arm and she asked, "Don't you love me any more?" He then blushed, and she said, "Dear, you must not be so easily embarrassed and afraid of your feelings."

After the young man left the room, he assaulted a ward orderly. The nature of the message sent by the mother as an example of inconsistent or "double-bind" communication is studied in detail by Jones (1983). But the mother's actions are also a good example of a confusing double message where an action runs contrary to the message that is verbalized by the mother. She says one thing, but her action of stiffening "says" something distinctly contrary. But do actions speak as loud as words? Sometimes they do, and the message conveyed by an action must be taken account of in the careful analysis of an argument. What about the case where the father who smokes says to his son, 'You must not smoke. It's very bad for your health.' Is the son justified in feeling that his father's argument is inconsistent? This problem is a complex one and best studied under the heading of an *ad hominem* argument. Suffice it to note here that sometimes arguments may not be outright inconsistencies, but an inconsistency can be derived by the addition of further assumptions. If the father is really arguing as follows, then he is inconsistent:

Example 5.23

(1) Nobody should smoke, because smoking is bad for health. I smoke.
(2) If I smoke, my act is justified. In other words, my action of smoking may be interpreted as meaning that I advocate smoking.
(3) Therefore, I should smoke.
(4) But if nobody should smoke, I should not smoke.

If this is a fair representation of the father's argument, then the argument is inconsistent; for (1) and (4) imply 'I should not smoke', but (2) and (3) imply 'I should smoke'. But do actions speak as loud as words in this case? In other words, is premise (2) being asserted by the father? This is the problem of the *ad hominem* fallacy.

The lesson for the moment is that some arguments do contain a contradiction, but only if further assumptions are added. In such a case, one must be careful to inquire whether these additional assumptions are reasonably attributed to the arguer before prematurely claiming that his argument is inconsistent. However, in some cases, the attribution of these additional assumptions is fairly uncontroversial. Consider the following two assertions:

Example 5.24

(5) Kevin always tells the truth.
(6) Kevin lied about his age on Saturday.

127

The additional propositions we need here to show that (5) and (6) are an inconsistent set are the following two:

(7) If Kevin always tells the truth, Kevin told the truth on Saturday.

(8) If Kevin lied about his age on Saturday, then Kevin did not tell the truth on Saturday.

As you can see, the collective set (5), (6), (7), and (8) is one from which a contradiction can be deduced by valid arguments. Now (7) and (8) are probably acceptable assumptions as part of the background of the assertion of (5) and (6) by an arguer in most contexts. If, in the particular context, they are acceptable, then we can say that (5) and (6) amount to an inconsistency. But we need to be careful. Premature and unfair allegations of inconsistency are often made and accepted uncritically, as Chapter 6 will show.

5.7 COMPOSITION AND DIVISION

Other logical constants that determine the validity of arguments are the terms 'all' and 'some'. For example, the following argument is valid because of the semantics of 'all' and 'some':

Example 5.25

All rodents are mammals.
Some rodents lurk around docks.
Therefore, some mammals lurk around docks.

By contrast, the following argument has a form that is not generally valid:

Example 5.26

All rodents are mammals.
Some mammals have horns.
Therefore, some rodents have horns.

The reason example 5.26 fails to be a valid argument is that the first premise makes a claim about all rodents, but it does not make a claim about all mammals.

Care is needed, however, in distinguishing between the collective

128

and distributive use of terms. The sentence 'Rodents are mammals' would normally be rightly interpreted as meaning 'All rodents are mammals'. Here we may say that the term 'rodents' is being used *distributively,* meaning that a property is being attributed to each rodent. However, in the sentence 'Rodents are widely distributed over the earth', the term 'rodents' is being used *collectively,* meaning that a property of the class of rodents as a whole is referred to.

Confusion between the collective and distributive use of terms can result in the *fallacy of composition,* which argues incorrectly that what may be attributed to a term distributively may also be attributed to it collectively:

Example 5.27

A bus uses more gas than a car.

Therefore, all buses use more gas than all cars.

The fallacy implicit in this argument arises from interpreting the conclusion collectively. Because there are many more cars than buses in the world, it is false that buses (collectively) use more gas than cars, even if it may be true that buses (distributively) use more gas than cars.

In other instances, the fallacy of composition can have to do with part–whole relationships:

Example 5.28

All the parts of this machine are light.

Therefore, this machine is light.

Or this fallacy can have to do with functional relationships:

Example 5.29

All the players on this team are good.

Therefore, this is a good team.

Both types of arguments fail to be generally valid because the properties of the parts do not necessarily transfer to the properties of the whole made up of those parts.

The fallacy of division is the opposite type of argument and has variants similar to those of the fallacy of composition:

Example 5.30

This machine is heavy.

Therefore, all the parts of this machine are heavy.

Example 5.31

American Indians have reservations in every state.

The Navaho are American Indians.

Therefore, the Navaho have reservations in every state.

Because the first premise is a collective, rather than a distributive, statement, example 5.31 fails to be a valid argument.

Care is needed in evaluating argumentation that fits the schemes for composition and division. Instances of these argumentation schemes are not all fallacious:

Example 5.32

All the parts of this machine are iron.

Therefore, this machine is made of iron.

This argument is not fallacious, although it appears to have the structure of the argumentation scheme of composition.

The key here is the critical question of whether the property in question is one that composes (or divides) over the type of collection or distribution in the example.[3] In example 5.32, the answer is affirmative because it is universally true that, when all the parts of an entity like a machine are made of a particular substance, then the whole entity is also made of that same substance. Hence there is no fallacy of composition in this case.

The argumentation scheme appropriate for example 5.32 is the following:

All the parts of X have property Y.

Therefore, X has property Y.

The critical question for this argumentation scheme is, 'Does the property of Y compose from the parts of X to the whole?' In other words, the question is whether the following conditional is war-

3 See Woods and Walton (1977).

ranted in the case in question: If all the parts of X have property Y, then X has property Y. The answer to this type of critical question is affirmative in some cases and negative in others.

If the answer to the relevant critical question is affirmative, then the argumentation scheme for composition (or division) can justify a particular argument as correct or reasonable. However, if the answer is negative, then the argument is incorrect and can be criticized as an error or fallacy of composition or division.

5.8 SUMMARY

A valid argument is one in which the premises can never be true while the conclusion is false. The premises and conclusion of an argument are propositions, which are either true or false. The conclusion of an argument is usually marked by an indicator word like 'so' or 'therefore'. If not, according to the principle of charity one should choose whichever proposition, as conclusion, makes the argument strongest. The premises are the propositions that back up, or give reasons for, the conclusion of an argument.

It is useful to be familiar with the common forms of valid argument studied in this chapter. An argument is determined to be valid or not by certain key terms called *logical constants,* meaning that they can be clearly defined in a fixed or constant way. In this chapter, the constants were the propositional connectives 'and', 'not', 'or', and 'if–then'. In Section 5.7, the constants 'all' and 'some' were also briefly discussed. It is because of the rules that govern the meaning of these constants that argument forms are determined to be valid or invalid. If an argument has a valid form, then it must be a valid argument. Therefore, valid forms of argument are useful semantic building blocks in both constructing new arguments and reconstructing old ones in pragmatic sequences of argumentation.

It is because the validity of the forms of argument MP, MT, HS, and DS are determined by the meanings of the connective words 'not', 'or', and 'if–then' that deductive logic is a branch of semantics. Semantics has to do with truth and falsity, and the meanings of these connective words determine which forms of argument are valid by the rules for the connectives that stipulate relationships of truth and falsity. Using these rules, we can generally prove that a particular argument form is valid.

131

We have learned to recognize several very common, valid forms of argument. Familiarity with these forms is very useful for many purposes in constructing and evaluating arguments. However, two of the most important uses we have studied in this chapter are proving that an argument is valid and proving that a set of propositions is inconsistent. Each of these is a valuable capability.

Linking arguments together in a deductive chain of argumentation is a way of making proofs absolutely airtight. Because each step follows from the previous step in the sequence of deductions, it may be rightly said that deductive logic, when correctly applied to arguments, leaves no room for dispute or controversy. Once the premises are postulated or accepted, if an argument is valid, the conclusion may be shown to follow inexorably. Similarly, if a set of propositions is inconsistent, deductive logic can show beyond all shadow of doubt that the set is, indeed, inconsistent by using a sequence of conclusions to deduce a contradiction.

However, sometimes different arguments have the same form. Also, the same argument may have different forms. Nevertheless, if any form of an argument is valid, then that argument is shown to be valid.

So we have seen that deductive logic has a formal nature. The study of deductive logic involves an ascent to generality because, at the theoretical level, it involves the study of the forms of argument. In practical logic, often called informal logic, each argument must be studied on its own merits. Each case is unique. But in formal logic, if two cases have the same form, then their particular differences may be ignored, at least at the formal level. Even so, applying formal logic to particular arguments is a practical or informal task. This is so because it is usually required by the principle of charity that an evaluator of an argument represent the argument by its most specific form, when a choice is possible.

Yet another use of valid argument forms is as an aid to help us determine which proposition is most plausibly meant to be the conclusion of an argument when no explicit indicator word is given. When we are given a set of propositions evidently meant to be an argument, yet no proposition of the set is clearly designated, or meant, as the conclusion, what are we to do? Until we determine the conclusion, the method of deduction cannot be brought to bear. Here, then, is another task of argument analysis. If every designation of a conclusion, except one, makes the argument invalid, then the

132

policy of giving an arguer the benefit of the doubt (principle of charity) suggests picking the one proposition as conclusion that makes the argument valid.

So deductive logic has many uses in the study of reasoned argument. It is in fact an indispensable tool. As a proof of validity of arguments, deduction leaves no room for doubt about the linkage between a conclusion and a set of premises.

Basically, however, we have not given the reader a method (algorithm) of deduction to prove the invalidity of arguments. The technique we used to show invalidity was the method of giving a counterexample. A counterexample is a counterpart argument that has the same specific form as an argument in question, where the premises of the counterpart argument are true while the conclusion is false.

Inconsistency is not, in itself, a fallacy. But if an arguer's set of commitments in a discussion show evidence of being collectively inconsistent, he can (and should) be challenged to defend his position by removing or explaining the apparent inconsistency. The usual way of doing this is to retract one of the commitments. In Chapter 6, cases in which an arguer is challenged on the grounds of apparent inconsistency will be studied.

In evaluating arguments that have the argumentation schemes for composition and division, it is critical to be aware of the distinction between the collective and distributive uses of terms. Arguments having these schemes are not always fallacious. But in order to test for this possibility, it is important to ask critical questions about the relationships between wholes and parts.

6

Personal attack in argumentation

The *argumentum ad hominem*, meaning "argument directed to the man," is the kind of argument that criticizes the arguer rather than his argument. Basically, it is a personal attack on an arguer that brings the individual's personal circumstances, trustworthiness, or character into question. The *argumentum ad hominem* is not always fallacious, for in some instances questions of personal conduct, character, motives, and so on are legitimate and relevant to the issue. However, personal attack is inherently dangerous and emotional in argument, and is rightly associated with fallacies and deceptive tactics of argumentation. Three basic categories of fallacy have often traditionally been associated with three types of *argumentum ad hominem*.[1]

The *abusive ad hominem argument* is the direct attack on a person in argument, including the questioning or vilification of his character, motives, or trustworthiness. Characteristically, the focus of the personal attack is on bad moral character in general or lack of truthfulness.

The *circumstantial ad hominem argument* is the questioning or criticizing of the personal circumstances of an arguer, allegedly revealed, for example, in his actions, affiliations, or previous commitments, by citing an alleged inconsistency between his argument and these circumstances. The charge 'You don't practice what you preach!' characteristically expresses the thrust of the circumstantial *ad hominem* argument against a person.

The last type of *ad hominem* argument is said to occur when the critic questions the sincerity or objectivity of an arguer by suggesting that the arguer has something to gain by supporting the argument he has advocated. This argument has sometimes been called *poisoning the well*, because it suggests that the arguer attacked has a hidden

---

1 For an account of the traditional categories of *ad hominem* fallacy recognized in the textbooks, see Govier (1983).

agenda – is supporting his side of the argument for personal gain or for other private and concealed reasons – and therefore cannot be trusted as a fair or reasonable exponent of an argument on this, or indeed on any, issue. As a reliable source, he is a "poisoned well," so to speak, for anything he says is suspect as reflecting his one-sided personal bias.

Sometimes the *ad hominem* argument is associated with the *tu quoque*, or 'You too!', rejoinder in argumentation. When a personal attack is initiated by one party, often the response is to fire another personal attack back against the first party by replying, 'You are no better!' The danger here is that excessive indulgence in personal attack can result in a dialectical shift, lowering the level of a critical discussion to that of a personal quarrel, with disastrous results for the logic of the argumentation.

The argument against the person is not always logically unreasonable or fallacious. But when it is wrong, it can be a dangerous and very serious error. Certainly, it is not hard to appreciate how personal attack on an individual's character or circumstances can often be vicious and unwarranted. Such an attack should be severely criticized when it can be shown to be unwarranted. The argument against the person can be a powerfully convincing or influential form of attack, however, when it is successfully deployed by a clever arguer. The argument against the person is, in fact, a very common form of argument, for example, in political debates. It could even be said to be the most powerful kind of argument in politics. And it is very important to be on guard against it and to know how to handle it reasonably. The whole of Chapter 6 will be devoted to the argument against the person.

In this chapter, we shall consider, first, the abusive *ad hominem*, then the circumstantial variety, and finally the "poisoning the well," or bias-imputing, variant of *ad hominem* attack.

6.1 THE ABUSIVE *AD HOMINEM* ARGUMENT

In the abusive type of personal attack, a range of aspects of an arguer's person may be the focus. The attack may focus on the personal character or past actions of the arguer in question, or it may focus on his group affiliations, like his political or national allegiances, religious beliefs, or ethnic background. Very often, personal attack is directed against the ethics of an arguer, trying to suggest that he is dishonest, unreliable, or lacking integrity. In other cases, the personal attack brings into question the arguer's credibility or ability to enter into reasoned argument. For example, it may even be suggested that the arguer is insane or mentally imbalanced and that therefore no serious attention can be paid to his argument.

The following case is typical of one type of abusive personal attack in argument because it suggests a personal untrustworthiness based on previous (allegedly immoral) conduct:

Example 6.0

Richard Nixon's statements on foreign affairs policies in relation to China are untrustworthy because he was forced to resign during the Watergate scandal.

This argument against the person is open to critical reply because whatever we might believe about Richard Nixon's personal integrity or honesty in relation to the Watergate affair, it does not follow that his foreign policy statements on China are false or incorrect. From allegations or presumptions about someone's personal character, even if they are justifiable, one is not warranted in drawing the conclusion that certain specific statements he has made are false. In some cases, these statements may turn out to be true and based on good evidence and reasonable arguments advanced by the arguer, despite his personal shortcomings or misconduct.

The point to be made in this case is that the argument is weak. Although some reservations about Mr. Nixon's reliability as an ethical politician in light of the Watergate scandal may be justified, these reservations are not very strong grounds for rejecting his expertise in foreign policy issues concerning China, an area in which he was very strong and widely acknowledged to have vast experience. In this case, the transference from the premise to the conclusion is (at best) weak. But the danger is that the reference to the Watergate scandal is a powerful personal attack, which may lead one to whom example 6.0 is directed to dismiss any of Mr. Nixon's statements as worthless because they are seen as coming from someone who is either corrupt or inept in all political matters. This closed view of the issue would not allow Mr. Nixon or anyone else to argue for his statements on any case.

It is not that the abusive type of argument against the person is always worthless. But it is, in this case, a weak kind of argument based on plausible presumptions that cannot be too broadly transferred to another area. So the danger is in overreacting to it.

In the political arena, an arguer's integrity, personal convictions, and individual conduct can, in many instances, be a legitimate subject matter for dialogue. This is because we must place our trust in elected politicians to be our representatives, and we rightly expect them to be honest and not to give in to corruption. Partly for this reason, the *ad hominem* attack could justifiably be said to be the most common and most powerful form of criticism of an opponent in political arguments. Even so, the prevalence of so-called negative campaigning in recent elections has prompted commentators to remark that the excesses of personal attack as a popular style of argument are a sign of a lack of interest and critical judgment of the issues on the part of the electorate.

In 1986 campaigns for the U.S. Senate, the following instances of negative campaigning were prominent: One candidate accused his opponent of being "soft" on terrorism and drugs, and spent two million dollars on television ads depicting bloody victims of terrorist attacks being carried away on stretchers. His opponent claimed, in return, that this candidate was "confused" and lacked conviction.[2]

Another candidate accused an opponent of mismanaging union funds. The opponent replied by accusing him of drinking on the job. Yet another candidate labeled her opponent "antimale" and a "San Francisco Democrat" and tried to make her unmarried status an election issue. Commenting on this trend, *Newsweek* remarked that "by historical standards . . . today's dirtiest smear jobs look positively polite" but that, unfortunately for the level of political debate, "negative campaigning all too often works."[3] Indeed, George F. Will commented in *Newsweek* that only those candidates who are convinced they have a large lead against their opponents conclude that they are so far ahead that they do not need to use negative ads.[4] Will's objection is not to "criticizing the public record of public people," which he feels is acceptable in political argument,

2 Tom Morganthau and Howard Fineman, "When in Doubt Go Negative," *Newsweek,* November 3, 1986, pp. 25–26.
3 Ibid., p. 25.
4 George F. Will, "So Much Cash, So Few Ideas," *Newsweek,* November 10, 1986, p. 96.

but to the "reckless use" of a candidate's voting record.[5] For example, a candidate whose vote could be interpreted as a vote for "less-than-maximum funding level for a program for the handicapped" can lead to a commercial that makes claims about his voting "against the handicapped." Will concurs that, unfortunately, in recent years, these negative ads have worked.[6]

However, it is not only in negative campaign tactics in television commercials that personal attack is found in political argumentation. It is very common on all levels of political debate for politicians, especially in opposition roles, to strive to find some grounds for accusing their opponents of circumstantial inconsistency, hypocrisy, or lack of personal integrity. Arguing that an opponent is possibly guilty of conflict of interest, questionable tax deductions on a personal income tax return, or is otherwise vulnerable on questions of personal conduct of this sort, is an important part of current political rhetoric and can be strikingly dominant when the race between two parties is close.

Character can be relevant in an argument if the issue of the dialogue is related to the arguer's character. For example, if the issue is alleged defamation of character by one arguer of another, then the character of the arguer allegedly defamed is in fact the main issue on which the argument turns.

But when is character relevant to an argument? What matters in answering this question in a specific case is to determine what the issue of the discussion should be, first of all, and then to judge whether the aspect of character in question is relevant to the issue.

A move in argument can violate the negative rules of persuasion dialogue outlined in Section 1.4 if it asks an inappropriate question or is otherwise not relevant to proving the thesis at issue. Unfortunately, the abusive *ad hominem* argument often violates these rules because, at a particular stage, the discussion should not really be about the arguer's character. Such radical failures of relevance in *ad hominem* arguments have already been illustrated in examples 1.7 and 1.8. In a scientific discussion exclusively about laws of physics and their verification, attacks on the character or personal convictions of the arguer have no place. However, in a political debate,

5 Ibid.
6 Ibid.

138

questions of personal character and veracity can be highly relevant. A recent case has brought this to the forefront of controversy. Some background to the following example can be found in an article by Jonathan Alter:[7]

Example 6.1

Repeated allegations by reporters about the extramarital affairs of a presidential candidate raised public concerns about his character. Intensive press coverage of his personal life led to more rumors and suspicions of philandering, and the candidate was forced, by the bad publicity, to withdraw from the race. Previous U.S. Presidents had kept mistresses or had extra-marital affairs, yet the media had refrained from making these aspects of their personal lives public.

This case raised the question of how far reporters should go in public reporting and examination of personal questions of character, like sexual morality, in a presidential campaign. The question raised was whether matters of a candidate's sexual morality or other aspects of his personal life are relevant to public discussions of his suitability as a holder of political office.

One can see in this case how such personal matters could be relevant. If the candidate took a strong stand on family values, for example, it could legitimately be questioned whether his infidelity to his spouse brought the sincerity of his convictions on the family issue into question. Or if he concealed his extramarital affairs from his spouse, one might reasonably be entitled to question this candidate's veracity or reliability. In other cases, if a candidate shows evidence of lack of good judgment or wisdom in his personal life, there may be legitimate questioning of his ability to guide his country in a difficult and potentially dangerous situation that requires good judgment and an ability to function under pressure. This is all part of the democratic system of representation, in which officeholders are elected in the trust that they will show integrity by sticking to their principles, and judgment in running affairs of state.

Whether personal matters are relevant depends on the issue of the critical discussion or the subject of the inquiry. Ultimately, the

7 Jonathan Alter, "Sex and the Presidency," Newsweek, May 4, 1987, p. 26.

139

agenda of the dialogue is the key factor in evaluating the reason-ableness or fallaciousness of an *ad hominem* argument.

Despite all the reservations about personal attacks noted above, sometimes bringing questions of the personal character of an arguer into the argument is reasonable and legitimate. This can occur when the personal characteristics of the arguer are relevant to the issue under discussion:

Example 6.2

A very flattering autobiography of a famous movie star appears in print, written by the actor with the help of a professional writer. The actor is portrayed in the book as a kindly, moral, humanitarian saint, who has often helped people in need and championed charitable causes. In a book review, a critic points out the actor has well-documented criminal connections, has used his paid bodyguards to beat up women and men he took a dislike to, and has committed other vicious and cruel actions. The critic concludes that the autobiography is a one-sided portrait and that its fairness, objectivity, and accuracy are open to question.

In this case, the critic may have a good argument, depending on the reliability of the evidence of personal misconduct he cited and on the arguments in the book he criticized. Even though the critic has attacked the argument of the actor on the basis of his personal characteristics, his criticism could still be quite reasonable and justified.

The critic's argument in example 6.2 could be judged as reasonable, even though it is a personal attack on the actor, because the actor's character is the real issue in the argument. An autobiography quite properly has as its subject matter the character of the writer. When personal allegations are relevant to the issue, the argument against the person can be reasonable. Hence we must be careful not to condemn every seemingly abusive personal attack as a fallacious *ad hominem* argument.

It should be clear, then, that the expression *abusive ad hominem* argument refers to the fallacious or illicit use of the direct type of *ad hominem* attack that focuses on personal character, reliability, or veracity; for in some instances, arguments against the person can be reasonable.

6.2 THE CIRCUMSTANTIAL *AD HOMINEM* ARGUMENT

In contrast to the examples of direct personal attack on an arguer's reliability, veracity, or character, examples of the *circumstantial ad hominem* argument against the person are based on an allegation that the person's circumstances are inconsistent in his own advocacy of the position adopted in his argument. This kind of argument is more subtle because it uses the allegation of inconsistency as evidence that the arguer criticized may be a liar or a hypocrite, or even that he may be so logically incompetent that he cannot follow his own argument. This form of attack is extremely powerful in political debate because it suggests that the person attacked does not follow, in his own conduct, the principles that he advocates for others. The conclusion is that anyone who does not practice what he preaches is not a person worth listening to or taking seriously.

What is characteristic of this type of argument against the person is the citation of an inconsistency between his argument and his personal circumstances. In the examples cited in Section 6.1, no allegation of inconsistency was involved in the personal attack. The examples below involve the attempted refutation of an opponent's argument by citing an inconsistency between his propositions and his personal circumstances.

The type of personal criticism characteristic of the circumstantial *ad hominem* alleges an inconsistent relationship between an argument and the personal practices, position, or situation of the person who advocates the argument.[8] This sort of criticism can be a reasonable challenge in some instances, but it is easy to be confused about the correct conclusion to be drawn from this relative type of argument.[9] Consider the following dialogue:

Example 6.3

Parent: There is strong evidence of a link between smoking and chronic obstructive lung disease. Smoking is also associated with many other serious disorders. Smoking is unhealthy. So you should not smoke.

8 The concept of an arguer's position as a systematic network of coherent commitments has been developed very well by Johnstone (1978).
9 This idea that an arguer's position can be revealed through reasonable dialogue is an important part of the analysis of personal attack argumentation given in Walton (1985b).

Child: But you smoke yourself. So much for your argument against smoking.

Now it might be possible in this case that the parent has a good argument that smoking is linked to lung disease and is therefore unhealthy. Presuming that the child wants to, or should want to, be healthy, the parent's conclusion that the child should not smoke could be, in itself, a reasonable argument. The child has not even attempted to disprove or bring reasonable doubt to bear on this argument. Therefore, he may be too hasty in rejecting it.

On the other hand, the child does seem to have a point worth considering. The parent smokes and admits it. Is it not the case that the parent's advocacy of nonsmoking is inconsistent with his own practice of smoking? And is this personal inconsistency not a reasonable basis for criticising or at least challenging the parent's personal advocacy of his own argument? It is as if the child were saying, 'If your argument is worth anything, why don't you follow it yourself?'

So it seems that both the parent's argument and the child's counterargument are open to reasonable criticisms. Who, then, is right, or how should we settle the argument?

The first constructive step is to point out a certain ambiguity or confusion in understanding what the conclusion of the argument is. If you take the conclusion in an impersonal way as the proposition 'Smoking is unhealthy' or 'Anyone who wants to be healthy should not smoke', the argument may be very reasonable. At least, the child does not seem to be challenging this much of the argument. But if you take the conclusion in a personal way, as the parent saying, 'I am advocating nonsmoking as a policy of good personal conduct', then the argument becomes subject to criticism. Absolutely speaking, the argument is reasonable. Relatively speaking, it runs into trouble.

The problem here is to determine how much of the contextual information should count as part of the argument. Should the parent's smoking be included in the propositions that make up the argument? If so, do his actions commit him personally to the practice of smoking? If so, there is an inconsistency, or at least the addition of a plausible assumption that leads to inconsistency. Assume that the parent wants to be healthy. Then, if anyone who wants to be healthy should not smoke, it follows that the parent should not smoke. But the parent does smoke. And if this practice indicates a commitment to smoking on his part, his practice would suggest that it is all right for him to smoke. But that cannot be consistent with the statement that he should not smoke. The basic issue is, do actions speak louder than, or as loud as, words? If so, then the child has a point. The parent's words run counter to his action. Granted, sometimes such inconsistencies can be explained, defended, or excused. But surely it is not unreasonable to require that the parent owes the child a defense or explanation of his position.

On the other hand, taking the parent's argument in a more impersonal way, the conclusion 'Smoking is unhealthy' could be based on reasonable evidence. Therefore, the child's dismissal of the whole argument is a case of throwing the baby out with the bathwater. It is a hasty and premature dismissal.

To sum up, the basic error in the circumstantial attack in this case is the confusion between two interpretations of the conclusion of the argument. The conclusion can be interpreted in an absolute (impersonal) way, or it can be interpreted in a relative (personal) way. Interpreted one way the argument could be strong, while interpreted the other way it could be weak, or open to challenge and criticism. One form of the fallacy of circumstantial argument against the person is the confusion of the two interpretations of the argument, based on the assumption that both must stand or fall together.

This case suggests that it is important to distinguish between a circumstantial argument against the person and a possible error or weakness in advancing this argument. Criticizing a person's argument by challenging his own advocacy of the conclusion of his argument can be a legitimate argument against that person.[10] At least, it is a not unreasonable challenge or criticism to bring forward in some cases. However, to reject the argument totally on the basis of such a relative criticism may be a serious error. At any rate, this is certainly one important type of error that can be committed in arguments against a person.

These distinctions are reminiscent of some of the components of

---

10 The thesis that an argument against the person can be a legitimate form of criticism is defended by Barth and Martens (1977), by appealing to principles of the theory of reasonable dialogue.

argument discussed in Chapter 1, in which we showed that there are always two participants in an argument, a proponent and a respondent. In the case of arguments against the person, the proponent is the original advocate of an argument, for example, the parent, in example 6.3. The opponent in an argument is the critic who alleges that there is a circumstantial or personal inconsistency in the proponent's position. In example 6.3, the critic is the child. Therefore, we see that in studying weaknesses and errors in personal attack as a type of argument, we must look at both sides of the argument. In other words, we cannot just look at the arguments as a set of propositions, after the fashion of Chapter 2. We have to go back to components of argument as a two-person dialogue that we studied in Chapter 1.

In studying example 6.3, we need to distinguish among several stages of the sequence of dialogue. First, there is the original argument. Then there is the circumstantial criticism of this argument by a respondent. If that criticism is successful, and there are no good grounds for the proponent's reply, then the burden of proof has shifted against his side. However, if the proponent can successfully reply to the criticism, the shoe may come to be on the other foot and it is the critic who is found to have advanced a weak argument, itself open to criticism. In short, it could be either the attacker or defender of an argument who may reasonably be found open to criticism.

Finally, we must be careful to observe another important distinction related to the nature of argument as reasonable dialogue. Taken in an impersonal way, the conclusion of an argument is simply a proposition. However, in any reasonable dialogue, a conclusion is that of the one arguer who must prove it. Therefore, in criticizing an argument, the respondent may not just be claiming that the proposition in question is false or unproved. He may be arguing that the proposition cannot consistently be maintained by his opponent in argument. He may be arguing that his opponent's proposition is not consistent with other commitments which can be fairly attributed to the position of his opponent in the argument. Here, the critic is not necessarily challenging the conclusion of his opponent's argument per se. He may be challenging the opponent's own advocacy of that conclusion and questioning his premises.

One basic problem with many cases of personal argumentation is to evaluate fairly whether an arguer's personal actions may reasonably commit him to certain propositions. From the given context of an argument, we may be required to sort out which propositions an arguer may reasonably be said to have committed himself to.

One example has been cited so often in logic textbooks as a case of the circumstantial *ad hominem* fallacy that it can justifiably be called the classic example of the argument against the person:

Example 6.4

A hunter is accused of barbarity for his sacrifice of innocent animals to his own amusement or sport in hunting. His reply to his critic: "Why do you feed on the flesh of harmless cattle?"

The sportsman's reply to his critic is traditionally said to commit an *ad hominem* fallacy because it attempts to refute the critic through the critic's own special circumstances. Because the critic is not a vegetarian himself, the sportsman alleges that the critic is personally inconsistent with his own argument. Why is the sportsman's reply an incorrect argument against the person? The point is the same one made in relation to example 6.3. The sportsman fails to present good grounds for the impersonal conclusion that hunting is acceptable as a general practice. Instead, he argues against the critic's own special and personal circumstances. The sportsman's personal criticism may be legitimate, but insofar as it fails to refute the general issue raised by the critic, his argument fails to provide grounds for the impersonal conclusion it should address. So far, then, example 6.4 seems similar to example 6.3.

But there is an important new point to be raised in connection with example 6.4. Is the sportsman's personal criticism of his critic's situation a legitimate case of circumstantial inconsistency? To sort this out, let us take a careful look at the propositions that make up the argument. First, what practice is the critic objecting to? He objects to the sportsman's practice of sacrificing innocent animals for his amusement, that is, hunting. But what practice does the sportsman accuse the critic of engaging in himself? It is the practice of eating meat.

Now is there any inconsistency between eating meat and rejecting the practice of hunting game for amusement? Well, certainly there is no logical inconsistency. If I sit eating a rare filet mignon while criticizing the cruel practices of hunters who take joy in gunning down innocent animals, I am not logically inconsistent. I would be logically inconsistent if I obtained my filet mignon by gunning down an innocent cow, took joy in it, and then made it clear that I advocated this practice as a worthwhile sport. But it is quite possible that such activities played no part in my obtaining that particular steak for my dinner table, nor would I advocate them. The lesson so far is that we should be very careful in specifying exactly which are the propositions alleged to be inconsistent when we are advancing an argument against the person.

According to example 6.4, the sportsman claimed that there was a circumstantial inconsistency between the following two propositions:

(1) The critic criticizes the killing of innocent animals for amusement or sport.

(2) The critic himself eats meat.

There is no logical inconsistency between (1) and (2), nor any clear case of a circumstantial inconsistency either. As Augustus De-Morgan (1847, p. 265) neatly observed in connection with this classic example, the parallel will not exist until we substitute a person who turns butcher for amusement for the person who eats meat. What the critic objects to is not eating meat, but taking pleasure in killing animals for amusement or sport.

Therefore, there is an additional dimension to the argument against the person revealed by this case. The sportsman could be on reasonable grounds if he had challenged the critic for himself being a hunter. But that was not his reply. The sportsman fell short of giving solid justification of his charge that the critic is circumstantially inconsistent. On initial appearances, the critic could seem open to a charge of personal inconsistency. But by falling far short of establishing this charge, the sportsman commits another error; for his argument supports merely a superficial appearance of inconsistency, rather than a solid justification of this charge.

This much said, it should also be recognized that there is some connection between the practice of eating meat and the practice of hunting. For one thing, eating meat, in economic terms, makes the killing of animals profitable as a source of food.

Although there is a connection between eating meat and killing animals by hunting, it is an oblique rather than a direct one. Moreover, the sportsman's reply is in the form of a question. That is a

146

point in his favor because, strictly speaking, he is only questioning the consistency of his critic.

Now the critic eats meat, and let us say that he concedes this personal practice. What propositions do his actions reasonably commit him to advocating? Clearly they do not commit him to hunting game for amusement or as a pastime. But his actions do connect him indirectly to the slaughter of innocent farm animals and might thereby suggest some degree of acceptance of these practices. Or do they? The best way to find out would be to ask the critic. But short of that, there could be a reasonable but weak presumption that the critic's dietary practices do commit him, to some extent, to the acceptability of slaughtering animals for food. If so, there is some basis, a fairly weak one perhaps, for the sportsman's rejoinder as an argument against the person. The problem is to determine fairly in a particular case what propositions one's acknowledged actions or practices may commit one to.

This type of problem is related to the ethical problem of "dirty hands." Does indirect involvement in an activity represent a sponsorship or personal advocacy of all or some aspects or consequences of that activity that is stronger than passive involvement? Each case in ethics must be approached individually. So too in pragmatic logic, in which evidence is derived from the text of argument so that the issue can be resolved through reasonable dialogue. Although the sportsman's rejoinder can be criticized for two kinds of errors as an argument against the person, still it is a persuasive argument because it does rest on a connection that may be not altogether worthless as a partial basis toward constructing a circumstantial argument against the person. But by the standards of reasonable dialogue, it is a weak argument that is very much open to criticism.

One legitimate function of the argument against the person may be to shift the burden of proof in dialogue back onto an attacker. Sometimes this form of attack and reply is called the *tu quoque* (you too) rejoinder:

Example 6.5

A student accuses a businessman of selling weapons to countries that use them to kill innocent citizens. The businessman replies, "The university you attend has investments in these very companies that manufacture weapons. Your hands aren't clean either!"

The businessman in effect replies that the student's argument is hypocritical. He is saying, "You too!" He alleges that the student's position is inconsistent and that his practices support the very institutions that he condemns. In this case, the response to the personal circumstantial attack is a second personal circumstantial attack.

In analyzing example 6.5, we must remember the lessons of our analysis of 6.4. There is a difference between the proposition 'X sells weapons to countries that use them to kill innocent citizens' and the proposition 'X attends an institution that has investments in companies that manufacture weapons'. To condemn one activity while engaging in the other is not logically inconsistent. It is not even circumstantially inconsistent. But there is a significant connection between the two propositions.

The businessman's *tu quoque* reply can be criticized as a weak argument on the same two grounds as the sportsman's rejoinder was criticized. Even once we recognize that the businessman's reply is a very weak basis for an argument against the person, however, perhaps the reply should at least deflect some burden of criticism back onto the student to defend his own position as a critic. If so, then in some cases, the *tu quoque* reply is not an unreasonable form of argument against the person.[11]

Clearly the great danger with arguments against the person is uncritically taking them for much stronger arguments than they really are. Personal attack arguments are so powerful and upsetting that often the mere suggestion of a personal inconsistency can damage an opponent's argument out of all proportion to the impact it should logically be taken to have. While personal criticisms are sometimes not unreasonable, the danger of committing serious errors by overreacting to them in argument is very real indeed.

The first step in analyzing any circumstantial argument against the person is to determine and clearly state the pair of propositions that is alleged to be the source of the inconsistency. The next step is to ask whether these propositions are logically inconsistent. If they are not, then the next step is to ask whether they are circumstantially inconsistent. A set of propositions may be said to be *circumstantially inconsistent* for an arguer when his circumstances or actions clearly indicate his commitment to a set of propositions in the context of dialogue, and those propositions are collectively incon-

---

11 This example (6.5) is studied in more detail in Walton (1985b, pp. 63–6).

sistent. To establish a circumstantial inconsistency, we must justify from our reading of the given circumstances that the arguer so accused indeed has an inconsistent set of propositions in his commitment-store, that is, has adopted a position that is inconsistent. The key step in evaluating any such claim of inconsistency is for the evaluator to state clearly each of the individual propositions that are, taken together, supposed to comprise a circumstantial inconsistency in the position of the arguer being criticized. As we have seen, it is all too easy, in practice, for a critic to launch a powerful attack by citing a pair of propositions that may superficially seem to be inconsistent but are really not inconsistent at all, as the argument stands.

6.3 THE ATTACK ON AN ARGUER'S IMPARTIALITY

In some cases, an *ad hominem* argument is designed to attack an arguer's presumed impartiality by imputing a bias to the arguer. In such a case, the criticism alleged is that the arguer in question cannot be trusted to engage in fair argument because he has a hidden agenda, a personal motive or bias for pushing one side of the argument and ignoring the other side. The following *ad hominem* attack is a case in point:

Example 6.6

Bob and Wilma are discussing the problem of acid rain. Wilma argues that reports on the extent of the problem are greatly exaggerated and that the costs of action are prohibitive. Bob points out that Wilma is on the board of directors of a U.S. coal company and that therefore her argument should not be taken at face value.[12]

Here Bob's criticism seems to be that Wilma has a hidden motive for pushing for one side of the issue. He is therefore questioning her fairness as an arguer who has looked at all the available arguments on the issue. Is she telling the whole story or taking a balanced perspective? Bob is suggesting that, because she did not tell us at the beginning that she was financially involved with an American coal company, there is some question of her reliability or fairness as an arguer on this issue.

12 Example 6.6 was derived from a similar case discussed by Robert Binkley during a symposium, "Walton on Informal Fallacies," at the Canadian Philosophical Association Meeting in Winnipeg, May 26, 1986.

Of course, the basic point about all arguments against the person must be kept in mind in this case, as in the previous cases. Wilma's arguments could be based on good evidence. Even granted that she is on the board of directors of a coal company, it does not necessarily follow that her arguments must be wrong. So to argue would be a fallacious kind of *ad hominem* argument.

But it could be that Bob's conclusion is the weaker claim that we should question Wilma's impartiality in emphasizing the points that she stressed. Bob could be saying that we should be careful in taking Wilma's arguments as the whole story; for she has a financial stake in the outcome, and therefore a strong motive for concentrating on the arguments against taking action and ignoring the arguments for action against industrial polluters of the environment.

What Bob seems to be suggesting is that there is a reason for questioning Wilma's integrity or impartiality as a neutral investigator of the issue. If she had openly told us at the outset that she was taking the side of the industrial companies on the issue, then there would be no need for this type of criticism; for there is nothing wrong with arguing for your own side in a persuasion dialogue. But if the dialogue is supposed to be an impartial investigation (inquiry), rather than a dispute, then the situation is different. In this context, if one arguer has a hidden agenda to support one side of the dispute while appearing to be a neutral investigator, then it can be reasonable for the other arguer to question the alleged neutrality of the first arguer, if there is a good reason to suspect bias.

In this case, the basis of the *ad hominem* criticism is the allegation that a dialectical shift has taken place – a change from one context of dialogue to another. As we have seen, one type of reasonable dialogue is the persuasion dialogue, in which the thesis of one arguer is the opposite of the thesis of the other. But not every reasonable dialogue is a persuasion dialogue. Sometimes participants in an inquiry can investigate an issue without having definitely made up their minds or taken sides on the issue at the outset. And this inquiry type of argumentation is a different context of dialogue from that of the persuasion dialogue.

Thus the argument against the person in this type of case is a challenge to the trustworthiness of an arguer in keeping to the rules and objectives of the game of dialogue that the arguers are supposed to be engaged in.

Even more damagingly, Bob could be suggesting that Wilma is engaged in a third type of dialogue, the negotiation, or interest-based bargaining type of argumentation. Bob has indicated that Wilma is on the board of directors of a coal company. Therefore, he claims that she has a financial stake in the issue of acid rain. Bob may be suggesting, then, that Wilma is even more strongly subject to bias in her argumentation because she is covertly promoting her own financial interests by trying to convince others that acid rain is not a serious problem.

Although elements of both the abusive and circumstantial *ad hominem* types of argumentation are tangentially involved in example 6.6, neither personal abuse nor circumstantial inconsistency per se is the main target of the attack. Instead, Bob is arguing that Wilma is not really open to impartial inquiry, or perhaps even to two-sided critical discussion of the issue of acid rain, because she is bound by her financial stake in the matter always to press for one side of the argument only, no matter what the real evidence on the question may indicate. Hence this type of case is really more like the "poisoning the well" kind of *ad hominem* attack. It is an imputation of bias, and it essentially involves an allegation that a concealed dialectical shift has taken place within the argument.

Another instance of this *ad hominem* imputation of bias occurred during a debate on abortion in the Canadian House of Commons, during which the Speaker of the House made the following interjection:[13]

Example 6.7

I wish it were possible for men to get really emotionally involved in this question. It is really impossible for the man, for whom it is impossible to be in this situation, to really see it from the woman's point of view. That is why I am concerned that there are not more women in this House available to speak about this from the woman's point of view.

This argument is based on a true premise, namely that a man cannot personally experience unwanted pregnancy or abortion. And therefore, perhaps, it is correct to suggest that a man's experience in this area is inherently limited, at least from a personal perspective. But is it right to conclude that it is *impossible* for any man to see the

13 *House of Commons Debates of Canada*, Vol. 2, November 30, 1979, p. 1920.

issue from the woman's point of view? The danger here lies in the suggestions that men have nothing to say on this issue and that what they say is not credible because it must always be based on a lack of the required expertise and therefore on an inability to take part in serious deliberations on the issue.

The problem with this type of argument is that, by suggesting an inevitable bias on the part of an arguer because of his personal circumstances or characteristics, it tends to exclude that person from a role in any subsequent serious argument on the issue. But if the critic has the opposite personal characteristic, then she too is trapped in an inescapable bias. So what is the use of further dialogue?

This argument suggests that a man cannot help having a biased opinion on the issue of abortion or taking a one-sided view of the subject, simply because he is a man. A criticism of this argument is that the speaker cannot help seeing the issue from the other side, or at least taking a one-sided view of the subject, simply because she is a woman. Such an argument can always be stood on its head in reply. But once the reply is made, the argument has gone nowhere.

Sometimes the best reply to a personal attack is an opposing personal attack. But the danger is that you may get still another personal attack in reply, and so on. The resulting personal quarrel may be unproductive and not advance discussion on the issue of the dialogue.

Another problem with this style of argument against the person is that it can create a stalemate that stifles further discussion; for it is implied that neither side can help taking a personal, one-sided position in the argument. So, the message seems to be, what is the point of continuing the argument? But postulating the inescapability of personal bias can be a bad mistake, for it suggests the futility of honestly looking at the evidence and issues on both sides in a reasonable manner. Although alleging personal bias is justified in some cases, to suggest that one's opponent in argument is totally biased and hopelessly dogmatic is a particularly strong and dangerous form of personal attack. It should be criticized or challenged when it tends to subvert or close our minds to reasonable dialogue. Unfortunately, the argument against the person is often so effective and devastating that it is a conversation stopper, closing off the possibilities of objective argument and further reasonable discussion of an issue.

In the following case, the leader of a group of black Americans who claim to be the descendants of Judah living in a country occupied by white devils is quoted as saying whites are "evil, wicked liars and murderers" whose "tricks must be removed."[14] This hard line toward disbelievers is reflected in further statements attributed to the leader of this cult:

Example 6.8

The dictionary defines devil as an adversary of God. If you are an opponent of mine, then you would be classified as a devil.

The problem with this point of view is that, by classifying all white persons as "evil, wicked liars" and "devils," no room is left for any presumption that further reasonable dialogue can be carried on with any arguer who has the personal characteristic of being white. The reason is that all white people, as "devils" and "liars," cannot be trusted to take part in serious or honest dialogue because they are inherently unreliable and unreasonable. When this point of view is reached, there is no room left for argument, because reasoned argument presupposes an arguer who is, at least to some degree, open-minded, serious, and trustworthy in collaborating in joint dialogue.

The bias type of argument against the person is so effective in undermining argument and discrediting an opponent that it is aptly called "poisoning the well," in many instances. The term is supposed to have originated with Cardinal Newman, when he was confronted by the argument that, as a Catholic priest, he did not place the highest value on the truth. The allegation was that, because Cardinal Newman was personally biased toward the Catholic position, he could not be relied upon as a source of fair or impartial argument. Cardinal Newman's reply was that this accusation made it impossible for him, or any other Catholic, to successfully or reasonably carry forward any argument on any subject or issue. In effect, then, the presumption was created, by the personal allegation, that any further argument advanced by Cardinal Newman would be automatically discredited. Hence the appropriateness of the term "poisoning the well."

Though it may be legitimate in some cases to raise the question of an arguer's commitment to a certain general position or ideology,

14 "Yahweh's Way," *Newsweek*, November 10, 1986, p. 31.

the problem is that this form of attack can often be so powerful and overwhelming that it stops conversation altogether. By so strongly discrediting an arguer, it prematurely blocks off reasonable dialogue altogether. Often, personal attack heightens emotions, leading to rage and frustration, and thence to a desire to hit back at all costs, whether by fair or foul means. Usually this is not a good direction for an argument to take, and it may indicate an underlying dialectical shift.

6.4 NONFALLACIOUS *AD HOMINEM* ARGUMENTS

The previous examples have indicated that there are many ways in which criticism directed against the person can be fallacious. However, the last examples have suggested that in some cases, and to some extent, a personal attack against an opponent's circumstances or position may not be altogether unreasonable. Does this mean that in some cases arguments against the person could be reasonable? In Section 6.1, it was suggested that this is, indeed, the case. And if it is true, it means that we must not reject an argument against the person without giving good reasons.

We saw that example 6.3, from one point of view, could be interpreted as a weak but basically reasonable criticism. Another example will illustrate a reasonable use of the circumstantial argument against the person as a move in argument. Consider the following dialogue:

Example 6.9

George: The notorious problems we have been having with postal strikes means that there is no longer reliable mail service provided by the government. I think we ought to allow private, for-profit mail-delivery companies to compete on an equal footing with the Post Office.

Bob: But George, you are a communist.

Let us suppose that in this case George is an avowed communist and has based his previous arguments on many standard communist principles and positions. Now, in many cases, calling your opponent in an argument a communist could be a fallacious type of *ad hominem* attack. However, in this instance, Bob seems to have a reasonable point. If George is an avowed communist, and communists are for

154

state control and against private enterprise, then how can George consistently argue for a for-profit mail service run by private enterprise? It seems like a legitimate question. Of course, George may be able to resolve the ostensible inconsistency in subsequent dialogue. But surely Bob is justified in challenging the consistency of George's position at this point in the dialogue. If so, then in this case, Bob's circumstantial argument is not fallacious. It is a reasonable use of the *ad hominem* argument to challenge George's position.

If arguments against the person can sometimes be reasonable, we must carefully analyze them to set out criteria that will enable us to distinguish between the incorrect (fallacious) and reasonable instances of *ad hominem* argumentation. First, let us address the reasonable type of person-directed criticism in argument.

A personal attack can be a reasonable criticism of an arguer's position by showing that his concessions or commitments are inconsistent with the propositions asserted in his argument. Some might say that such an attack is, or can be, specious because it misses the real point of looking to the external evidence and instead concentrates on the internal relationships of the arguer's position. For instance, in example 6.9, some commentators might say that Bob would be better off to evaluate George's proposal of private mail service on its own merits, rather than raise the internal question of whether the proposal is internally consistent with George's own political position. What does George's internal position matter to anyone else, compared with the very important issue of whether mail service should be public or private? This point of view has some justification, for external evidence should very often have priority, and if we are distracted from that external evidence by purely personal (internal) considerations, that is the very climate in which the personal attack creates the most mischief in argument.

However, internal matters of an arguer's position can sometimes be important too. If George really is inconsistent in his position and confused – a communist who advocates free enterprise – then it is very important for George to sort out his own position. First, if George's position does truly contain a logical inconsistency, then it cannot be right. Second, there may be many other readers or listeners affected by George's argument who may be moderately sympathetic to some forms of communism, and who may be quite irritated and concerned about postal strikes and reliable mail services.

For these people, it may be very important to think through the whole issue in much the same way that George is trying to think it through. Even those who strongly reject any communist political ideals may be concerned about how a communist could deal with the problems posed by mail strikes. So the internal question of the consistency of George's position on this issue may be very important for George and many others as well. ,

Third, internal evidence can be enough to swing the balance of acceptance to one side of an argument or the other when external evidence is lacking or cannot be brought to bear on an issue. On a complex and controversial moral or political issue like state control of services, there may be no clear external, factual, or scientific evidence that would definitely resolve the controversy. Although internal evidence derived from an arguer's position may always be weaker than external evidence, sometimes, when it is hard to decide on a controversial topic, weak evidence may be enough to shift the burden of proof. In such a case, if an arguer adopts a position that is open to a criticism of inconsistency, that may be enough to shift the burden of proof against his case. Such an arguer will be put on the defensive, and his credibility as an advocate of his side of the argument may then be questioned.

Fourth, in some cases a successful argument against the person can bring into question an arguer's impartiality, sincerity, or trustworthiness. This may be a weak form of argument, but it may be enough to alter the burden of proof on a controversial issue. And therefore it can be a reasonable criticism.

On controversial issues, hard evidence that can be directly brought to bear on a disputed proposition may be lacking. In such a case, reasonable dialogue may be the only available way of deciding to accept a conclusion, short of deciding by random choice or by following one's dogmatic inclinations. Here, understanding the arguer's positions both pro and con may help one to arrive at a more intelligent or reasoned decision on how to make a commitment, if a decision must be made. If an arguer's position is open to fair criticism of internal inconsistency, that could be a good reason for anyone to withhold acceptance of the arguer's conclusion based on that position.

In short, sometimes arguing against an opponent by using his own concessions against his argument can be fair and reasonable, within limits. Such an argument may show that the arguer's position

156

is inconsistent and may thereby show that the arguer is not a credible advocate of the conclusion he purports to advance. However, an argument against the person does not show that his conclusion is necessarily false, in itself. At best, it shows that the position backing up the argument is open to challenge. In example 6.9, George's conclusion that private companies should be allowed to compete with the Post Office might, for all we know, be true. George may even be able to give some good reasons for it that anyone, even an anticommunist, would wish to take into account. Even so, Bob's criticism is a reasonable argument against the person in reply if it shows that this conclusion does not square with George's own political philosophy. That may be a good criticism, but of course it does not necessarily imply that George's conclusion is false. So to argue would be an incorrect use of the argument against the person. In short, then, an argument against the person can sometimes be a reasonable criticism, but only within carefully drawn limits.

Traditionally, the argument against the person, or so-called *ad hominem* argument, has been called a fallacy in the discussions of many textbooks.[15] However, it is more useful to make the following distinctions, which allow for the argument against the person to be a reasonable criticism in some cases and an inadequately reasoned or supported criticism in other cases.[16] A *personal attack* (*personal allegation*) is said to have been advanced in argument where one arguer uses some personal allegations relative to the motives, circumstances, actions, and so forth, as a basis to criticize an opponent's argument. This form of attack can have three forms: the direct (abusive) personal attack, the circumstantial personal attack, and the attack on an arguer's impartiality. Such an attack becomes a *personal criticism of an argument* when evidence is given by the arguer to back up his personal attack on the argument criticized. For this criticism to be reasonable, the evidence must fulfill various requirements.

The more subtle and complex type of personal attack is the circumstantial type, in which care is needed to identify the nature of the alleged circumstantial inconsistency. A *circumstantial attack against the person* occurs when an arguer questions the consistency of another

15 See Govier (1983) and Walton (1985b).
16 A deeply and carefully reasoned defense of the argument against the person as a kind of criticism that can be reasonable in some contexts of dialogue is given by Johnstone (1978).

arguer's position. A *circumstantial criticism* is advanced when the questioning arguer (1) pins down a specific set of propositions and gives some evidence that the other arguer is committed to these propositions as part of his argument or position and (2) gives some reason to show that there is a danger of inconsistency, either circumstantial or logical, in these propositions. A *circumstantial refutation* occurs when a circumstantial criticism is successfully backed up by showing that the set of propositions in question is part of the other arguer's set of commitments and does imply a logical contradiction by valid arguments. Various forms of errors occur in direct and circumstantial personal attacks when criticism is inadequately supported and therefore fails either as a reasonable criticism or as a successful refutation of the argument in question. There are several types of failures, which we will turn to in the next section.

As a form of criticism, argument against the person has the effect of challenging an arguer's position and thereby putting his case on the defensive. All controversial argument is really a dialogue, and there are always two sides to a dialogue. The effect of an *ad hominem* reply in dialogue is to bounce the ball back into your opponent's court. However, the ultimate resolution of an argument against the person as a criticism that is successful, or itself open to criticism, is often highly dependent on the subsequent dialogue that takes place between the critic and the defender of the argument. Thus a good personal criticism may be successful if it opens up the channels of dialogue in articulating or exploring two opposed positions on a controversial issue.

Some arguments are more open to personal criticism than others. Consider the following argument:

Example 6.10

Skeptic: All arguments are relative to beliefs that can be challenged. Hence no argument is reliable.

This argument is open to the following personal, circumstantial reply to Skeptic: "What about your own argument (example 6.10), Skeptic? Is it reliable?" If Skeptic tries to insist that his argument is reliable, he is clearly in danger of personal inconsistency, for he has just maintained that *no* argument is reliable. How can he consistently make an exception to his own argument without being illogical? On the other hand, if Skeptic concedes that his own argument in example 6.10 is indeed unreliable, he is also in trouble on grounds of circumstantial inconsistency. Can he really be a sincere and competent participant in reasonable dialogue if he is advocating an argument that he knows to be unreliable? Either way, Skeptic is hoisted by his own petard.

So some arguments, like example 6.10, are especially vulnerable to the circumstantial argument against the person as a form of criticism. In such cases, the argument against the person is the most reasonable and appropriate type of criticism to bring forward. In these cases, the argument against the person can successfully refute the argument. However, in many cases the argument against the person is inherently weaker. It is not a refutation in such cases, but nevertheless it can often be a reasonable form of challenge to the argument and can successfully shift the burden of proof against it.

6.5 REPLYING TO A PERSONAL ATTACK

The argument against the person is not a total refutation in most cases, but a kind of argument that can be replied to by further argument that shifts the burden of proof back onto the attacker. Thus the argument against the person is often a *defeasible criticism,* meaning that it is inherently open to a rejoinder that could defeat, or at least ward off, the criticism. One way to reply to an argument against the person is for the respondent to come back, *tu quoque,* with a parallel personal argument against his critic. However, it should be realized that such arguments are inherently defeasible because it is always possible that an arguer can claim that his personal circumstances are different from those of his critic in some respect, which would destroy the parallel cited.

In example 6.3, the child's criticism of the parent's inconsistency in smoking while advocating nonsmoking turned on the presumption that the parent is not treating himself and the child on the same basis. The parent smokes but then tells the child he should not smoke. The child, by his allegation of circumstantial inconsistency, is in effect accusing the parent of treating his own circumstances and those of the child he criticizes on an unequal basis. But notice that it is possible that the parent could cite some relevant difference between his own circumstances and those of the child. Suppose the parent informs the child that he, the parent, is suffering from AIDS, a terminal disease, and that smoking will not significantly affect his

159

prognosis or prospects for health; whereas, the parent might maintain, smoking in the child's circumstances could radically affect his prospects for a healthy life.

The prospect of new information about the personal circumstances of an arguer entering into the dialogue, in the case of an argument against the person, is made possible because this type of criticism is often more like a questioning than a decisive refutation of an arguer's position.

The following case will illustrate how question–reply dialogue is the natural context of the argument against the person, and how this defeasible argument is subject to the reply that the defender's situation is different from that of his attacker:

Example 6.11

Parliamentarian A: Can you assure the public that there will be no increase in interest rates tomorrow?

Parliamentarian B: This is a ludicrous question coming from the Honorable Member who was a minister when his previous government was pushing interest rates up to 20 and 25 percent per annum.

B's reply is a circumstantial personal attack. B alleged that during the period when A's party was in power, there was a 20 to 25 percent increase in interest rates. Given A's personal track record in this regard, B alleged, it is ludicrous for him to request assurance that there will be no rise in interest rates. In other words, B is replying with the classic *tu quoque* circumstantial argument that A does not "practice what he preaches." One reason that this example of the use of the argument against the person is novel and interesting, however, is that the argument is used in reply to a question. It is a combination of two traditional types of informal fallacies, which shows how the argument against the person can be used in dialogue to attack a question powerfully.

What B is arguing is that A has no right to ask this question, because if A were in B's situation, he could not answer the question himself. How reasonable is B's reply?

To begin with, there do appear to be good grounds for criticizing B's reply as not conducive to the goals of reasonable dialogue. The reason is that B's clever personal attack effectively avoids the real issue of interest rates by attacking A and thereby avoiding the necessity of answering the question. By attacking A's question, he has shifted the burden of reply back to A's side of the argument, thereby appearing to make A somehow vulnerable to his own criticism. From this point of view, B's reply can be construed as evasive, or at any rate as a failure to answer the question. But that is not the end of the matter.

If a question is not fair or contains a loaded presupposition, it is generally reasonable to allow the answerer to reply by questioning the question instead of giving a direct answer. In such a case, a failure to answer the question need not be a wrongful evasion.

Now one might observe here that A's question is fairly aggressive. A certain degree of short-term fluctuation in interest rates has become rather normal in the recent economic climate. Therefore, a question requesting assurance that there will be no increase in interest rates on a specific day may not be all that reasonable, relative to the context of this particular dialogue. Moreover, it would probably be politically unwise for Parliamentarian B to guarantee that there will be no increase on any particular day in the future. For one thing, he most likely has very little or no control over this specific fluctuation or stability. So he dare not answer 'yes', but if he answers 'no', he also concedes something that may appear negative or may be open to further criticism. The question is not as forcefully aggressive as the celebrated spouse–beating question, but it is sufficiently aggressive that one can see the resemblance.

Observing the aggressiveness of the question, then, a critic could argue that B's not answering the question should not be judged unduly evasive. By replying with a circumstantial citing of rising interest rates during the questioner's own time of power, B's reply could be interpreted as quite justifiably criticizing the presumptions of the question. And if B feels, with reason, that he cannot directly answer the question without being unreasonably forced to damage or undermine his own position or that of his party, then he should have the right to challenge the basis of the question. Indeed, some might say that B is doing the right thing in this case as a critical reasoner, instead of submitting to a question that has implications that could be misleading.

Since the argument against the person can be a reasonable way of criticizing an arguer's position, B's questioning of A's question can be defended as a reasonable reply. Although B did not answer the question, and although his reply was a personal attack, it does not follow that B has committed an error or given a bad reply in the dialogue.

This case at once illustrates the wisdom of being careful not to give in too easily to the temptation to shout "Fallacy!" without looking at each side of an argument carefully and individually on its merits. Now that we have considered how B replied to A, it might be useful to go even further in the dialogue to ask how A might reasonably respond to B's reply. Consider the following hypothetical extension of the dialogue:

> *Parliamentarian A:* When the previous government was in power, the world inflationary pressures were at their peak. The high interest rates, at that time, affected all currencies and were not due to our fiscal policies in particular. At present, the fiscal situation is very different, and it is possible for the government to keep interest rates down.

By this reply, A is arguing that his initial question was reasonable and that the parallel drawn by B between his own situation and the previous situation of A's government is not reasonable.

It is as if B is arguing, 'When you were in the same situation, you did the very thing you now criticize me for doing, and so you are inconsistent', whereas A is arguing, 'I was not in the same situation as you, so my criticizing your action is not inconsistent'. So the issue of whether the allegation of circumstantial inconsistency can be supported depends on the similarity between the two situations, the particular circumstances of A and B. Ultimately the resolution of the reasonableness of the personal attack as a reply in the dialogue depends on the evidence of whether the personal situation of both arguers is similar in the relevant respect.

What our evaluation of example 6.11 has shown is that each case of an argument against the person must be examined in light of the personal circumstances alleged to be parallel. Thus the argument against the person is defeasible as long as there remains the possibility of the defense that the two sets of circumstances are different in some significant respect.

This is perhaps not too surprising because as we saw in Section 6.2, the resolution of an allegation of circumstantial inconsistency may depend on how an action is to be described. But this in turn may depend on the particulars of the situation in which the action was alleged to be carried out.

6.6 CRITICAL QUESTIONS FOR AN
AD HOMINEM ARGUMENT

The *argumentum ad hominem* is essentially a negative kind of argumentation – it is a form of attack or criticism that is applied by one participant in dialogue against the argument of another participant. An *ad hominem* attack can be applied to any kind of argument but is especially appropriate and effective when external (objective) evidence for the argument is weak or lacking. In such a case, the *ad hominem* criticism attacks the internal, or subjective, support of the argument by questioning the reliability, veracity, internal coherence, or impartiality of the arguer himself.

The following check list of critical questions should be answered in evaluating any argument against the person:

1. Is the argument against the person posed in the form of a question? If so, and the respondent has made a reply to the question, is the reply relevant? Note that, even if the attack is made in the form of a question, the respondent may not necessarily be guilty of fallacious evasion if he fails to give a direct answer to the question. In the sportsman's rejoinder, for example, a better answer is to question the presupposition of the question that the defender's position is inconsistent by virtue of his practice of eating meat. In some cases, a defender might also, for example, want to question the presupposition that he does eat meat. More information on the reasonableness or unreasonableness of questions is given in Chapter 2. For the present purpose, it is enough to see that if the question is unreasonable or unfairly aggressive in the dialogue, failure to answer it should not necessarily be evaluated as a fault or error on the part of the respondent.
2. Is the argument against the person a direct or circumstantial attack? If it is a direct attack, check critical questions 3 through 7. If it is a circumstantial attack, check points 8 through 17.
3. What is the critic's conclusion? Is he only questioning the arguer's contention or is he claiming that it is false? Note that the latter claim is stronger and requires stronger evidence.
4. Is there a rejection or questioning of the arguer's impartiality? If so, is reasonable evidence given? Are the reasons given strong enough to support the claim?
5. Has the critic rejected the arguer's reliability on one issue when his reliability on another subject has been questioned? If so, are the two topics closely enough related to each other to warrant the argument against the person as a strong argument?
6. Does the argument against the person tend to close off further dialogue by "poisoning the well"? If so, can it be "stood on its head" in reply?
7. How relevant are questions about personal character to the issue of

the argument if the attack turns on questions of the personal character of the arguer?

8. In evaluating any circumstantial argument against the person as a reasonable or unreasonable criticism, one must first of all attempt to identify the propositions that are alleged to be inconsistent. What are these propositions? Clearly identify them from the given corpus of the argument.

9. Are the given propositions logically inconsistent? Collect together the set of propositions alleged to be inconsistent, and investigate whether they are logically inconsistent as they stand. To show that they are logically inconsistent, you must deduce a contradiction from them by valid arguments. If this cannot be done, go on to critical question 10.

10. Are the given propositions circumstantially inconsistent? If there is no logical inconsistency, then evaluate whether there are reasonable grounds for the claim that there is a circumstantial inconsistency in the defender's position. What sort of evidence does the given corpus offer for a claim of circumstantial inconsistency? Is the case strong or weak? Who is alleged to have committed the inconsistency? Often a group is referred to in an *ad hominem* allegation, for example a profession or a political party. If some members of the group have engaged in certain practices, it need not follow that the defender is one of those members or accepts all their policies.

11. How well specified is the defender's position? Could further dialogue spell out that position more specifically in relation to the conclusion at issue? Does the defender's position commit him to certain propositions that could lead to a propositional inconsistency, even if he has not explicitly accepted these propositions in his argument?

12. If the allegation of inconsistency is weak, what is the connection between the pair of propositions alleged to be the basis of the conflict in the defender's position? If the parallel is weak, or nonexistent, does that mean that the personal attack can be classified as erroneous? See the four types of shortcomings of the argument against the person outlined in Section 6.7.

13. If there is an inconsistency that can be established as part of the defender's position, how serious a flaw is this contradiction? Can the defender explain or resolve it very easily without destroying his position? What could be a plausible reply for the defender?

14. Does the defender have a legitimate opportunity to reply to the personal attack? Most arguments against the person can be answered by further dialogue, so it is important not to allow the criticism to be a conversation stopper if the accused party could respond. Remember that most arguments against the person are not conclusive refutations, but they can reasonably shift the burden of argument onto the defender to reply.

15. Could the arguer who has been attacked by a circumstantial argument against the person cite a relevant difference in the two sets of personal circumstances alleged to he parallel in the attack?

16. If the defender has in fact replied to an *ad hominem* attack with another *ad hominem* attack in reply, is there enough of a parallel to justify shifting

the burden of proof back onto the attacker? In such a case, has a question been evaded or the issue avoided?

17. If a defense against an *ad hominem* attack involves a denial of inconsistency by taking a hard or dogmatic stance on the language used to describe the situations at issue, ask whether the terms used are being defined in a one-sided manner. Is the defender being consistent in his use of terms?

These seventeen critical questions must be considered in evaluating arguments against the person. In any given case, some questions on the list will be more significant than others. Many violations of the rules of persuasion dialogue are possible on both sides in disputed arguments against the person, but certain important errors are listed in the next section.

6.7 IMPORTANT TYPES OF ERROR TO CHECK

Several distinct types of errors or shortcomings can be made in mounting a personal criticism against an arguer's position. The most basic type of error is to argue that there is a circumstantial inconsistency or questionable impartiality in an arguer's position, and then conclude from that personal criticism that the conclusion of the argument criticized must be false. This was the basic error in the child's argument in example 6.3. The child argued that the parent was circumstantially inconsistent – the parent argued against smoking, but his own practice was to smoke. Then the child concluded from that relative circumstantial inconsistency that the conclusion of the parent's argument could be absolutely dismissed. However, the mistake in this approach is to overlook the possibility that the parent's conclusion might be true. For as we noted, it might be possible that the parent could produce good evidence that smoking is linked to chronic lung disease, and is therefore unhealthy. The child's strong rejection does not leave enough room for this reply.

This first type of error is an extreme form of shortcoming in an argument against the person which may be called the *basic ad hominem fallacy* because it takes the strong stance that the argument criticized is totally refuted and that its conclusion is absolutely false. However, an argument is only rarely open to this type of strong refutation as a basic *ad hominem* fallacy. Most arguments against the person are defeasible.

The second important kind of error occurs when the critic questions an argument by citing a plausible appearance of inconsistency in a circumstantial attack but does not do enough work to make the inconsistency explicit. In this case, the critic may not have claimed to completely refute the argument he has attacked, but nevertheless, if he has not explicitly made a good case for a specific inconsistency, his argument may still be much weaker than he considers it to be.

The classic case of this second type of shortcoming, however, is the sportsman's rejoinder, 'Why do you feed on the flesh of harmless cattle?' As we saw in studying example 6.4, there is no contradiction in eating meat and decrying the barbarous practice of hunting for sport or amusement. However, because there is a connection between these two actions, one might be tempted to conclude erroneously that the sportsman's rejoinder has strongly challenged the meat eater's argument position by showing a circumstantial inconsistency in it. If the sportsman purports to have strongly replied to his critic by his circumstantial attack, then he has committed this second type of error. The propositions he cites are in fact not even close to being circumstantially inconsistent. Much more argument would be needed to back up his criticism adequately. In this case the attack is in the form of a question. But the case for circumstantial inconsistency is so weak that the question is open to vigorous challenge and should not reasonably be taken to shift the burden of proof.

This second kind of shortcoming, although less severe than the first, is still an error to watch for. It is the error of taking a personal attack to be a personal criticism without giving enough evidence to shift the burden of proof required for a reasonable criticism. This shortcoming, like the first one, is a case of an argument that is taken to be stronger than its support merits.

The third type of error occurs when the issue of the personal attack is, or becomes, irrelevant to the proper issue of discussion in the dialogue. It is this third type of error that is most often associated with the direct (abusive) personal attack. When an arguer's personal motives are questioned, it may be difficult for the critic to resist launching into an unwarranted or irrelevant personal attack on the character of his opponent.

The direct personal attack need not always be unreasonable in argument, but the more emotional and abusive it becomes, the more likely it is to become a diversion from the real issue, or even a shift to a different context of dialogue. Such attacks may fail either because they are altogether irrelevant to the issues or because their relevance is too weak to sustain the strong rejection of an opponent's argument. In example 6.0, there might be some reason to question Nixon's integrity because of his resignation during the Watergate scandal. However, that issue is only weakly relevant to the trustworthiness of Nixon's statements on foreign policy in China. To strongly reject those arguments because of some doubts about his character could be a mistake if Nixon's policy arguments were based on long experience and solid evidence.

The fourth type of error is to discount the reliability, integrity, or capability as a reasoned participant in argument of the person attacked so heavily that no room is left for further reply or discussion. This violation is premature closure of the dialogue by "poisoning the well."

Any circumstantial or direct personal attack raises the question of the integrity or sincerity of the arguer who is attacked because, if someone does not practice what he preaches or has a hidden agenda, it becomes an open question whether he is being a hypocrite, not saying what he truly believes. And we saw in Section 6.3 that in some cases the personal attack even directly criticizes the impartiality, honesty, or reliability of an arguer by citing his questionable personal motives. We saw in several examples that this type of personal criticism can be reasonable, but that it is a weak form of argument that can go wrong if the attack is pushed forward too aggressively. When this happens because the arguer is too strongly rejected as incompetent or untrustworthy, the fourth type of error has occurred. This type of shortcoming, like the first two, occurs when a criticism, in this case of an arguer's reasonableness or impartiality, is taken for a stronger criticism than the case warrants. For example, we noted that in example 6.6 it would be an error for Bob to conclude that Wilma's arguments on acid rain must be worthless despite the evidence she presented for them because she is on the board of directors of a coal company. Although Bob may be right to question Wilma's impartiality, it does not necessarily follow that her arguments are completely worthless and should be totally rejected from any further hearing or consideration.

All four types of errors are variants of the same kind of fault – taking an argument against the person to be a stronger criticism than the evidence given to back it up really warrants. The argument

167

against the person can be a reasonable argument in some cases. But the problem is that it is such a powerful argument in everyday dialogue that there is a strong temptation to be overcome or bullied by it, instead of carefully examining how the attack was mounted. More soberly considered, the argument against the person is a form of criticism that requires careful justification and the inclusion of many steps to be backed up enough to shift the burden of proof strongly. The critical questioner must not go on the defensive too quickly in the face of this type of attack and instead be prepared to pose specific critical questions in reply to the *ad hominem* attack.

6.8 SOME CASES FOR FURTHER DISCUSSION

Three further examples will illustrate some additional problems and dimensions of difficulty that concern the distinction between personal morality and expressed political policies of a person in political argumentation. Each example of these three cases poses a specific problem for the reader to reflect on. Consider, first, the following:

Example 6.12

A minister of Parliament admitted saving a large amount of money through a "quick-flip" tax shelter. However, his own political party had long been vociferously critical of the "tax dodges for the wealthy" allegedly favored by their conservative opposition. This minister belonged to a socialist party that had been very critical of the wealthy who take advantage of tax loopholes. Indeed, the minister explicitly said that he had been long opposed to tax breaks like the one he personally took advantage of.

The conservative leader of the opposition called this behavior hypocritical, because it was a case of preaching one thing and doing another. He argued that this tax "scam" was undertaken by a member of a government that claimed to be the "champion of the little guy," yet who was "first at the trough" to take advantage of a tax loophole.

The socialist minister defended the position, however, that his actions and principles were not inconsistent. By taking advantage of tax breaks, he claimed, he was "operating within the system," and at the same time, he maintained, he was being consistent all along and was still arguing that the system should be changed. His position was that he was operating within the law, and therefore need have no qualms about taking advantage of the tax laws, even though he was against those laws. He cited the difference between legality and personal morality as vindicating his consistency of position.

The leader of the opposition disagreed, insisting that the minister had damaged his own credibility and integrity, and the credibility of

168

his party as well. He expressed the view that a government minister must personally maintain his expressed standards of ethical conduct and not contravene them by his own personal actions, or else suffer a loss of credibility as a political spokesman.

The basic problem with this example is that, although the leader of the opposition would appear to have a strong case for a criticism of circumstantial inconsistency by the guidelines listed in Section 6.6, still the minister being criticized has some grounds for rebuttal. In effect, he is accusing his critic of a confusion, an equivocation between matters of public policy and private morality. Does he have a way out?

He might have argued that legal rules or political policies are forged through compromise and majority pressures. And therefore, he might argue, in a pluralistic democracy with freedom of thought and religion, questions of personal morality and conscience are private matters, and may be different from public policies one adheres to. This distinction has been persuasively cited in politics, as the next example illustrates.

As background to the following case, the reader might like to consult articles by Kenneth L. Woodward and Mario M. Cuomo:[17]

Example 6.13

A Catholic politician running for a high federal office declared that she supported freedom of choice on the abortion issue, even though, as a Catholic, she personally opposed abortion. She argued that her personal views were not in conflict with her position on public policy. A Catholic bishop criticized this stance as illogical, replying that he did not see how a good Catholic, who should be against the taking of human life, could vote for a politician who supported abortion. She replied that as a Catholic she did not personally support abortion, but that she felt she has no right to impose that view on others, who might have different religious viewpoints. She stated that her political support of freedom of choice concerning reproduction was logically consistent with her personal opposition to abortion because of the separation of church and state.

This case poses a kind of paradox; for if one is committed to deeply held moral principles concerning ethical conduct or religious belief,

17 Kenneth L. Woodward, "Politics and Abortion," *Newsweek*, August 20, 1984, pp. 66–7, and Mario M. Cuomo, "Religious Belief and Public Morality," *New York Review of Books*, Vol. 31, No. 16, October 25, 1984, pp. 32–7.

that personal conviction cannot be completely irrelevant to one's political stances on matters of public policy. Yet if public policies are matters of group agreement and concessions, which may have to involve some degree of tolerance and compromise, there may be room for explanation of apparent practical inconsistencies between personal and political commitments to social policies.

Questioning the arguer's motives can be a weak but reasonable form of criticism of an argument in some cases. However, this form of challenge can be carried to excess, and it is in just such a case that an irrelevant attack constitutes an incorrect type of argument against the person. The following example provides a case for how an initially reasonable *ad hominem* criticism can go wrong. Such cases often degenerate into direct personal abuse, indicating a dialectical shift:

Example 6.14

The subject of debate in the U.S. Congress in 1813 was the New Army Bill, a proposal to raise more troops for the war against England. The majority, led by Speaker of the House Henry Clay, argued that an invasion of Canada with these additional troops would help to win the conflict. Josiah Quincy, speaking for the opposition on January 5, 1813, argued that the additional troops would be insufficient, that an invasion of Canada would be unsuccessful and immoral, that a conquest of Canada would not force England to negotiate, and finally that the bill was politically motivated, "as a means for the advancement of objects of personal or local ambition of the members of the American Cabinet."[18]

In his speech, Quincy backed up his last argument that the advocates of the bill were not to be trusted because of their hidden motives. He cited facts to support his allegation that the most outspoken supporters of the bill were motivated by personal ambition. This last argument, then, is clearly a personal attack on the motives of the bill's supporters. Could it be a reasonable argument against the person?

The answer is that it is a weak form of argument. But even if the other arguments advanced by Quincy could be stronger, this personal argument also has some legitimate weight, if Quincy has

18 *Annals of the Congress of the United States, Comprising the Period November 2, 1812, to March 3, 1818, Inclusive,* Washington D.C., Gales and Seaton, 1853, pp. 540–70, cited in Brinton (1985, p. 56).

given good reasons to support his contention that the advocates of the bill are behind it, to a significant extent, because it favors their personal interest; for when a country is at war, the interests of the country should be foremost in the deliberations of Congress. If personal interests play a role in someone's argument, then he may not be taking a balanced and impartial approach to the issue of the larger fate of the nation. Thus his impartial judgment may reasonably be questioned, in such a case. Quincy's conclusion is not that the bill should be defeated exclusively because of his personal criticism, but that the opinions of the other party should carry less weight than they would apart from his criticism of his opponent's personal position on the issue.

However, when Quincy went on in his speech, he is reported to have called his opponents "toads, or reptiles, which *spread their slime on the drawing room floor.*" Here he has gone too far and resorted to direct personal abuse. In short, then, criticism of an arguer's motives can be a reasonable if weak argument in some cases. But when it is carried too far, the argument can cease to be a relevant one, and it can become an abusive personal attack that is not justifiable in reasonable dialogue.

7

Appeals to authority

The *ad hominem* attack is the negative use of personal argumentation to undermine or destroy the credibility of a person in a critical discussion. An opposite type of tactic is the *argumentum ad verecundiam*, which uses the opinion of a respected authority or expert on a subject as positive personal argumentation to support one's own side of an argument. The *ad hominem* criticism attacks a person as an untrustworthy source, whereas the *ad verecundiam* cites a person who is especially reliable and authoritative as a source of advice.

In certain respects, however, these two types of argumentation are similar. Both are appeals to personal sources of opinion that center on the internal position or credibility of a particular individual as a reliable source of knowledge. Both types of argumentation can be contrasted with the appeal to external or objective knowledge that comes from scientific evidence like experimental observations, the kind of knowledge that comes from nature, not from a personal source.

Appeals to expert opinion can be a legitimate form of obtaining advice or guidance for drawing presumptive conclusions about an issue or problem when objective knowledge is unavailable or inconclusive. However, authority-based arguments can become questionable or fallacious when they are misused as tactics to try to beat an opponent into submission or silence by appealing to an inflated respect or reverence for authority.

The phrase *argumentum ad verecundiam* literally means 'the argument from modesty', and it was John Locke who evidently first used this phrase to refer to a kind of error or deceptive tactic that can be used by one person in discussion with another.[1] In the chapter entitled "Of Wrong Assent, or Error" of his *Inquiry Concerning Human Understanding* (1690), Locke described the *argumentum ad verecundiam* as a sort of argument that a person can use, in reasoning

---

1 Hamblin (1970, p. 159).

172

with another person, to "prevail on the assent" of that other person or to "silence his opposition." This way of prevailing is to allege the opinion of a third person who has "gained a name" and settled his reputation in the "common esteem" with some kind of authority. According to Locke, "When men are established in any kind of dignity, it is thought a breach of modesty for others to derogate any way from it, and question the authority of men who are in possession of it."[2] Thus anyone who does not "readily yield to the determination of approved authors" may be portrayed as impudent or insolent by the arguer who is using the *argumentum ad verecundiam* to prevail on his assent in an argument.

Locke did not claim that all appeals to authority in argumentation are fallacious, however.[3] The fallacy he described is the misuse of an appeal to an authoritative source to try to prevail unfairly or to "silence the opposition" in a discussion. Locke's approach will be supported by the conclusions of this chapter. There can be legitimate appeals to a third-party authoritative source when two people reason together in a critical discussion. But fallacies can occur when one party presses too hard in deploying authority to try to suppress the critical questioning of the other party.

7.1 REASONABLE APPEALS TO AUTHORITY

Although appeals to authority can be erroneous, as we have seen, it must be recognized that some can be reasonable and legitimate in argument. For example, suppose you have a toothache, and you go to your dentist for advice. He replies as follows:

Example 7.0

This tooth is badly decayed, but not beyond repair. I propose to replace the decayed portion with a filling immediately.

Your dentist's advice in example 7.0 is the judgment of a suitably qualified expert in his field. In asking for his advice, therefore, you have appealed to an expert authority. However, it by no means follows that by acquiescing to his proposal you have committed a fallacy. It could be that his advice is eminently reasonable, and you would be wise to take it and act on it soon.

2 This passage from Locke's *Essay* is quoted in full in ibid.
3 Ibid., pp. 159–60.

173

That does not mean that, if you have any reason to question his judgment, advice, competence, or qualifications, you should not get a second opinion; for any appeal to authority is best treated as fallible, a form of plausible argument. But it does remain that some arguments based on the say-so of authorities can be highly reasonable, even excellent, arguments. The point is, then, that appeals to expertise are not intrinsically fallacious, even if they can be erroneous in some cases, when misinterpreted, taken too seriously, or taken uncritically.

It is important to realize that the term 'authority' contains an important ambiguity. One meaning is that of *administrative authority*, which is a kind of right to exercise command over others or make rulings binding on others through an invested or recognized position or office of power. A second meaning of authority refers to expertise in a domain of knowledge or skill, which may be very different from administrative authority in many instances. Wilson (1983, p. 13) calls the authority of expertise *cognitive authority*, a relationship between two individuals when what the one says carries weight or plausibility, within a certain domain or field of expertise, for the other.

The two kinds of authority are very different in nature, even though in some instances the same individual may possess or convey both kinds. Take the example of a physician who certifies a person as fit to possess a driver's license according to the legally required standards determined by a physical examination. In making such a judgment, the doctor is arriving at a conclusion based on medical expertise. His pronouncement is therefore based on his cognitive authority as a medical expert. However, his ruling is also an instance of the exercise of administrative authority, for it is his being a licensed physician that confers on him the right, and perhaps also the obligation, to make this official and binding pronouncement.

It is important to make this distinction because there is often an immediate feeling of resentment or hostility to the idea of authority. By confusing the two meanings of 'authority', we may be led to exaggerate our feeling that authority of any sort is somehow fallacious or contrary to reasoned argument and scientific investigation.

Good scientific method is based on the idea of reproducible evidence. In other words, it is better to do an experiment yourself rather than rely on the say-so of someone else who has done it and claimed certain results. But does that mean we should always mistrust and reject the word of an authority as fallacious? It need not, if our reliance on cognitive authority is regarded only as a means of supplementing experimental investigation in those cases when an immediate decision is required and independent experimental investigation is not possible or practical:

Example 7.1

The captain of a ship surveying for wrecks in the South China Sea discovers a heap of antique porcelain in a submerged wreck and has it hauled aboard. It is blue and white Chinese porcelain that might be old and valuable. There is only one way to be sure. The captain calls in an expert, an authority on Chinese ceramics. The expert surveys the find and pronounces his opinion: "Definitely eighteenth century. Probably late Ming and Traditional Period Chinese porcelain." On this advice, the captain continues to probe the wreck for further treasure.[4]

In this case, subsequent study of the porcelain will determine whether the expert was right. But at the moment, the captain must make a decision whether to continue his search. So if he has chosen a well-qualified and reliable expert on porcelain, his reliance on this cognitive authority as a source of advice could be a reasonable conclusion in making a decision on how to proceed at this point.

Of course, later scientific investigation of the findings may or may not bear out the expert's judgment. But in the absence of this scientific confirmation, the captain may be making a good decision by acting on the presumption that the expert is right.

In contrasting the uses of subjective versus objective sources of evidence in reasoning, it is well to be clear that, in some cases, testing an appeal to expertise by experiment may not be practically feasible or wise:

Example 7.2

On a very cold day in northern Canada, a mother runs outside when she is told that her daughter has her tongue stuck to a metal flagpole.

Mother: I've told you a hundred times not to put your fingers or your

4 This example is loosely based on the content of an article by John Dyson, "Captain Hatcher's Fabulous Sunken Treasure," *Reader's Digest*, November 1986, pp. 63–7.

tongue on very cold metal. I told you that, if you did, you would get stuck to it. Why did you put your tongue on the flagpole?

Daughter: I wanted to see if it was true.[5]

In this case, the desire to test the logic of mother's argument by experiment might indicate a laudable interest in scientific investigation. But at the same time, it suggests the wisdom of paying attention to a subjective source of advice if it is based on valuable experience, when experiment may not be practical in the given situation.

This case also illustrates that not all reasonable appeals to authority are based on expertise in a narrow, well-defined domain of professional experience. Some appeals of this sort can be based on a claim that one is in a special position to know about a particular situation or set of facts. For example, if foreign policy requires making a decision about political conditions in a certain foreign country, it may be a good idea to consult with people who have recently lived in that country. Such people may not be experts in the sense of being political scientists. But they may be in a special position to know about current political conditions in that country. Because they are in a special position to know, from the point of view of those attempting to formulate foreign policy relative to these conditions, the advice of these consultants could reasonably be given a special status akin to expert judgment. Again, their opinions should not be treated as the "absolute truth," and they may be questioned in many cases. Yet in dialogue, some judgments of those who are in a special position to know, by virtue of their experience in relevant matters, may be taken as more plausible than the judgments of those without the requisite experience.

In this chapter, we are concerned primarily with cognitive authority. Cognitive authority is always relative to a domain of knowledge or experience in which the expert's judgment can be given greater weight or burden in argument than the layperson who lacks equivalent experience or knowledge in this domain. But the asymmetry that gives rise to the expert–layperson relationship is defined not only by the expertise of the expert, but also by the ignorance of the one who uses expert advice. The general practitioner who consults the specialist is taking the advice of an expert,

5 This example is a paraphrase of some of the dialogue in a cartoon strip by Lynn Johnston, "For Better or Worse," *Winnipeg Free Press,* January 3, 1987.

but his relationship to the specialist may be quite different from that of the medical layman who consults the same specialist on the same question.

The reason that appeals to authority have been traditionally mistrusted in science as a source of argument is that such appeals are inherently subjective. The expert bases his judgment on "rules of thumb" and accepted methods for carrying out procedures that he and other experts have found to be useful in their practical experience of working in their special area. But it may be difficult, or in some cases even impossible, for the expert to translate his practical experience or judgment into "hard evidence" that can be explicitly and completely described to a layperson. Since the expert's judgment is really based on his professional training, long experience, and practical know-how, his conclusion is, in an important respect, an individual and subjective judgment, from the point of view of the layman who acts on his advice.

However, science has traditionally questioned the subjective appeal as "good evidence" or "hard evidence" in confirmation of hypotheses. This is because it is important for scientific hypotheses to be confirmed by experimental verification that is reproducible and that can be confirmed objectively by empirical evidence or mathematical calculations. Hence appeals to expertise, being essentially subjective and judgmental, have often been systematically rejected as a reliable source of knowledge.

There are good reasons for a certain mistrust of evidence obtained by appeal to authority. The strongest form of argument is the deductively valid argument. The acme of scientific knowledge is the axiomatic system, in which the only proof of a hypothesis is the deduction of that hypothesis by valid arguments from clear or well-established propositions called 'axioms'. A weaker form of argument is inductive confirmation. A hypothesis is said to be inductively confirmed if it is based on evidence that is highly probable. Both types of evidence are objective. But the appeal to expertise fits neither of these patterns and, as we have seen, is inherently subjective. Therefore, an argument based on the appeal to expert judgment should be rejected or discarded if deductive proof or inductive confirmation of the proposition in question can be given.

Moreover, because appeals to expertise are based on plausible reasoning, in practice they should be generally treated as arguments that can shift a burden of proof, but are inherently weak and subject

177

to questioning. Experts can be subject to the same kinds of bias and prejudice that were studied in connection with arguments against the person in Chapter 6. If an expert has something to gain by taking one side of an argument, or is even being paid to argue for one side – as frequently happens in courtroom disputes – then pointing out this potential for bias may be a legitimate criticism.

The law allows that expert testimony (e.g., that of a ballistics expert) can be a reasonable form of evidence to be considered in a trial. Thus legal standards of evidence accept appeals to scientific expertise as necessary and reasonable in many cases. However, there do remain many questions about how expert arguments in court should be evaluated. And as we will see, there are many problems here, and some dramatic cases in which arguments from expertise have gone quite wrong in courtroom decision making.

Another area that has increased acceptance of the concept of expert reasoning as a distinctive and intrinsically reasonable form of argument is the development of expert systems in the field of artificial intelligence. Expert systems are computer programs that duplicate the skills of an expert in a well-defined area of expertise. Expert systems are widely used in medical diagnosis, geology, electrical troubleshooting, and many other areas of science and industry. For example, expert systems that incorporate the knowledge of senior automotive engineers who have helped design, or are familiar with, particular motor vehicles are used to advise mechanics who work on that type of vehicle. It is a way for one expert (the mechanic) to take advantage of the specialized skill and experience of other experts by asking questions and receiving programmed answers from a computer terminal. These developments have tended to counteract the older ideas that appeal to expertise is inherently erroneous or fallacious, now that the practical usefulness of expert systems has been well established.

7.2 THREE COMMON ERRORS IN CITING EXPERT OPINIONS

First, if the appeal to authority is on an issue outside the field of the expert cited, then the appeal can be criticized as an erroneous argument. The topic of the following argument is economics:

178

Example 7.3

This alarming defense spending will lead to economic disaster. According to Einstein, heavy defense spending in a country is a sign of political instability that is not consistent with sound fiscal policies that can yield lasting financial recovery from a recession.

Einstein was a great physicist, but using the prestige of his name in an appeal to settle an argument on economics is highly questionable. Because some individual is an acknowledged expert in field A does not necessarily imply that his pronouncement in field B should also be treated as a highly plausible or authoritative proposition. Einstein was often consulted by the media on issues in religion and politics after he had achieved celebrity status as a scientist. But like many academic specialists, he often tended to be somewhat naive and idealistic in moral and political matters outside his field of expertise. The fact that his opinions were taken so seriously and often printed as headlines was in many cases a source of puzzlement, difficulty, and embarrassment for him.[6]

The problem here is that there is a sort of halo effect with experts. If someone is acknowledged to be a prestigious expert in a field of specialization, then that halo of authority often carries over into any pronouncement made by that expert, even if it is in a totally unrelated field or topic.

Here, then, is one common type of error in appeals to expertise in argument. If the expert's field is A, but the issue he is cited as pronouncing upon is another field B, then the argument from authority should be questioned. The problem is that many fields of expertise are extremely specialized. To achieve eminence, a specialist may have to restrict his research and learning to a narrow area. Therefore, the expert may have even less time or fewer resources than the layperson to accumulate knowledge about areas of controversy or opinion outside his field of expertise. Appeals to expert opinion are highly sensitive to subject matter, because of the narrowness of specialization. Hence they can be highly fragile outside a narrow domain.

Second, sometimes the appeal to expertise is so vague that the name of the expert is not even cited or the relevant field of expertise identified:

6 Ronald W. Clark, *Einstein: The Life and Times*, New York, Avon Books, 1971.

179

Example 7.4

According to the experts, corporal punishment has a traumatic effect on a child's later development. So parents should never spank a child under any circumstances.

The problem here is a severe lack of documentation of the argument from expertise. When the pronouncement of "experts" is left this vague, it would be a serious error to accord it much weight in the argument. The appropriate reply is to ask who are the "experts" and what is their field of specialization. However, because of the power of any appeal to expertise in argument, such questions often go unasked. Often the mere phrase "according to the experts" is enough to silence opposition and end the argument. The fact is that we may be so intimidated by the authority of technical or specialized fields of expertise, that the mere phrase "according to experts" may inhibit reasonable dialogue or further questioning.

Third, sometimes an error of appeal to expert opinion in argument occurs when the name of the so-called expert is identified, but the person cited is no real authority at all. Often the person cited is a powerful opinion leader simply because of personal popularity or prestige. We are all familiar with advertising testimonials in which a famous actor or baseball star endorses some product, like a car or chocolate bar. These appeals are sometimes not appeals to authority at all, but are more simply appeals to popularity. But when they are appeals to authority, one may well question whether the person appealed to is a legitimate expert:

Example 7.5

A famous comedian recommends a particular brand of soft drink on the basis that it contains no sugar and is therefore a good way to maintain a healthy diet and take off weight.

In this instance, the comedian may have no expert credentials in any field related to nutrition, health, or weight loss. Nevertheless, his recommendation of this soft drink over another type of drink may carelessly be given credibility on the basis that he is a trend setter who seems to know what he is talking about. However, if you really want reliable advice about your health, a comedian might not be the best person to go to. The danger here is that of being unduly influenced by the advice of a person who is no expert at all.

7.3 EXPERT TESTIMONY IN LEGAL ARGUMENTATION

The use of expert testimony in the courts has increased to the extent that, nowadays, most major trials involve some kind of expert testimony. Medical specialists, psychologists, ballistics experts, statisticians, and scientists of all sorts may be called in to a trial to give evidence on all sorts of questions. One of the most notable cases in the United States concerned evidence introduced by scientific experts in the case of Wayne Williams, who was convicted of child murders in Atlanta in 1982. A main factor in the conviction was scientific evidence based on microscopic analysis, which matched fibers from the carpet in Mr. Williams's bedroom with fibers found on the bodies of the victims. The statistical odds of the match presented by the scientific experts was thought to be convincing evidence by the jury, and it led to the conviction of Mr. Williams.

Appeal to expert testimony is generally accepted as a form of legal evidence, but there are many questions about what the standards and limits of this kind of evidence ought to be. Until recently, the standard in the United States, based on the case of *Frye v. United States* (1923), was that any technique or theory to be used as legal evidence must be "sufficiently established to have gained general acceptance in the particular field in which it belongs."[7] However, this ruling, by keeping to demonstrable evidence, has been criticized for excluding newly developed scientific techniques. This pressure to include new and promising scientific developments, however, has led to a liberalization of standards of expert testimony, which seems to give too much power to the expert, in some cases.

According to Imwinkelried (1986, p. 22), expert testimony is now admissible in many states that is based on theories or techniques that are not generally accepted in a field:

Example 7.6

When trying accused child molesters, for example, many courts now permit psychiatrists to testify that the psychological problems of an

---

7 Imwinkelried (1986, p. 22).

alleged victim are evidence that abuse has in fact occurred. The notion that abused children develop characteristic "syndromes" can be useful to clinicians making diagnoses or prescribing treatment; as care-givers, they are concerned primarily with the patient's current state of mind.[8]

Under the *Frye* ruling, such evidence might not have been admissible because a "syndrome" is not used by a scientist to make factual determinations. It is used only by psychologists to guide therapy. Now, however, this type of testimony could be used.

Thus according to Imwinkelried (1986) there has been a gradual lowering of standards concerning the introduction of expert testimony in the courts, and the result is that experts are freely allowed to draw conclusions without being challenged. The problem is that, under the newer, liberalized standards, lawyers, judges, and juries are put in the position of having to try to assess the merit of a scientific theory, even though they are not experts in the field. Imwinkelried (1986, p. 23f.) cites the technique of voiceprint analysis produced by the second spectrograph. At first, this technique seemed a reliable way to identify a ransom caller from a telephone tape, but as criminals learned to disguise their voice over the phone, the technique became less reliable. Yet according to Imwinkelried (1986, p. 24), few lawyers tended to question the reliability of the technique, and if the general acceptance of the technique could not be challenged, the testimony was typically allowed to stand as evidence.

One response is for a lawyer to bring in another expert who will oppose the evidence of the first expert. The result is what has been called the "battle of the experts" in court. In some areas of psychiatry, for example, in which theories are not exact or universally accepted, it may not be difficult for a lawyer to find an expert who will draw a conclusion opposite to that of the opposing side's expert.

In fact, expert witnesses are chosen by an attorney in a partisan manner. That is, the attorney typically pays the expert a fee to testify and chooses an expert that, he thinks or hopes, will give testimony that will support the attorney's side of the case. The expert is not obliged to appear in court like the lay witness or bystander, for example. The opinion of the expert witness is his private property, and he is free to sell it or give it away.

According to Younger (1982, p. 8), the expert used by an attorney

---

8 Ibid., p. 22.

in court is usually a so-called house expert, often used previously by the law firm. Younger notes that many law firms have a "stable" of experts, ten or fifteen doctors, who are used as witnesses:

> These are doctors who prefer to be in court. They are very good at it; they enjoy it. They all look like Spencer Tracy; they make an infallible impression upon the jury and each side then produces somebody drawn from that group of experts. In the normal situation, you just call up somebody, you work things out financially, and the expert appears in court.

Hence it may be an oversimplification to think that the expert witness who testifies in a court of law is entirely neutral. The selection of such witnesses by the lawyer reflects the realities of the adversarial system of legal argumentation.

On the other hand, there are checks and balances in the adversarial system, because the opposing lawyer is free to attack the testimony of an expert and to introduce his own expert witnesses. When this happens, it is up to the judge or jury to decide which side's expert testimony is more credible or stronger. However, the lawyer can do much to aid this decision by questioning the other side's experts.

Weber (1981) has set out advice on how a lawyer can attack the other side's expert testimony in a trial. According to Weber (p. 303), such a cross-examination requires careful preparation and study of the expert's qualifications and, if possible, advance study of any reports or documents submitted as evidence by the expert. Then the lawyer must carefully devise a plan of attack. Weber (p. 303) even refers to checklists for cross-examination of an expert appropriate to the type of case and expert. For example, he (p. 312) gives a checklist for cross-examination of an economist. This is a list of questions that can be used to question the expert's track record, qualifications, sources of information, and the fallibility of judgments in his field.

The courts will sometimes even allow a lawyer to cross-examine an opposing expert witness with the goal of establishing bias based on the expert's financial interests. Three permitted forms of this type of cross-examination are cited by Graham (1977, p. 50): (1) financial interest in the case at issue on grounds of remuneration for services, (2) hope of continued employment, or (3) prior testimony for the same attorney or same party. Graham (1977) argues that this type of evidence, including facts about the percentage of

183

livelihood a person gets for acting as an expert witness, should be regarded as relevant to establishing bias, and the scope of cross-examination of an expert in court should include these areas of inquiry.

Cross-examination of an opposing witness by an attorney in court is a practical art of question–answer dialogue that lawyers learn by practice, and many lawyers can become very skilled at the art. Much of this skill involves attacking the weak points of the expert's argument and exposing them to a jury. For example, Weber (1981, p. 305) advocates that the questioner try to expose bias by showing whether critical information came from a potentially biased source like the plaintiff, his wife, friend, attorney, or boss. Or if the expert is projecting into the future, the lawyer could ask whether it is true that no one can guarantee the future. These techniques of cross-examination clearly involve using the kinds of complex questions and arguments against the person outlined in previous chapters. That, of course, does not mean that the lawyer using these techniques is necessarily resorting to bad or deceptive argumentation. But it does show the adversarial nature of the use of expert opinion in legal argumentation in the trial setting.

7.4 HOW EXPERT IS THE AUTHORITY?

Clearly, some experts are more authoritative than others on a particular topic or issue. Let us say that I want to get an expert opinion on whether I ought to have gall bladder surgery. Dr. Smith has had twenty years' experience as a gall bladder surgeon and has published a book and numerous articles on the subject. His work is highly regarded by other gall bladder specialists and often cited by them in articles on this subject in the leading medical journals. Dr. Jones is a psychiatrist who is an expert on bulimia and is director of a weight-control clinic.

Now both Dr. Smith and Dr. Jones are medical doctors. Both are therefore experts in medical matters. But in making up my mind about whether to have gall bladder surgery, clearly I would be well advised to attach more weight to Dr. Smith's recommendation than to Dr. Jones's.

Another question to be raised is whether the claimed area of specialized expertise is a recognized area of specialization within the field or just a topic of interest for the scientist or practitioner in that field. This question has arisen in connection with the issue of whether doctors should be allowed to advertise their services (for example, in the yellow pages of the telephone directory) by stating their interest in a special disease or particular type of medical problem. Should a psychiatrist with a special interest in adolescent mental health, for example, be allowed to advertise this interest in the yellow pages?

According to the current standards of the College of Physicians and Surgeons in Manitoba, Canada, for example, this form of advertisement would not be allowed, because adolescent mental health is not presently a recognized area of medicine. According to the registrar of the college, even though a practitioner with a predominantly adolescent clientele might have more working experience with the special problems of adolescents, "it is an interest, as opposed to a qualification."[9] In other words, a physician would not have to pass a special qualifying examination to be licensed in this area of specialization, as he would, for example, to become a specialist in anesthesiology or internal medicine. It is a good question, therefore, to ask whether a claim to specialized expertise within a field is based on a recognized area of subspecialization with special qualifications or is only an area of special interest. A familiarity with an area of special interest may make an expert's advice more valuable than that of another expert who lacks such a familiarity. But even so, an important distinction can be made between an interest and a qualification.

Generally speaking, then, some experts are much more expert than others on a specific problem or issue. So even if an opinion is correctly quoted as the pronouncement of a qualified expert, it is a separate question how seriously the opinion may be taken as an authoritative statement.

One problem here is that someone cited as an authority may look to an outsider like an impressively credentialed expert – a senior scientist who is head of an established institution – but to those in the know, his reputation may be less than glorious. This person may be an expert, but not the best expert on the question.

Shepherd and Goode (1977) conducted a study to question whether scientists cited as experts by the press are in fact the scientists

9 Anonymous, "Medical Advertising Views Sought," *Winnipeg Free Press,* January 27, 1986.

who have done the research on the subject in question. The scientific controversy they investigated was the issue of whether marijuana causes brain damage. They found that of the ten marijuana researchers most frequently cited in the scientific literature, only one was one of the ten authorities most publicized in the press. Of these ten press authorities, seven were found not to have published anything at all in the scientific literature.

What Shepherd and Goode's findings suggest is that the press tends to seek out the administrative head of an institute or faculty rather than a working researcher as an authoritative spokesperson. In other words, why quote a mere working scientist when you can quote the head of the organization?

The problem here is that, for those of us who are unfamiliar with a field, any expert may sound good because we are not in a position to know who are the real authorities in a specific area of research. It may be hard to question an expert's credentials or authority, or to ask for a second opinion. But in some cases we may be well advised to persist in our search for the best expert advice possible. The fact that an expert has spoken may not be the final word.

A researcher who is busy contributing to the leading edge of scholarship in his field does not want or need publicity in the popular media and probably does not have time for television bookings or interviews with journalists. Instead it is the "quote-meister" we most often hear from, that most-quoted authority whose name is already familiar to the public. According to Alter (1985, p. 69), the news media have developed a habit of relying heavily on a few sources who are often quoted as experts:

Example 7.7

"Round up the usual suspects," the editor or producer snarls as deadlines loom. Reflexively, a story involving feminism becomes a story quoting Gloria Steinem or Susan Brownmiller. Starved for a cogent quote on science (any science)? Get astronomer Carl Sagan on the line. None of this is necessarily a reflection on the "usual suspects" themselves; they are usually genuine resources in their fields. Still, the impression conveyed is of a world that contains only a handful of knowledgeable people.[10]

10 Alter (1985, p. 69).

Alter mentions several celebrities who are usual media favorites. Alan Greenspan is often quoted on economic issues, Alan Dershowitz on legal affairs, and Gloria Steinem on anything to do with women's issues, for example.

Now the various "quote-meisters" so heavily relied upon by the media are, in most cases, genuine experts in their fields. That is not the problem. The problem, according to Alter, is that there are good reasons to believe, in many instances, that these people are not the best or most informative experts that could be consulted on a specific problem or controversy. The quoted person so favored by the press is more likely to be chosen because he is provocative and cooperative, rather than because he is the best expert. And the problem with provocative authors or personalities is that they are popular precisely because they are animated and trenchant. They are the people who tend to avoid making scholarly qualifications or reservations and are therefore more colorful and quotable because they "shoot from the hip." In other words, they become quotable precisely because they show a style that is contrary to the more careful qualifications of sound scholarship. In short, then, there are grounds for suspecting that these much-quoted experts may be far from the most genuinely authoritative experts on a particular issue. They are popular to reporters because of media deadlines and their quotability.

Consequently, many appeals to expertise utilized by the media on topics of popular controversy should be carefully evaluated. They may be reasonable appeals to expertise, but they may also be very weak arguments because the authorities cited are not the best experts on this particular question.

A good way to verify expert advice is to get a second opinion. But in some cases experts disagree or contradict one another. Particularly on controversial issues, experts may strenuously disagree.

Many famous cases of the "battle of the experts" have occurred in criminal trials, where so-called expert witnesses are called in by both sides to give testimony on matters of evidence. Ballistics experts give evidence on weapons. Pathologists may be called in to give expert testimony on questions of the cause of death or wounds. Psychiatric experts may be called in by both sides to testify that the defendant either was insane or was in control of his actions. Because each side can call forth experts that support his side of the argument, conflicts of expert testimony are notorious in many criminal trials.

In one famous case (Regina v. Roberts), a man was convicted of murder mainly on the basis of physical evidence found at the scene of a woman's murder. According to expert testimony hair found on the scene matched samples of the defendant's hair. Mr. Dieter von Gemmingen, an analyst from the Center of Forensic Scientists, was the expert who testified that the hair samples were similar, based on his experience of more than five hundred investigations involving hair analysis. A summary of the nature of the evidence presented in Mr. von Gemmingen's testimony is presented in example 7.8:

Example 7.8

On the basis of scientific intuition developed over thirteen years of experience, an expert can use the comparison microscope to compare pigmentation granules from two hairs, and determine by overwhelming probability that two hairs came from the same person. Hence one can arrive at a scientific conclusion that it is very unlikely the two hairs are not from the same person, even though the expert cannot put a probability number on it.[11]

On the basis of this expert testimony, the defendant was found guilty. After spending several years in prison, the defendant was finally able to get a hearing for an appeal for retrial on the basis of new evidence.

The new evidence was the testimony of another expert, Dr. Robert Jervis, a professor of nuclear physics and radiochemistry, who had done research in radiochemical techniques for twenty-six years. Dr. Jervis had developed a new radioactive technique to detect and measure trace elements in hair samples. Dr. Jervis presented evidence summarized as follows:

Example 7.9

Irradiation and measurement of isotopes found in hair samples can be used to run computer tests to determine amounts of trace elements in the hair. On the basis of these tests it was concluded that it was very unlikely that the hair samples found at the scene of the crime matched those taken from the head of the accused man.

11 A more complete analysis of this case (*Canadian Criminal Cases,* 34, 1977, pp. 177–83) is given in Walton (1984, pp. 198–214).

On the basis of this new expert testimony, the defendant's appeal was granted, and he was released from prison.

One interesting aspect this case illustrates is how dramatically experts' conclusions can conflict. In this case, the second expert's argument was found to be the stronger, no doubt largely because it was based on a more up-to-date scientific technique that had been developed, established, and recognized by scientific experts in the field; for the defendant's attorney brought in a third expert, who supported the method of neutron activation analysis of hair. And the judge indicated in his remarks that he found it plausible that neutron activation is a more reliable method of analysis than microscopic examination. The plausible conclusion to draw, then, is that the new evidence introduced by the more reliable method is enough to overturn the presumption that the defendant was guilty beyond reasonable doubt. And that, in fact, was the conclusion drawn by the judge.

This case illustrates the danger of relying on an authority whose techniques may be out-of-date. It also illustrates the problem of attempting to deal with the appeal to several authorities who contradict each other.

7.5 INTERPRETING WHAT THE EXPERT SAID

Another area of concern in judging arguments from authority is the question of correctly interpreting what the authority has said. It is always better if the expert cited can be quoted directly. Most often, however, experts are not quoted, and instead their opinion is reported. However, there are several problems with this. For one thing, experts characteristically use technical, specialized terms (jargon) that may be difficult to translate into nonmisleading layperson's language. Second, real experts often make qualifications and special exceptions. Their advice may be based on certain contingencies relative to a particular situation or problem queried. Overlooking these subtleties can lead to many errors or oversimplifications.

Some of these potential errors are indicated by the following list of critical questions:[12]

12 The points in this checklist are given in a more inclusive list of errors in the citing of sources warned of by DeMorgan (1847, pp. 281–5).

1. Is the expert's pronouncement directly quoted? If not, is a reference to the original source given? Can it be checked?
2. If the expert advice is not quoted, does it look like important information or qualifications may have been left out?
3. If more than one expert source has been cited, is each authority quoted separately? Could there be disagreements among the cited authorities?
4. Is what the authority said clear? Are there technical terms used that are not explained clearly? If the advice is in layman's terms, could this be an indication that it has been translated from some other form of expression given by the expert?

Even if we are sure that we have gotten right what the expert has said there may still be further room for questioning an appeal to authority.

In legal cases, lawyers have to learn how to question experts effectively. Although the lawyer may not be a trained physician, nevertheless, he must actively cross-examine expert witnesses giving medical testimony. This means that the able attorney must become somewhat acquainted with the medical facts relevant to a case and use this knowledge effectively. In other words, the expert's say-so cannot be altogether accepted at face value in every case. Sometimes the layperson must persist with intelligent questioning of the expert in dialogue.

An example is the following specimen of dialogue cited by Cohen (1973, p. 543f.), in which a lawyer cross-examined a medical expert during the course of a murder prosecution:

Example 7.10

Q: Dr. Exe, in the study of psychiatry isn't it more beneficial in formulating an opinion as to a person's state of mind on a particular or a given day to conduct an examination of him as soon thereafter as possible?

A: That is true.

Q: So that if a person committed an act on March 23, 19___, an examination conducted of him three days later or two weeks later would be more beneficial to the psychiatrist in evaluating and forming an opinion than an examination conducted fourteen months later?

A: It doesn't necessarily follow. No. It depends on the situation, the type of reaction and the type of patient we are dealing with.

Q: Well, as a psychiatrist, you yourself, would you not prefer to examine a patient closer in point of time to the incident than fourteen months later?

A: I'd like to examine him five minutes after the crime.

Q: So then you do agree that it is better to examine closer in point of time than at a remote period of time?

A: I would agree that it would probably be better.

Q: And is it not true that mental diseases and their manifestations are subject to change?

A: Very much so.

Q: And a person may display symptoms of a particular disease or mental condition of an active psychosis one day or one week and then the next week or the next month that sickness may be in remission?

A: May be either way, yes.

Q: Right?

A: Yes.

Q: Now, are you aware of the fact that Dr. Zee examined John Small three days after the incident?

A: Yes, sir, I am aware of that.

Q: And do you concede, Doctor, that John Small's mental condition three days after the incident would not necessarily be the same condition as it was on the day that you examined him?

A: That is true.

Q: If he had a mental condition such as schizophrenia and if he received medication, if he received therapy and he had consultation and it was over a ten-month or twelve-month period, in your opinion, would that condition change?

A: Again, it depends on the condition and the type of condition. Not all people improve under treatment and not all people stay static without treatment.

In this dialogue, the defense attorney has shown that the psychiatrist who has testified for the prosecution has a weak case for an accurate diagnosis of the defendant; for as the attorney's questioning showed, the psychiatrist did not examine the defendant until fourteen months after the time of the crime. This line of questioning opens up the possibility that the defendant's condition may have improved during these fourteen months. The jury, then, can be left with this implication.

Notice how the lawyer's questioning works. He is not an expert, but by asking intelligent and relevant questions, he can pin the expert down to making commitments. Once the expert has made a statement, he is then committed to it. It is part of his position, and he cannot then retract it or go against it on pain of contradiction. The lawyer knows this and uses it effectively by organizing his questions in a well-planned order so that the dialogue moves toward a conclusion favorable to the defense argument.

Therefore, experts can be questioned, and if the appeal to authority is to be a valuable part of reasonable dialogue, the word of an expert must sometimes be questioned. In fact, sometimes experts even contradict themselves. When this happens, their statements must be questioned very carefully.

7.6 ARGUMENTATION SCHEME FOR APPEAL TO EXPERT OPINION

Because it is only a plausible, and therefore often a weak, form of argument, appeal to expertise has, in the past, often been mistrusted as a fallacious form of argument. And to be sure, if the appeal to authority ignores better evidence for a conclusion based on harder evidence, it can be fallacious. Nonetheless, in many cases, appeal to the expertise of a legitimate authority can be a reasonable argument.

The expert consultation dialogue is a subspecies of the knowledge elicitation dialogue and is different from the type of dialogue called the *inquiry*. The inquiry is proof-seeking and both (or all) parties to the inquiry are (relatively) ignorant. In the expert consultation dialogue, one party, called the "layperson," is ignorant and the other party is an expert in a certain discipline or topic area. The goal is for the nonexpert party to get pertinent advice from the expert. The initial situation is a need for expert advice, and informed (intelligent) action is a benefit or potential outcome of the expert consultation.

However, the most characteristic, primary context of argumentation in which the *argumentum ad verecundiam* is a problem is the persuasion dialogue. In this type of dialogue, the goal of the proponent is to persuade a respondent that the proponent's thesis (point of view) is true (right), but when the proponent appeals to the opinion of an expert, he brings in a third party to the context of the argument. Typically, two participants – let us call them Black and White – are engaged in persuasion dialogue, and one of them attempts to back up his side of the argument by citing the opinion of an expert authority. Let us say that White backs up his argument by claiming that an expert, Green, has vouched for the proposition that White is maintaining. This move in the persuasion dialogue has been advanced by White with the objective of persuading Black. Or let us say that White's strategy is evidently to put forward his argument strongly and forcibly so that it will be overwhelming against Black's side.

Once such a move has been made, it implies the existence of a secondary knowledge-elicitation dialogue between White and the expert Green, whose advice or opinion has been used in argument by White. The existence of this secondary context of dialogue can be inferred, because every *ad verecundiam* type of argument from expert authority involves a secondary dialogue between the expert and the solicitor of the expert's opinion. The critical questions appropriate for this secondary dialogue are given in Section 7.5.

The type of reasoning built into an expert system is *knowledge-based reasoning*, meaning that it draws its premises from a set of facts and rules (or frames) called a *knowledge base*. There is nothing inherently illicit or fallacious in this type of reasoning. Nor is there anything fallacious or illicit per se in the use of conclusions drawn by an expert (or expert system) in order to solve a problem, answer a question, or back up an opinion in argumentation. Argumentation based on solicitation of an opinion from knowledge-based expert sources is a species of plausible reasoning that has a legitimate function of shifting a burden of proof in interactive argumentation (dialogue).

The scheme for the appeal to expert opinion in argumentation is the following:

> E is an expert in domain D.
> E asserts that A is known to be true.
> A is within D.
> Therefore, A may (plausibly) be taken to be true.

A use of this scheme by a proponent in argumentation can be judged to be weak, erroneous, or insufficiently documented if one or more of the premises is inadequately supported. However, there are several specific errors that can be committed, corresponding to failures to answer the various critical questions listed in Section 7.7.

7.7 CRITICAL QUESTIONS FOR THE APPEAL TO EXPERT OPINION

Like other types of argumentation we have studied, the problem is to sort out the fallacious or questionable instances from the more reasonable instances of the uses of the appeal to expert opinion. The following six critical questions must be kept in mind when evaluating any appeal to authority. A reasonable appeal to authority must satisfy all the requirements cited in these six questions. And if a particular requirement is violated by an appeal to authority, then the appeal should be criticized or questioned in this regard. If the argument is weak, as presented, but advanced in the context of dialogue in such a way as to silence any of these critical questions preemptively by imputing a breach of modesty, on the part of the respondent, the argument is fallacious.

The first question is whether the judgment put forward by the authority actually falls within the field of competence in which that individual is an expert. Some cases are clear violations of this. If the expert is a physicist and the judgment is about religion and has nothing to do with physics, then such an appeal should be rejected for being of questionable value or relevance. In some cases, the appeal is so vague that the name of the would-be expert is not even given. One should criticize this type of case by asking for more documentation of its claim to expert authority.

In other cases, the relevance of a field of experience to a particular issue may be harder to judge. For example, suppose the issue is the health value of taking vitamin C. The views of a famous biochemist may lay some claim to expert value. But perhaps the judgment of a medical doctor who has done research on this topic would be more authoritative. Here, each case must be judged on its own merits from the information given. But one must be careful to question the credentials of an expert authority in relation to the specific issue. If the expert's field is only indirectly related to the issue, that could be grounds for caution and critical questioning of the claim.

The second main question with regard to any appeal to authority is whether the cited expert is actually an expert, and not merely someone quoted because of his prestige, popularity, or celebrity status. Several critical subquestions are relevant to establishing whether someone can reasonably be called a legitimate expert in a particular field:

1. What degrees, professional qualifications, or certifications by licensing agencies does this person hold?
2. Can testimony and evaluations of colleagues or other experts be given to support his status?
3. Does the expert cited have a record of experience in the field or particular technique being discussed?
4. What is this individual's previous record of predictions or successful accomplishments in this field of expertise?
5. Can evidence be given of publications or other projects that have been evaluated, refereed, or reviewed by other authorities?

By responding to these five critical subquestions, the proponent should be able to give some reasons why the authority cited qualifies as a legitimate expert. But many of the more superficial appeals to authority that are commonplace in everyday reasoning simply fail to pass this test. Instead, the would-be authority is often cited more for reasons of celebrity status or personal popularity. In this case, the individual cited may not be an expert at all.

The third critical question is that of how authoritative a particular expert is. Even if the individual cited is a legitimate expert in the field in which the question lies, there still remains the question of how strongly the appeal should be taken as a plausible argument. Because someone is quoted as an expert on some controversy or problem by the media, that should not mean that the final word has been said, even if this person is truly an expert. An appeal to authority can be reasonable (nonfallacious) yet weak, as arguments go.

The fourth question is whether there is disagreement among several qualified authorities who have been consulted. Here there are several methods that may be used to resolve the disagreement. Usually, further dialogue among the experts is the best method, when this is possible.

If there is inconsistency among well-qualified experts whose advice has been appealed to, then the *ad verecundiam* is certainly open to question. However, such a case of inconsistency need not always be an indication of fallacy, for sometimes the inconsistency can be dealt with by further critical discussion or clarification. However, it is, in general, a requirement of a successful appeal to authority that known pronouncements of other qualified authorities be consistent with the cited proposition as advocated by the expert appealed to. If not, the inconsistency must be resolved or further questions raised.

The fifth question is whether objective evidence on the cited opinion is presently available, and whether the expert's opinion is consistent with it. First, we noted that the appeal to authority is no substitute for objective evidence in the form of experimental or direct scientific confirmation of the proposition at issue. If this sort of evidence is available, it should be given preference to the say-so of an authority because inductive confirmation is generally a stronger form of argument than plausible reasoning. But second, we also noted that, when experts disagree, they should be able to defend their position by citing objective evidence in their field. By this means, as we saw, inconsistencies between expert pronouncements can sometimes be resolved through further dialogue.

The sixth question is whether the expert's say-so has been correctly interpreted. It must be in a form that is clear and intelligible. Yet it must not be only a simplistic rewording of what the expert said that may overlook necessary qualifications or exceptions. Preferably, the expert should be quoted directly. If not, it could be reasonable to question whether his view has been presented fairly and accurately. The four subquestions listed at the beginning of Section 7.5 are the specific methods of answering this sixth type of critical question.

Much depends here on the given argument. If further dialogue is possible, questions of interpretation can be pursued. If not, the evaluator may have to go on the basis of the given corpus. However, in this event, an argument from authority may be rated as weak or unreliable if it overlooks or omits responding to any of these six major critical questions.

An appeal to expert opinion in argumentation commits the *ad verecundiam* fallacy if the context of dialogue shows that it is an instance of Locke's type of strategy of being overly aggressive in trying to prevail on the respondent to prevent him from advancing critical questions. This fallacy is a violation of the negative rules of persuasion dialogue given in Chapter 1. It is a failure of the proponent to defend his point of view by argument – a type of systematic (and often very clever) tactic to evade the obligation of presenting proof for a contention. Instead, the proponent tries to close off the dialogue prematurely in his own favor by browbeating the respondent to yield to the authority of revered experts, approved authors, or others who are held high as opinion setters in common esteem. This tactic is a suppression of argument that deceptively aims to close off the process of legitimate dialogue prematurely and to defeat the respondent by a short-cut to persuasion.

Reasoned use of expert opinion can be a legitimate and helpful way of introducing external evidence into a critical discussion to shift a burden of proof, when direct access to technical or specialized knowledge is not available for practical purposes. This chapter has shown the many errors encountered in the appeal to authority that make it an inherently weak type of plausible argumentation that can go seriously wrong. Appeals to authority can be weak and undocumented. When pressed too hard in a persuasion dialogue, they can even commit the *ad verecundiam* fallacy.

8

Inductive errors, bias, and fallacies

In a deductively valid argument, if the premises are true, the conclusion must be true. Deductive validity is a very strict standard of argument. If an argument is deductively valid, it is impossible for the premises to be true while the conclusion is false.

In an inductively strong argument, if the premises are true, it is probable or likely that the conclusion is true. If an argument is inductively strong and the premises are true, it is logically possible that the conclusion could be false. So inductive strength is a less strict standard of argument than deductive validity. Inductive strength is a matter of probability.

Probability and statistics have an acknowledged place in scientific reasoning and experimental methods, but even outside these specialized contexts, the use of inductive argument is an important part of most reasonable dialogue. For example, the use of statistical arguments seems to play an increasingly significant role in political decision making on virtually any subject of discussion.

Of the many different kinds of inductive arguments, we will single out three for discussion in this chapter. The first type, the *inductive generalization,* is an argument from premises about a specific group or collection of individuals or things to a more general conclusion about a larger group or collection. Traditional logic textbooks have often stressed the perils of hasty generalizations, for it has been rightly perceived that inductive generalization is associated with significant and common fallacies.

To give an example of an inductive generalization, suppose I have looked at books shelved in various parts of the reference room of the library, and I have observed that each book I have looked at has a call number beginning with an R. I might then conclude by an inductive generalization that most or all the books shelved and cataloged in the reference room have numbers beginning with an R. My premise is based on my observation of a few books, a specific set of books. My conclusion is generalized to the larger group of books in the reference room.

A second type of inductive argument singled out for discussion in this chapter is the statistical argument. A *statistical argument* is an inductive argument in which the degree of probability of the strength of the argument is either given as a specific percentage (number) or in which a nonnumerical statistical term is used. These statistical terms include expressions like 'most', 'many', 'nearly all', 'a few', 'rarely', 'almost', 'least', 'at least', 'never', and so forth. To determine whether an inductive argument is a statistical argument, you must examine the conclusion to see if the claim is statistical. Such a judgment is relative to the context of dialogue, but normally the presence of a statistical term in the conclusion is the best indicator.

The inductive generalization about the call numbers of books in the reference room is a statistical argument because the conclusion uses the term 'most'.

The third type of inductive argument we will be concerned with in this chapter is the *causal argument*. Judgments of causality are of basic importance both in scientific and in less structured contexts of reasoning about the world. However, exactly what it means to say clearly that a causal relationship exists between two events is a question that has proved notoriously difficult to answer. Indeed, the concept of causality is so elusive that scientists often try to avoid the language of cause and effect altogether. Such attempts have largely proved unsuccessful, however, most notably in the applied sciences, for disciplines like medicine and engineering are essentially practical in nature. In these contexts, the practical language of cause and effect is altogether unavoidable because the whole intent and nature of the subject is to manipulate causal variables.

We will not try to offer an analysis of the causal relation in this chapter, any more than we will try to offer an analysis of probability or induction. Our goal will be the more modest one of understanding some basic and useful criticisms of inductive and causal arguments. When statistical claims are the basis of conclusions arrived at by causal or inductive argumentation, it is useful to ask certain basic types of critical questions about how these conclusions were arrived at; for statistical evidence is nowadays a very common basis of argument in many contexts of everyday reasoned dialogue.

8.1 MEANINGLESS AND UNKNOWABLE STATISTICS

The *error of meaningless statistics* occurs when a statistical claim uses a term that is so imprecisely defined that the use of a precise statistical figure in the claim is meaningless. The error of meaningless statistics is, therefore, a linguistic problem, even though it is, of course, also a problem in inductive reasoning and statistics. A classic illustration is the following statement, made by then Attorney General Robert F. Kennedy, in a speech in Athens, Georgia in 1960:[1]

Example 8.0

Ninety percent of the major racketeers would be out of business by the end of the year if the ordinary citizen, the businessman, the union official, and the public authority stood up to be counted and refused to be corrupted.

One can appreciate the sense and good intent behind this statement, but unfortunately, the exact figure of 90 percent is misleadingly imprecise. The use of this number gives "punch" to the statement, but if we stop to think about it, how could such a figure be arrived at reasonably? You might try to devise a precise cutoff point in terms of a criminal's income, say fifty thousand dollars. But even if that cutoff point could be justified, finding out a particular criminal's income could be difficult, even dangerous. The term 'major racketeer' is extremely vague. One could well imagine the considerable controversy about whether a particular person should reasonably be described as a 'racketeer', 'major racketeer', or even a 'minor racketeer'. Moreover, the use of this term might vary with different contexts. A major racketeer in Sioux City, Iowa, might be described as a minor racketeer in New York City.

The *error of unknowable statistics* occurs when a statistical claim requires evidence that is practically or logically impossible to verify. In this type of fallacious claim, the terms used by the arguer may be sufficiently clear or precise, but the problem is that it is implausible that evidence could be available to support such a precise statistical and numerical hypothesis as the one given. A classic illustration is the following claim attributed to Dr. Joyce Brothers:[2]

1 Reported in Seligman (1961, p. 146).
2 Dr. Joyce Brothers, *This Week*, October 1958, cited in ibid., p. 147.

Example 8.1

The American girl kisses an average of seventy-nine men before getting married.

The critical question to ask in relation to this sort of statistical claim is how anyone could possibly compile this sort of information. It is extremely dubious that any girl would keep an exact tally of the number of times she kissed a man before she got married. Even if anyone did try to keep track, there are good possibilities of remembering wrongly. And even so, what reason would we have for thinking that respondents to a question or poll on this subject would answer truthfully? Many women would be insulted by such a question, and no doubt refuse to answer it at all. Once you think of it, the claim is absurd because it would be practically impossible to get enough reliable data to support or refute the claim with anything like enough confidence to yield an exact statistical figure.

With any statistical claim, you should ask how the data were collected. Sometimes just asking this question can point to problems, especially when a precise number is given. Suppose you are presented with the statement that 33.87 percent of all forest fires are intentionally set. Initially, this statement may seem much more plausible than if it said that only some, or a few, forest fires are intentionally set. But if you reflect on it, how could you obtain reliable data to support the precise figure of 33.87 percent? By their nature, the causes of many forest fires must remain unknown. And once again, if you think about it, even if the cause of a fire is known, for example a cigarette, there must be many cases when there would be no way to know whether the burning cigarette was tossed somewhere to start a fire intentionally. Here the difficulties of determining an exact ratio of types of causes juxtaposed with the exact figure of 33.87 percent strongly indicate the practical impossibility of verifying the statistical claim, as stated. This is a case in which we can reasonably question whether the argument commits the error of unknowable statistics.

A famous example of unknowable statistics comes from the claims often given in newspapers concerning the rat population of New York City:

Example 8.2

According to Seligman (1961), newspaper feature writers have claimed for years that there are eight million rats in New York City. This

201

sounds impressive, but how would you know that this figure is correct? Seligman interviewed the rodent and insect consultant for New York City and was referred to two studies. The investigators counted rats in certain areas, and then extrapolated from these findings to figures for the whole city. But how could one be confident that even the original counts could be accurate or representative of the rat population of an area? The problem is that rats do not tend to be cooperative. They tend to stick to inaccessible places, like sewers, and they are not willing to stand around and be counted. According to the insect and rodent consultant, "You can count a rat on the eighth floor of a building and then another on the seventh floor, and then another when you get to the sixth – but after all, you may just be seeing the same rat three times."

The problem here is one of spurious accuracy. An exact statistical figure makes the claim look impressive, but the practical difficulties of getting the evidence required to support it make it clear that the use of an exact figure is spurious. Even if rats in buildings could be counted by using some form of electronic surveillance, there is no plausible reason for thinking that it would be practical to devise or use such a technique. And the account given by the newspaper feature writers yields no reason to believe that the collection of such evidence is possible.

Unknowable and meaningless statistics have traditionally been called statistical fallacies, but the term 'fallacy' seems appropriate only if the statistical argument is so badly flawed in its underlying pattern of reasoning that it is beyond recovery. However, the real error with the kinds of statistical arguments studied in this chapter is the failure to indicate proper doubts, critical questions, and reservations. The error lies in presenting a weak argument as one that is stronger than the evidence warrants.

For example, the statistician who made the claim that there were eight million rats in New York City could have made a valid statistical extrapolation from rats in a specific area that he really did observe. But the fault lies in reporting the estimate without adding a confidence factor or estimate of reliability to indicate that the figure given is, at best, a rough estimate. Too often the media fail to put in estimates of confidence, or fail even to indicate in any way how the specific figure was arrived at. Given this lack of information, the use of a specific figure conveys a false and unwarranted sense of accuracy that should be questioned as a serious error.

The error of unknowable statistics concerns the lack of, or impossibility of access to, data for certain claims, whereas the error of meaningless statistics concerns the vagueness of the definitions of terms used in some statistical claims. But both errors involve the use of exact figures in which such precise claims are impossible to support reasonably without important qualifications.

The fact that it is not easy to eliminate important biases in statistical polls about significant political or economic matters can be appreciated if you ask yourself how you would determine the current rate of unemployment in your country at the moment. The obvious answer would be to phone a number of homes and ask how many people are in the household and how many of these are currently unemployed. What could be simpler?

However, a statistician would know that there are many biases that could be built into your procedure. It is known, for example, that more women would be respondents to your phone call than men. So gender might be a bias in your results. Other known forms of bias in this type of sampling would include income, age, education, and rural versus urban residence. So a statistician would have to build in a procedure for adjusting for all these kinds of bias in the poll.

Another problem you would have to solve is how to define 'unemployed person'. Does an actor who is between jobs count as 'unemployed'? Does a mother who has not seriously considered going back to work count as 'unemployed'? Let us say you define 'unemployed person' as an individual who is presently not working but who is seriously trying to find work. Then you have partly solved your problem of definition, and the mother not seriously considering going back to work is not defined as an unemployed person. But you still have the problem of applying your definition to a particular person. Suppose the actor between jobs has tried to find more work to fill in but will take on assignments only that he finds artistically satisfying. Should we classify him as a person who is "seriously trying to find work" or not? This is a problem of interpretation that may significantly affect the unemployment figure arrived at.

Statisticians who take sample surveys of the labor force to give official unemployment figures have devised careful guidelines to define their terms and eliminate biases. But it is not the simple job it may appear to be, and when making a decision based on a figure

203

of current unemployment, to know what the figure really means it may be helpful to know, or to ask about, the assumptions and definitions on which the figure was based.

If a vague term is used in a statistical claim, then the critical questions to ask are how the claimant defines the vague term and whether the definition offered is a reasonable one that can be justified. But if reasons can be given to show that the term is vague to the extent that its use in the claim makes the exact statistical figure given impossible to justify, then the error of meaningless statistics has been committed. If reasons can be given why statistical verification of a statistical claim is impossible, then the error of unknowable statistics has been committed. In each case, the burden of proof is on the critic to show why the claim is fallacious.

8.2 SAMPLING PROCEDURES

The conclusions derived from polls, surveys, and many other common kinds of statistical generalizations are based on the reasonableness of a process called a sampling procedure. A sampling procedure is a way of drawing elements from a certain population having a certain property and then generalizing from the properties of the elements in the sample to the properties of the things in the whole population.

For example, suppose you want to estimate what proportion of the Canadian people are in favor of a bilingual Canada. It would be impractical to try to poll all Canadians, so the usual approach would be to select a sample of Canadians and then ask them the question. The reasonableness of sampling as a way of making generalizations depends on the presumption that the sample selected is representative of the population in the distribution of the property in question.

To understand what is at stake in a sampling procedure, think of a large urn full of marbles and the problem of determining the color of the marbles in the urn. Let us say that we do not have the time or resources to take all the marbles out and count them, and we cannot see into the urn. However, when we take out a handful of the marbles from the top of the urn, we can easily see that half the marbles in the handful are black and half are white. Using the handful as our sample, we could conjecture that half the marbles in the urn are black and half are white. The marbles remaining in the urn taken together with the marbles in the sample would constitute the population we are making our generalization about.

In this instance, the basic assumption underlying the reasonableness of our sampling procedure is that the proportion of black to white marbles in the sample represents the proportion of black to white in the whole population. In other words, we are working on the assumption that the marbles in the urn are mixed up so that the proportion of black to white marbles is uniform throughout the whole urn. For example, if we have good reason to believe that most of the black marbles are concentrated toward the bottom of the urn, our sampling procedure would be highly questionable.

The basic type of sample is called a simple random sample, or simply a random sample. A *simple random sample* is defined as one in which each sample of the same size has an equal chance of being selected. For example, if the urn contained five marbles, and the sample is to contain two marbles, then there are ten different possible pairs of marbles that constitute samples. Now suppose that more of the black marbles are known to be concentrated at the bottom of the urn. Then if a sample did not have an equal chance of being selected from the bottom, it would not be a random sample.

Sampling can be a reasonable way of estimating that a property is likely to be distributed throughout a population in a set proportion of instances provided a certain basic assumption is met. We could say that the *assumption of representativeness* is met when the sample selected is representative of the whole population in relation to the distribution of the relevant property or properties throughout that whole population. However, the problem for statisticians is that, in practical terms, it may not be easy to obtain reasonable assurance that the assumption of representativeness is adequately met in particular cases. In reality, the possibilities of bias are very significant because real populations can be less homogeneous and more variegated than one might initially think. It seems that simple random samples are not always appropriate and that more complex types of sampling procedures must be devised to make representative generalizations.

For example, suppose we want to find the average weight of one elephant in a herd, but we can weigh only a few elephants. But suppose the herd is composed of adult and baby elephants. In this case, there are two *strata* in the population, adults and babies. Therefore, the sample must fairly represent both strata. Here statisticians would speak of a *stratified random sample,* in which independent random samples are drawn from each *stratum,* or level, in the population. Once again, the sample must meet the assumption of being representative of the variations in the whole population.

It is important to remember that sampling is basically an inductive form of reasoning. If the sample is representative, then the population will be likely to have the same proportion of relevant properties. But by the very nature of sampling, we never know for sure what relevant properties the population has as a whole. Our conclusion is based on reasonable probability. According to Campbell (1974, p. 142), the most important basic concept of sampling is this: "If sample items are chosen at random from the total population, the sample will tend to have the same characteristics, in approximately the same proportion, as the entire population." But Campbell warns us that in order to have confidence in this basic assumption, we must have proper respect for the word 'tend'. Sampling is a way of making a reasonable estimate based on probabilities. It is not meant to be a substitute for direct observation of the properties of a whole population. In evaluating any generalization based on a sampling procedure, it is important to know how the sample was selected. We now turn to some problematic cases in which the sample for a statistical claim was inadequate or poorly chosen.

8.3 INSUFFICIENT AND BIASED STATISTICS

The *criticism of insufficient statistics* should be raised when the sample selected is so small that the generalization to the whole population may be virtually worthless. For a generalization to be worth serious consideration, the sample must be sufficiently large.

One problem here is that claims may be made on the basis of a sample when no information at all is given on sample size. We may be told, for example, that a test group of children who brushed with Brand X had 60 percent fewer cavities than those who brushed with Brand Y. This claim might be quite true, but if each group consisted of five children, any generalization based on this claim would be meaningless. There is just too much chance of error. Perhaps the five children who brushed with Brand X just happened to have good teeth and were generally healthy, whereas the other five subsisted largely on chocolate bars and soft drinks during the test period. With such a small sample, there is no way to rule out the many possibilities of chance or coincidence that might affect the two groups of children. The use of the words 'test group' or 'controlled study' may sound impressive, but a little reflection about the size of the sample should lead us to question this sort of generalization. Until we know the size of the sample, we should not be prepared to place any confidence in this sort of claim.

In general, how large should a sample be? It is difficult for a statistician to answer this question in general terms, for it depends on several detailed factors in a particular case. One such factor is that, when there is more variation in a population, a larger sample size is required. According to Campbell (1974, p. 148), the more varied the population is, the larger the sample size should be, other things being equal. For example, a small blood sample is usually acceptable as a good sample because the chemical composition of blood throughout a person's body does not normally vary much in relevant respects. However, to cite another example given by Campbell (p. 148), eight men in a bar would not be an adequate sample to determine the political leanings of a whole country. Of course, it would be a nonrandom sample as well.

To avoid the problem of inadequate statistics, two critical questions should always be considered. First, we must ask whether information is given, or can be produced, on the size of the sample. In many cases, such information is simply not given. But second, if the information is given, we must question whether the size of the sample is adequate to sustain the generalization that has been made. If the sample is very small, the question should be raised whether it may be so small as to be worthless.

The *criticism of biased statistics* should be raised when the assumption of representativeness may fail to be met, not because the sample is too small, but because the distribution of the property in the generalization may not match the same distribution in the sample. In our previous illustration of the marbles in the urn, suppose that all the black marbles happen to be located near the bottom of the urn. But then suppose the handful of marbles chosen as a sample is scooped up from the top of the urn. Such a sample would not be representative of the distribution of colors of marbles in the whole urn. It would be a biased sample. Consider the next example:

207

Example 8.3

In 1936, the *Literary Digest* mailed out ten million ballots in a political poll to try to predict whether Franklin Roosevelt or Alfred Landon would win the upcoming election. According to the two million three hundred thousand ballots returned, it was predicted that Landon would win by a clear majority. The names for the poll were randomly selected from the telephone book, lists of the magazine's own subscribers, and lists of automobile owners.[3]

In this famous case, it turned out that Roosevelt won by a 60 percent majority. What went wrong with the poll? The problem was that the sample selected tended to be from higher-income groups. People in the lower-income brackets tended not to own telephones or cars. This biased sample yielded incorrect results because, in the election, there was a strong link between income bracket and party preference. So despite the enormous size of the sample, it turned out not to be representative of the population of voters in the relevant respects.

It is very common for statistical claims and generalizations to be used as evidence for a causal conclusion. Some of the most important statistical errors and weaknesses in argument arise in connection with causal conclusions drawn from statistical premises. In the next sections, we turn to a study of these arguments.

8.4 QUESTIONABLE QUESTIONS AND DEFINITIONS

When data are collected by polls or surveys that direct questions to the respondents, the exact wording of the questions may be significant. According to Moore (1979, p. 20), it is surprisingly difficult to word questions so that they are entirely clear to the respondents. Moore cites the case of a survey that asked about "ownership of

---

3 This classic case is outlined in Campbell (1974, p. 148) and Giere (1979, p. 214). A more detailed analysis is given in Freedman, Pisani, and Purves (1978, pp. 302–4). According to their account, Roosevelt won by a landslide of 62% to 38%. According to their analysis, the names and addresses for the survey came from sources like telephone books and club membership lists, which tended to screen out the poor. They note that, in 1936, there were eleven million residential telephones and nine million unemployed. Freedman, Pisani, and Purves conclude (p. 303) that there was a strong selection bias against the poor in the *Digest* survey. They add that, in 1936, the political split followed economic lines, and the poor voted overwhelmingly for Roosevelt.

stock" and found that most Texas ranchers owned stock. However, for all one can know, the kind of stock they were referring to was probably not the kind traded on the stock exchange. This particular question ran a large risk of committing the fallacy of equivocation (outlined in Chapter 9) when the respondents were ranchers.

All statistical claims are based on assumptions about the meanings of the terms used in the claims. The numerical figure that results from a poll or other statistical study can be highly influenced by exactly how a term is defined. For example, statistical claims are often made about the poverty level in a country. How 'poverty' is defined can be very crucial in determining what figure is arrived at to represent the number of poor persons at a particular time.

The usual way of defining 'poverty' is by specifying a cutoff income level. If this definition is used, one should ask whether it takes into account inheritances, insurance payments, gifts, or money from the sale of property. A retirement couple living comfortably in their owned home and with a modest income from investments could be classified as a poverty family, by some definitions.

One could more carefully compose a definition of 'poverty' by setting some minimal standards of nutritional adequacy on diet and then calculating the cost of minimally adequate nutrition at current food prices. From the assumption that a low-income family should spend a third of its income on food, one could then arrive at an income figure to determine the poverty level. One can see, however, that such a definition makes some basic assumptions that could be open to reasonable argument.

We can see, then, that in the course of argument, statistical claims are open to the use of loaded definitions of the kind we studied in Chapter 7. Indeed, in connection with the example of defining 'poverty', Campbell (1974, p. 16) reports grim amusement at the "numbers game" played on the poverty issue by political economists in recent times. To play the game, Campbell observes, all one needs is a friendly definition of poverty – friendly to one's own side of the political argument.

Another problem is that what qualifies as meeting the definition or criterion of an object of study in a sample of a population may change in a different time, place, or situation. This may occur even if there is no good ground for disputing the definition itself. Although the definition of the type of individual to be studied may be clear and reasonable, figures may be biased by the way these individuals are selected. Two research statisticians, Dr. Alan Fisher and Dr. Wendy North, have suggested that apparent improvements in survival rates for lung and breast cancer cases may be an illusion resulting from improved techniques of earlier detection.[4] The problem stems from the practice of reporting survival rates in terms of the percentage of cancer victims who live for at least five years after they have been diagnosed. As techniques for earlier diagnosis have improved, a bias is introduced into the survival rate statistics that makes the patients appear to live longer. Thus, as time goes on, the figures for survival of cancer keep improving. The optimistic interpretation of these figures so often given is that a cancer patient's chances for survival are now much better because of improved diagnosis and treatment. But critics claim that these statistics can be deceiving because the sample identified as meeting the criteria for a cancer patient has also changed over the years.

If this type of criticism is justified, what sort of error does it reveal? The problem is not so much with the definition of the terms used by doctors to describe or identify types of cancer. It is that improvements in screening programs for cancer have meant that the populations selected as having a diagnosis of a particular type of cancer have changed significantly over the years. How the sample population is chosen has varied at different times. The shift is in selecting the individuals that meet the definition.

Moore (1979, p. 20) notes that bias can be introduced into a sample survey by slanting the questions in the direction of the conclusion the survey taker wants to prove. For example, the question 'Do you favor banning private ownership of handguns in order to reduce the rate of violent crime?' would be a loaded question because it would tend to draw positive responses from those respondents worried about violent crime.

These cases are examples of statistical errors in reasoning because they relate to polls and other statistical methods of collecting information. But clearly their implicit dangers are types of weaknesses and faults we are already familiar with under the headings of loaded questions and question-asking problems (Chapter 2).

Sometimes surveys can be very controversial because the questions asked must be reasonably simple. If the questions are too complicated, they will undoubtedly confuse many respondents, who

4 Fisher and North (1986, p. 6).

are then likely to respond in a misleading way; but if the questions are too simple, they may also be open to criticism for that very reason.

In a recent forty-one-question survey for the Prayer Book Society conducted by Gallup, the following questions were asked of a sampling of Episcopalian clergy and laity:

> Do you believe that the gospel miracles are mostly historical facts, mostly the gospel writers' interpretation or mostly legends? (Choose one).
>
> Would you approve or disapprove of a merger of the Episcopal (Anglican) Church and the Roman Catholic Church?
>
> In general, do you think the Episcopal Church is too "trendy" or too old-fashioned?[5]

Episcopal church leaders were described as "seething" over these questions because "they reduce complex theological and sociological issues to simplistic yes or no answers." Church leaders took the position that the questions were phrased in such a way as to produce answers that would support the agenda of the Prayer Book Society. Although Gallup conceded that he received a great deal of criticism of the questions in the returned questionnaires, he said that he was "not uncomfortable" about the poll.[6]

In this case, whether the questions can be fairly criticized as unreasonable depends on the theological position of those church leaders who were supposed to respond to them. The reasonableness of this first question, for example, depends on the Episcopalian doctrine of the gospel miracles and how central that doctrine is to the Episcopalian theology. Suppose that most Episcopalians accept the position that the gospel miracles were writers' interpretations based on historical facts as transmitted through legends and other oral traditions and sources. Then the instruction 'Choose one' appended to the first question certainly forces the respondent to choose an answer that must fail to represent reasonably the full spectrum of his beliefs as an Episcopalian. From the position of that respondent, then, the question may fairly be criticized as an instance of the unreasonably dichotomous black and white question.

5 Marjorie Hyer, "Episcopal Wrath Quick to Descend on Gallup Poll," *Winnipeg Free Press*, June 22, 1985 (originally from the *Washington Post*).
6 Ibid.

Commenting on the second question, Reverend John R. Frizzell, Jr. of St. Alban's Episcopal Church in Annandale, Virginia, replied, "Clearly, anyone who takes seriously the words of our Lord that 'there shall be one flock and one Shepherd' is committed to the reunion of the church . . . yet the questions do not even recognize the complexities of reunion."[7] What Reverend Frizzell's comments suggest is that the second question may be introducing bias into the survey by its slanted style. The question could then be criticized as loaded because it would tend to draw positive responses from Episcopalians; for all Episcopalians would, at least in principle, be committed to the proposition that there should be a church reunion in virtue of the biblical injunction that "there shall be one flock." The bias imposed on the question by this general commitment might tend to produce affirmative answers without due consideration of all the complexities inherent in the question of a merger with another specific denomination like the Catholic church.

Finally, the third question is a good example of a faulty black and white question (the fallacy of unreasonable dichotomy studied in Chapter 2), presuming, as seems reasonable, that many of the respondents would want the option of answering that the church is "old-fashioned" in some respects but too "trendy" in others.

To sum up, then, we can see that many of the same kinds of errors and criticisms studied in Chapter 2 on question asking are also relevant in the context of the statistics drawn from polls, surveys, and opinion sampling. Broadly speaking, with any generalization based on collecting data from a sample, it is always a good idea to inquire into the precise wording of the question or questions that were used. The questions may not be clear. But even if they are clear and exact, they may still be open to critical questions or reasonable objections.

8.5 THE *POST HOC* ARGUMENT

The traditional *post hoc* fallacy is said to be the unjustified argument which concludes that one event causes another event simply because there is a positive correlation between the two events. Let A and B stand for events or states of affairs that may obtain at a certain

7 Ibid.

time.[8] Then the *post hoc* fallacy is said to occur when it is concluded that A causes B simply because one or more occurrences of A are correlated with one or more occurrences of B. The full Latin name for this traditional fallacy is *post hoc, ergo propter hoc,* meaning 'after this, therefore, because of this'. Consider the following example:

Example 8.4

Every time I wash the car, it starts to rain shortly afterward. Therefore, my car-washing activities are causing outbursts of precipitation in the clouds.

The reason this kind of causal inference has been viewed as a fallacy is that an association or correlation between repeated occurrences of two events can, in some cases, turn out to be a coincidence. Therefore, to leap too quickly to infer a causal connection between two events on the basis of their single or repeated correlation could turn out to be an unfounded conclusion.

The initial problem with the *post hoc* fallacy, like the other so-called fallacies we have studied, is that the argument from a correlation to a causal relationship is sometimes a reasonable type of argument. In fact, if there is a positive correlation between two events, this can be very good positive evidence that there is a causal relationship between them. Even so, errors in *post hoc* reasoning can occur where an arguer leaps too quickly to conclude that one variable A causes another variable B when the only evidence given is that there has been a positive correlation between occurrences of A and occurrences of B. It seems, then, that positive correlation is not enough, by itself, to establish a causal relationship conclusively. The error implicit in *post hoc* reasoning, therefore, may be in overlooking factors other than positive correlation that may be important in evaluating a causal relationship between two events.

There are so many kinds of errors implicit in the hazardous process of arguing from correlation to causation – as we will see in the Sections 8.6 and 8.7 – that it is difficult to avoid them. Certainly,

---

8 In other chapters, we have used the letters $A, B, C, \ldots$ to denote propositions. However, in this chapter, we depart from that practice and let the same letters stand for states of affairs (sometimes also called events). Just as propositions are true or false, states of affairs have as their defining property that they obtain or do not obtain at a particular time.

we can see why tradition labels *post hoc* argumentation as fallacious. If it is basically reasonable to argue from correlation to causation, why is this form of reasoning so heavily subject to bias and error? Is there some underlying reason for our propensity to commit the *post hoc* type of fallacy? The reason may be ultimately connected to the Kantian point of view that causality is based on a selective interpretation of external events as filtered through the perceiver's framework of logical reasoning. An individual's causal expectations can serve to fill gaps in a perceived sequence of events by imposing a logical completion on the sequence, based on familiar causal patterns or routines. Because such causal orderings are based upon (1) a selection of remembered events, and (2) upon a combination or sequential ordering of them drawing on familiar expectations drawn from similar cases in experience, they are subject to occasional mistakes, perceptions of apparent causal connections subject to correction, when seen from a different point of view.

This type of error has been studied by Trankell (1972), who suggests that our causal judgments are inevitably based on a personal interpretation of data because the logical completion mechanism that fills in causal gaps are based on patterns of earlier experiences. The following case from Trankell (1972, p. 18) illustrates the seriousness of the kind of mistake that can be made in reasoning based on plausible completion of a series of real events:

Example 8.5

A taxi carrying a lawyer along a busy city street was forced to come to a fast stop behind another taxi, which had also stopped quickly. Through the car window, the lawyer saw that the back door of the taxi in front had swung open, and at the same time, he noticed an older man fall through the open door and lie unconscious on the street. The next day, reading about the accident in the newspaper, he found that his observations had been wrong. What had really happened was that the old man had crossed the street without looking, and the car in front braked to avoid hitting him, resulting in a collision that knocked him down.

In this case, what the lawyer had actually perceived was the open door of the car and the man lying on the ground. However, he made sense of these perceptions by combining them into a natural

214

causal sequence. However, evidence from other sources subsequently made it clear that the lawyer's plausible completion of what he saw was based on an erroneous interpretation of the real sequence of events.

Because of this natural psychological tendency to fill in a "logical completion" of causal links between events as we see them, the urge to fall into *post hoc* errors is powerful. Even so, it is an exaggeration to suggest that all reasoning from observed correlations to causal conclusions is inherently fallacious.

It is misleading and simplistic to look at *post hoc* reasoning as a fallacy, for four basic reasons. First, arguing from a correlation to a causal conclusion is not inherently incorrect or fallacious. Sometimes it can be a reasonable type of argument. Second, when this type of argument should be subject to critical questioning, it is not because of a single fault. Rather, there are several distinct types of gaps or weak points that can be implicit in arguing from evidence of correlation to a causal conclusion. Third, when one of these gaps is pinpointed, it is characteristically not a kind of fault that refutes or destroys the argument as "fallacious." More typically, it calls for a critical question that points out a need for more study, or further support of the claim, in order to clarify the nature of the relationship between the two factors in question. Fourth, when one of these specific questions is raised, it typically points out a weakness in the argument that can be remedied. So the criticism is that the evidence for a causal link is not as strong as it may have initially seemed. Thus the argument is not necessarily "fallacious." Most often it is better seen as an argument that is weak but not worthless, an argument that needs further backing in order to fulfill its burden of proof in the discussion.

8.6 SIX KINDS OF *POST HOC* ERRORS

There are several factors to be taken into account in causal reasoning, and consequently there are several kinds of *post hoc* weaknesses, shortcomings, or errors that are important to recognize.

The first type of *post hoc* error can occur when the number of positive correlations between the events in question is too small to rule out coincidence. A classic example is given by Fischer (1970, p. 166):

215

Example 8.6

On the fatal night of the Doria's collision with the Swedish ship, Grisholm, off Nantucket in 1956, the lady retired to her cabin and flicked the light switch. Suddenly there was a great crash and the sound of grinding metal. Passengers and crew ran screaming through the passageways. The lady burst from her cabin and explained to the first person in sight that she must have set the ship's emergency brake.

In this case, event B, the sinking, followed event A, the flicking of the switch, but this correlation would be extremely weak evidence, at best, that there may be a causal relationship between A and B. In fact, in this situation, there is plenty of evidence to show that the real cause of B is not connected to A at all. To conclude a causal relationship from a single instance of one event occurring with another is a weak type of argument that runs great risk of error.

A second type of error concerns the possibility of getting the causal relationship backward. Sometimes we know that there may be some sort of causal relationship between events A and B, but we are not sure which way the relationship should go. For example, there is definitely a positive correlation between personal wealth and ownership of stocks and bonds. But is it the stocks and bonds that cause the wealth, or is it that the acquisition of wealth leads to the investment of it in stocks and bonds? Probably both factors are at work to some extent in many cases. So here, we know that there is a correlation between A and B, but it is not clear whether it is better to conclude that A causes B or that B causes A.

A classic example of this second type of error is given by Huff (1954, p. 98):

Example 8.7

The people of a certain island had observed perfectly accurately over the centuries that people in good health have body lice and people in poor health do not. They had traditionally concluded that lice make a man healthy.

What happened here is that when a person became ill with fever, he came to have a higher body temperature. The lice did not find this comfortable and departed. Observing this, the people of the island concluded that lice make a person healthy. But they could,

216

more correctly, have concluded that being healthy is a causal factor in providing suitable conditions for body lice.

This second type of error can occur because correlation is always symmetrical, meaning that if *A* is correlated with *B*, then *B* is always correlated with *A*. Causation is different, however. Sometimes if *A* causes *B*, then *B* may also cause *A*. But sometimes the causal relationship does not go both ways.

Consider the following example from Damer (1980, p. 69): 'It's no wonder that Phillip makes such good grades and always does what the teacher asks. He's the teacher's pet.' Damer notes it is more likely the case that Phillip is the teacher's pet because he does what the teacher asks. In other words, the causal relationship is just the other way around from what is stated in the argument.

However, in this particular case, it is quite plausible that the causal relationship goes both ways. Because Phillip is a cooperative student and a hard worker, the teacher gives him special attention and respect. But the converse causal relationship is also likely to be at work. Because Phillip gets special attention and respect from this teacher, he may tend to be especially cooperative and hard working in this teacher's class.

Therefore, given that there is a correlation between *A* and *B*, it may not be established whether it is better to conclude that *A* causes *B* or that *B* causes *A*. And the two conclusions are not mutually exclusive in every case. There may be a reciprocal, or feedback (circular), type of mutual causal relationship between *A* and *B* in some cases.

A third type of causal error occurs when it is overlooked that two states of affairs *A* and *B* are correlated because there is some third factor *C* that is the cause of both *A* and *B*:

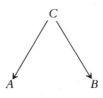

Here, there may be a genuine correlation between *A* and *B*, yet it may be quite incorrect to conclude that *A* causes *B*; for it may be, in reality, that C causes A and C causes B. Thus C, which may account for the association between A and B, may also make it clear that there need be no causal relation between A and B. The following example from Zeisel (1968, ch. 9) illustrates this type of case:

Example 8.8

It was found that married persons ate less candy than single persons. A second look at the data showed that if married and single individuals of equal age were compared, the correlation vanished. Hence it would be misleading to conclude that getting married causes less candy consumption in an individual. Age is the operative factor in both increased likelihood of marriage and decreased candy consumption.

This example also illustrates the practical nature of causal relationships. Suppose the candy manufacturers were able to prevent people from getting married. Would that result in a massive increase in candy consumption? No – to increase candy consumption they would have to keep people from getting older. And preventing them from getting married would not keep them from getting older. Thus causation is a practical matter. To say that A causes B means that if you can change or manipulate A, then you can change the occurrence of B as well. Correlation between A and B does not always mean that there is a genuine causal relationship between them.

In some cases, it is not clear how the causal relationship works, but the particular form of the relationship concluded in an argument can and should be questioned. Observing that a college student is both severely obese and severely depressed, an observer might conclude that the obesity is causing the depression. However, it may well be that there is a reciprocal causal relationship and that the depression is a causal factor contributing to the student's tendency to overeat. But then again, as Damer (1980, p. 70) observes, in this type of case, a more plausible conclusion is that there may be an underlying physical or psychological problem that is a common cause of both these effects.

This type of case shows that, if there is a positive correlation between two states of affairs A and B, it may be hasty and premature to conclude that A causes B, and it may be equally erroneous to conclude that B is the sole cause of A. It could be that both A and B are caused by some third factor, a common cause, and the failure to recognize the possibility or plausibility of this factor could be a serious bias or misrepresentation of the case.

A fourth type of error is to overlook the complex chain of linkages in a causal sequence. It may be that A causes C but that the causal relationship between them is more clearly brought out by observing that there is a third causal factor B intervening between A and C:

$$A \longrightarrow B \longrightarrow C$$

In a case like this, C may more correctly be said to be *indirectly* caused by A. The causal relationship between A and C may be said to be *complex* (*recursive*):

Example 8.9

A motorist observes that, whenever he applies the brakes, his defroster fan starts to squeak. He concludes that the brakes must somehow be connected to the fan mechanism.

The real explanation of what has happened is that the braking caused deceleration of the car, which in turn caused the loose fan motor to tilt and squeak. So while it was correct to say that the braking caused the squeaking, it was fallacious to conclude that the braking directly caused the squeaking.

Sometimes the sequences of causal linkages between two states of affairs can be quite complex. In example 8.9 the sequence could be described as a relationship between four states:

$$\text{Application of brakes} \longrightarrow \text{deceleration of car} \longrightarrow$$
$$\text{fan tilting} \longrightarrow \text{fan squeaking}$$

So in some cases, there may be a number of intervening causal variables between two states of affairs. Failure to appreciate these intervening factors is a kind of fallacy of oversimplification.

The following case illustrates that sequences of states of affairs taken as causal variables are often more complex than a situation initially suggests. It was found by a study of admissions data that rejection rates were much higher for women than for men at the University of California at Berkeley. This statistical finding seemed to indicate that being a woman causes one to be rejected at Berkeley. Consequently, the graduate school at Berkeley was accused of discriminating against women. However, Bickel, Hammel, and O'Connell (1977) showed that, if you looked at the figures for each of the eighty-five departments individually, you could see that the probability of admission was just about the same for both sexes, or even somewhat higher for women. What had been overlooked is that women tended to apply for admission to the more popular departments, which also happened to be the departments with the higher rejection rates.

What initially seemed to be the conclusion to be derived from the data was a causal relationship between being a woman and being rejected at Berkeley:

Being a woman ⟶ being rejected at Berkeley

But a closer look at the situation seemed to indicate that the real causal relationship was between a third variable (applying to a popular department) and the outcome of being rejected at Berkeley. Yet, as it happened, being a woman was associated with the variable of applying to a popular department:

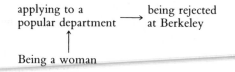

The error here was to overlook the intermediate variable. Instead of there being a direct causal relationship between two variables, A and C, as it initially appeared, there was a more complex sequence of relationships. It just happened that A was correlated with B, and it was really B that caused C. But by overlooking the intervening step, the situation seemed to indicate a causal link between A and C. Now if being a woman were to be causally related to applying to a popular department then there would be a causal sequence of the form $A \rightarrow B \rightarrow C$. But to conclude that A directly caused C without mentioning or taking into account the middle variable B would be a serious error of causal reasoning.

We must be careful not to mix up the last two types of causal errors. In the third type of error, the initial two states that seemed to be causally related were not causally related at all, in the sense that one caused the other. The third factor C caused both A and

B. But it turned out to be false, in that type of case, to say that *A* caused *B* (or that *B* caused *A*). The fourth type of error was quite different, however. The two initial states were not directly causally related. But it did truly turn out that the one variable (indirectly) caused the other. Hence the two types of fallacies are distinct. The third error involves getting the attribution of causality wrong, whereas the fourth error only involves oversimplifying the nature of the causal relationship.

Considerable care is needed here because, in some more complex cases, both types of errors can be involved. The following case is related by Croxton and Cowden (1955, pp. 9–10):

Example 8.10

A meteorologist discovered that the fall price of corn is inversely correlated with the severity of hay fever cases. Should we conclude that there is a causal relationship between severe cases of hay fever and a drop in the price of corn? Two other factors suggest some second thoughts. First, the price of corn tends to be low when the crop is large. Second, when weather conditions favor a bumper crop of corn, they also favor a bumper crop of ragweed. It seems fair to conclude that the price of corn and the suffering of hay fever victims are related, but they are not directly causally dependent on each other.

To get a grasp of this example, we have to look over the sequence of causal linkages between all the pairs of causal variables:

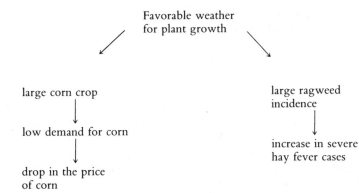

Basically, this example is a case of the third type of error. The favorable weather is a common causal variable behind the initial variables of the drop in the price of corn and the rise in severe hay fever cases. It would be false to say that either one of these initial variables causes the other.

However, the fourth type of error is involved here as well; for the favorable weather is indirectly causally related, by two intervening variables, to the drop in the price of corn. Also, the favorable weather is indirectly related to the severity of hay fever cases, once we realize that the favorable weather causes an increase in ragweed growth. In this case both the third and fourth types of errors are combined. To analyze the case properly, we need to sort out the involvement of each type of error.

A fifth type of causal error involves extrapolation beyond a given range of cases. Sometimes there is a positive relationship between two variables A and B within a certain range of cases, but then the relationship falls outside that range:

Example 8.11

It is often observed that rain is good for the crops. Within a certain range of conditions, this causal relationship holds – the more rain, the better the crops. But if there is too much rain, it can have a negative effect on crop yields.

In this type of case, it is correct to say that, in some circumstances, a positive correlation between A and B means that A causes B. The problem is that, in other circumstances, it may come about that A does not cause B, or even that A is counterproductive for B. The relationship, in this case, is nonlinear.

8.7 BIAS DUE TO DEFINING VARIABLES

A sixth kind of error in arguing from a statistical correlation to a causal conclusion has to do with how the events or items studied in the correlation are classified and defined; for in some cases, an apparent trend or causal link may turn out to be merely a statistical artifact created by a shift in the way the variables are defined or identified. The classic case of this type of problem concerns recent criticisms of the reporting of cancer survival rates.

The message given out by the media in recent years is that we are winning the battle against cancer, because early detection and new methods of treatment have resulted in increased survival rates.

Statistical presentations of these results show significant increases in survival rates for many types of cancer, including lung, colon, prostate, and breast cancers, from the initial period of 1950–4 to the recent period of 1977–81. However, numerous respected researchers have criticized the validity of these statistics. This criticism is based on the contention that the real survival rates may not have changed at all, and that the apparent improvement may be due only to a shift in the way 'cancer patient' is defined over the years.

Fisher and North (1986) identify six types of bias in reporting cancer survival rates:

1. *Lead time bias.* Advances in cancer detection have led to increasingly earlier diagnosis. *Lead time* (Fisher and North, 1986, p. 6) is the extra time added on to a patient's survival due solely to earlier detection, and not to a later time of death. Critics claim that lead time biases cancer statistics because compilation of current survival rates contains greater lead time than cases compiled in the past.

2. *Length bias.* Newer methods of detection now identify greater numbers of cancer patients with slower growing types of cancer than before. The patients with slower-growing cancers tend to have a more positive prognosis and to live longer, even over and above the factor of lead time. According to Fisher and North (1986, p. 6), length bias is like comparing two different diseases – a slow-growing disease with a positive prognosis versus a fast-growing disease with a negative prognosis.

3. *Overdiagnosis.* The newer detection methods identify cancer patients with small, harmless tumors or tumors that get smaller on their own. Using the older methods of detection, these individuals were not even identified as cancer patients. Today's practice of counting these patients introduces a favorable bias into cancer statistics.

4. *Patient self-selection.* People who often volunteer to be tested for cancer by recent detection methods tend to have better results of treatment, for several reasons. They tend to be more health conscious, better educated, and more compliant with physicians' orders and to have higher incomes. These people may be able to obtain better quality treatment and therefore better prospects for survival.

5. *Stage migration.* Better detection of the spread of cancer (metastases) means that cancer patients are classified differently at different stages of the development of cancer.

6. *Increased reporting of nonfatal cases.* Better reporting of nonfatal cases by physicians in recent times may make for a false improvement in survival rates because the recording of cancer deaths has not changed over the years.

Some of these criticisms of bias relate to a kind of *post hoc* error. Others are similar to the general kinds of problems with defining terms in inductive reasoning already encountered in Section 8.4.

But in discussing these six types of bias in cancer statistics reporting, it is important to separate two questions: (1) Is there a real improvement in survival rates? (2) Is the improvement in survival rates due to the improved medical treatment of cancer? Question (2) presumes an affirmative answer to question (1). And question (2) relates to *post hoc* reasoning and singles out a special kind of new *post hoc* error.

Question (1) relates to a combination of (a) biased statistics and (b) how the term 'cancer patient' is defined. Thus question (1) combines the problem of biased statistics and the problem of loaded definition in the same criticism. The claim is that the shifting definition has introduced a bias into the way the sample for study has been selected.

Probably the basic worry about the presentation of cancer statistics that seems to suggest an improved survival rate is the concern that the apparent improvement may not be due to improved treatment methods in recent times. Thus the basic problem is one of *post hoc* argument. All six forms of bias point to a generally reasonable requirement of any argument from correlation to causation – the change in the variable alleged to be caused should not be solely due to the way the variable is defined or classified; the problem that can arise is that changing standards of the variable as defined or classified can occur over a period of time, thereby introducing a possibly hidden bias into the statistical correlation. The meaning of terms can change over the years; procedures for identifying an item or determining a condition can change as scientific procedures of identification and classification improve. An apparent causal link may only be due to such a shift in terminology.

One can easily see how this type of unduly optimistic interpretation of statistics can be tempting, when research support is needed or when the media may overlook subtleties in reporting statistical findings. Yet to document the precise extent of the bias may itself require a scientific study.

8.8 *POST HOC* CRITICISMS AS RAISING CRITICAL QUESTIONS IN AN INQUIRY

As a study becomes more advanced, and further data are processed, initial correlations that suggested a causal relationship may become subject to criticisms as knowledge of other operative variables may begin to appear. Thus the initially postulated relationship may not be as simple as the earlier knowledge of the situation made it seem. Instead of being a simple two-place causal relationship between two variables, the newer data may suggest that there are other factors, which were previously in the background, that are causally related to A and B. And therefore a fuller description of the causal network of events may require dropping the original, simple causal relationship as a hypothesis and moving toward a more complex set of linkages of several events.

This need not mean that the original postulation of a simple two-place causal relationship between A and B was necessarily a fallacy or a blameworthy error. In light of the available evidence at that time, it may have been a reasonable presumption. Although it was a good place to start, the initial presumption may have to be given up in light of the new information and rejected in favor of a new hypothesis.

Of course, the dogmatic course of insisting on the original, simple presumption even in the face of, or despite, the new information could be a fallacy. But that is because there is a failure to allow further discussion, or change one's argument, even in the face of new evidence or critical questioning.

Instead of putting down an argument by condescendingly claiming that it commits a *post hoc* fallacy, it is more constructive to raise specific questions about the strength of the argument from the correlation to the causal conclusion. Such a criticism is more constructive because it may suggest specific critical questions. Answering these critical questions could strengthen the causal argument through subsequent critical discussion that introduces new evidence. Consider the following news item:

Example 8.12

A Canadian researcher has cited statistics that children from poor families are two and one half times as likely as children from affluent families to die from infectious diseases and twice as likely to die from accidents. The professor concludes that the effect of poverty on health is profound and that poverty is an "invisible killer" more deadly than cancer.[9]

9 "Research Ties Illness to Economic Status," *Winnipeg Free Press*, February 8, 1987.

225

This argument is one from correlation to causation and could perhaps be criticized as a *post hoc* fallacy, but it is more appropriate to pose certain questions about the argument. How is 'poverty' defined? Could the reverse causal relationship be at work to a significant extent? That is, could health problems like anemia, learning disabilities, and mental retardation be causes of poverty, rather than poverty causing the health problems? And could more specific factors be linked to both poverty and health problems that could serve to explain the correlation to some extent? That is, if someone who lives in a poor neighborhood dies of a bullet wound, it could be partially correct to say that his death was "caused" by poverty; for perhaps if he had lived in a better neighborhood, he might not have been shot. But this could also be misleading, for the more specific cause of death should not be overlooked, namely the shooting.

Each of these critical questions suggests a way in which the correlation between poverty and health could be explored and studied in certain directions in order to clarify the real strength of the causal connection between the two variables.

What these cases bring out is that a dialogue or inquiry can proceed by opening questions, or suggesting possible causal relationships at the opening stages of the inquiry. But later on, as the inquiry proceeds and more evidence comes in, these relationships may be firmed up, repudiated, questioned further, or even made more complex by the discovery of factors that had not previously been identified. To leap ahead and ignore or preempt the natural and reasonable order of dialogue by drawing a causal conclusion too firmly or too quickly could be a *post hoc* error. On the other hand, it may be natural and reasonable, at the early stages of the investigation, to advance causal connections as hypotheses that may later on turn out to be refuted. This in itself is not inherently fallacious or incorrect, provided the hypothesis is corrected by further evidence.

The following case also illustrates how initial observation of a plausible connection often suggests a causal link between two variables and how further studies may raise questions and criticisms, thereby opening the way to study other possibly related factors:

Example 8.13

At a conference on the bond between humans and pets in Boston in 1986, researchers reported that pets can lower blood pressure in humans, improve the survival odds of heart patients, and even penetrate the isolation of autistic children. According to a report in *Newsweek*[10] researchers at the conference reported on the beneficial effects of pet companionship. Studies showed that women who had owned dogs as children scored higher on self-reliance, sociability, and tolerance tests than petless women. Men who had owned a dog "felt a greater sense of personal worth and of belonging and had better social skills." Children with pets also showed greater empathy.

These correlations cited by the reported studies could be based on good research, but questions remain concerning what causal conclusions should be drawn from them. How confident can we be that loving interaction with a pet is actually the cause of improvement in the health or well-being of a human companion?

Animal ecologist Alan Beck of the University of Pennsylvania is quoted by the *Newsweek* article (p. 65) as saying that, while early work assumed a positive relationship between people and pets, later studies have raised some criticisms. One critical question cited is whether pets produce the empathy in children, or whether parents who tend to buy pets for their children are the kind of parents who would foster empathy in a child.

Another question is whether any kind of change in a nursing home, not specifically the arrival of a pet, may have a cheering effect on elderly patients. In other words, the effects on health could be due to other variables, which are associated with the introduction of pets into a situation. Perhaps elderly patients in a nursing home tend to be bored and have very little common to talk about. The introduction of a pet is a visible change that affects everyone and provides many interesting common events that affect everyone in the institution. But is the affectionate interaction with the pet here the *specific* cause of everyone perking up or would any change in routine that provides common material for interaction among the patients have an equally positive effect on morale? One could address this question only by studying the effects of further variables in the situation.

Questions in *post hoc* criticisms of causal arguments are therefore often reasonable and constructive. But they are often better viewed as questions that invite replies by the other participant in a critical

---

10 Sharon Begley and Karen Fitzgerald, "Freud Should Have Tried Barking," *Newsweek*, September 1, 1986, pp. 65–66.

discussion rather than as refutations of an argument or indications that the argument is fallacious. Indeed, these critical questions are usually very helpful to ask, because any causal conclusion or hypothesis runs the risk of becoming a correctable *post hoc* argument, if not properly qualified.

8.9 STRENGTHENING CAUSAL ARGUMENTS BY ANSWERING CRITICAL QUESTIONS

To understand the logic of causal reasoning in relation to the *post hoc* fallacy, we need to appreciate how most attributions of a causal relationship in controversies about causal claims have a highly practical nature. Characteristically, when it is alleged that one event or state of affairs A causes another one B, it is meant that, *in these particular circumstances,* A was accompanied by and produced B. Such a claim need not imply that, whenever you have A, you always get B, or even that, most times when you have A, you will probably also have B. For example, suppose it is claimed that Bob's lighting a match burned down a warehouse. What is meant is that the lighting of the match in the circumstances, at the time, caused the warehouse to be burned down. The particular circumstances may have included the facts that the warehouse was full of dry lumber on that day, that it was a hot day, and so forth.

Causality is always a practical kind of relationship between two variables A and B, because it states that, if A is introduced into a stable or normal situation in which, by assumption, no interfering new variables are introduced, then B will result. Thus a causal relationship always obtains relative to a *field,* a stable environment that can be presumed to be constant, or at least similar, from one case to another. When it is said that A causes B relative to a given field, it can never be ruled out, absolutely, that the change B has been affected or partly caused by some other intervening factor I, which is contained in the field but not known by the observer (Figure 8.0). This field-dependent property of causation is what makes causation practically useful in fields like medicine and engineering in which individual cases must be dealt with causally at the singular level.

This field-dependent characteristic shows why particular arguments based on causal inference, in most causal claims and arguments on controversial issues, are instances of plausible reasoning.

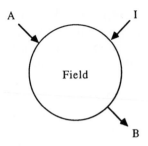

Figure 8.0. Causation as a field-dependent relation.

Causal arguments of these kinds often have to do with probability and induction, but they may be based more fundamentally on a judgment of plausibility than of probability. To see why, let us look at the basic argumentation scheme in which *post hoc* controversies occur.

The elementary argumentation scheme for arguments from correlation to causation is very simply given as follows:

(C) There is a positive correlation between *A* and *B*.

Therefore, *A* causes *B*.

In the simplest cases, the premise may only amount to the claim that *B* followed *A* in time, in one particular case. Now what are we to say about (C) as an argumentation scheme? Is it correct or erroneous?

The first observation, as we have already indicated, is that an argument that fits the scheme (C) can be a reasonable argument; for in many instances, a positive correlation, even a weak one that has only one instance, is a perfectly good and reliable indication that there may be a causal connection between two states of affairs. But the problem, as we saw when we examined instances of erroneous *post hoc* reasoning, is that there are too many ways that use of scheme (C) can go wrong. An instance of (C) can be erroneous when some other factor accounts for the correlation, showing that the apparent causal relationship between *A* and *B* is really spurious or misleading. Here we find the different types of *post hoc* errors.

However, we must resist the thesis that (C) is itself an incorrect type of argumentation. As a plausible inference, in some situations, an argument that fits the scheme (C) can be a quite reasonable kind of argument. The error arises when further information is brought in that may tend to undermine the plausibility of the use of (C) by suggesting gaps, thereby throwing the burden of proof back onto the proponent of (C) to account for other factors relevant to the argument. This leads to several types of critical questions.

What we should conclude, then, is that (C) can be a reasonable form of argument in some cases, but it is a form of argument that can be open to several kinds of critical questions. And we saw seven different types of critical questions that can be used to show that an argument of scheme (C) is weak or erroneous. A critic may respond to any causal argument of scheme (C) by indicating that failure to reply adequately to any of these questions brings out the weakness and vulnerability of the argument.

How can an argument from correlation to causation be made stronger? The proponent of the argument can strengthen it by responding to, or taking account of, these seven types of critical questions. Each of these questions (except the first) covers one of the characteristic errors previously studied:

1. Is there a positive correlation between A and B?
2. Are there a significant number of instances of the positive correlation between A and B?
3. Is there good evidence that the causal relationship goes from A to B, and not just from B to A?
4. Can it be ruled out that the correlation between A and B is accounted for by some third factor (a common cause) that causes both A and B?
5. If there are intervening variables, can it be shown that the causal relationship between A and B is indirect (mediated through other causes)?
6. If the correlation fails to hold outside a certain range of causes, then can the limits of this range be clearly indicated?
7. Can it be shown that the increase or change in B is not solely due to the way B is defined, the way entities are classified as belonging to the class of Bs, or changing standards, over time, of the way Bs are defined or classified?

Our confidence in any causal conclusion is always likely to be somewhat shaky because there are so many other practical factors in any situation that might be involved. In the basic argument (C), a critic can always suggest that there might be some other factor at work that might throw doubt on the causal relationship between A and B. But as each of the seven critical questions is adequately answered in the discussion or inquiry, the causal claim is strengthened. The respondent must specify which of these factors has not been established, or why the claim made for it is weak. By this means, the burden of proof is thrown directly onto the proponent. He must substantiate his causal argument by showing that some other factor is not also at work, like an intervening cause, a common cause, or simply coincidence.

When starting out with a correlation between two variables A and B, one may have a strong suspicion that there is a causal link between A and B that accounts for the correlation. As each of the seven critical questions of the argument from correlation to causation is adequately answered, that initial suspicion can become increasingly strengthened as an argument that fulfills its obligation in the discussion or inquiry. But it is not easy to establish conclusively that there is a causal link between two states of affairs. To establish conclusively that A causes B, an investigator must arrive at a clear theoretical understanding of the mechanism whereby A is causally related to B. Understanding this mechanism typically involves an understanding of the chemistry or physics, the underlying structural linkage between A and B as physical or causal processes. This means shifting the context of dialogue to that of a scientific inquiry.

So if all seven questions are answered, then an investigator may be able to say in practical terms that, in all plausibility, A is the cause of B. But the causal hypothesis cannot be conclusively confirmed with scientific precision until more is known about the underlying theory of the linkage between A and B. It is for this reason that the strengthened form of argument from correlation to causation remains a relatively weak (plausible) type of argument, in many instances, even if all seven critical questions are answered. Consider the following case:

Example 8.14

In 1925, pernicious anemia was a fatal disease that caused people to die because their bones mysteriously failed to produce red blood cells. By 1926, Dr. George R. Minot had found through clinical experience that feeding large quantities of liver to forty-five of his patients with pernicious anemia was followed by a great increase in red corpuscle count in each one. Moreover, each of these patients stated feeling better and, when kept on a diet of liver, survived to continue a healthy life.

With these results, anyone might conjecture reasonably that there could be a causal link between the consumption of liver and the

231

recovery from anemia. But as de Kruif (1932) tells us in his account of the story of Minot's work, many more steps were taken before a causal relationship was established.

Minot's first reaction, according to de Kruif (1932, p. 107ff.), was that a scientific doctor might suspect that this group of recovering patients could be a coincidence: "Minot was too cagey to trust such embryo statistics [and] knew the illness always had its ups and downs before killing its victims." Minot's reservations here relate to the kind of factor described by the sixth premise of the strengthened causal argument form. It could be that the recovery persisted only temporarily and did not continue for a more prolonged period. Subsequent study of these patients eventually put these doubts to rest.

Another concern was the worry expressed by the first premise. It could still have turned out that, with this limited number of patients studied, the apparent connection was coincidence. Subsequent studies of larger numbers of patients soon brought further evidence to bear against this reservation as well. Eating liver helped every pernicious anemic patient except those who had gone so far that they could not eat any solid food at all. But when pulped liver was poured into the stomachs of these patients through a tube, they began to recover, and after a week were greatly recovered.

At this point, it became more and more plausible that there was a causal connection between ingestion of liver and recovery from pernicious anemia. However, the precise nature of the causal connection was not fully established until laboratory studies tracked down the mysterious X factor in liver that went through the blood to start the bone marrow producing new red blood cells. Now we know that it was the vitamin B_{12} in liver that enabled this process to take place and caused the patients to recover.

In scientific inquiry, the technique used to study correlations between two variables when there is a suspected causal connection between them is the method of the controlled experiment. If there is an interesting correlation between two variables A and B, scientific experiments can confirm the existence of a causal relationship by studying A and B in different circumstances. If B tends to be followed by A, even in different circumstances after many trials, the claim that A causes B is made stronger. If B fails to obtain in circumstances where A is not present, the claim may be even stronger. As common causes for the correlation of A and B are ruled out, the claim becomes even stronger, as happens when all seven types of critical questions are answered. If all the questions are adequately answered, the claim for a causal relationship may be very plausible, and a critic is then put on the defensive to find counterevidence to criticize the plausibility of a causal conclusion. The burden is now shifted to the critic.

But even with all seven requirements strongly established, the conclusion that A causes B in a critical discussion is, at best, a practical hypothesis or presumption and should not be treated as a scientifically established fact. The only way that the hypothesis that A causes B can be certified as a scientific finding is by means of the theoretical clarification of the precise causal connection between A and B according to established laws in a rigorous scientific inquiry. Only then can we be confident of the existence of a definitely confirmed causal link between A and B.

In highly controversial cases, it is always dubious whether a strong inductive argument can be made for a causal conclusion:

Example 8.15

In examining data from 141 countries, Steffie Woolhandler and David Himmelstein found that infant mortality rates in 1979 were correlated with increases in military spending. From these statistical findings, they concluded that arms spending is causally related to infant mortality. They state, "It seems that bombs, both nuclear and conventional, may kill before they explode". They argue that, even after allowance for other relevant factors, their analysis confirms a significant correlation: "While correlation does not prove causation, we think it highly plausible that such a causal link does exist."[11] However, Dr. John Bailar, a biostatistician at the Harvard School of Public Health has criticized the conclusion of these two authors, saying, "The methods they've used are adequate for some kinds of description but simply are not up to the job of telling what causes what. It may be high infant mortality that causes military spending." Dr. Bailar also indicated that the approach of Woolhandler and Himmelstein could be used to show a link between infant mortality and the consumption of bananas: "Bananas are a greater staple of diet in a good many poor parts of the world, but that doesn't mean that bananas cause infant deaths."[12]

11 Steffie Woolhandler and David Himmelstein, "Militarism and Mortality," *Lancet*, June 15, 1985, pp. 1375–78.
12 Dr. John Bailor, as quoted in "Infant Death Link Found," *Winnipeg Free Press*, June 15, 1985, p. 70.

Could the statistical findings of Woolhandler and Himmelstein indicate that arms spending causes infant mortality? Their argument is of the form (C), which, as we have seen, can be a reasonable type of argument. However, (C) can be open to several types of critical questions, and therefore requires considerable strengthening to be substantiated as a scientific conclusion.

Has the argument been sufficiently strengthened in this case? We do not know without studying the Woolhandler and Himmelstein article more thoroughly, except to note that they claim that they have allowed for "other relevant factors." But observe also that Dr. Bailar's criticism that it may be the high infant mortality that causes the military spending is a query of the form of the third critical question as it applies to the argumentation scheme from correlation to causation. Thus our confidence in the plausibility of the conclusion suggested by Woolhandler and Himmelstein should be reserved until we are assured that they can provide adequate evidence that the causal relationship is not the reverse of what they conclude.

Dr. Bailar's parting remark about the bananas also suggests that we should not be too quick to interpret the correlation between arms spending and infant mortality as anything more than coincidence until we can be satisfied that other critical questions can be answered.

Further developments in this controversy will turn on the factors we have studied in relation to the seven critical questions. Statisticians have sophisticated methods for arguing about the degrees of probability we can reasonably attach to the correlations involved. But these arguments cannot, at this point in the inquiry, conclusively establish the existence of a causal connection between the two variables. At best, the causal conclusion must remain an argument based on plausible reasoning, and therefore subject to further criticisms and replies, until some underlying physical or causal link is found between the two variables.

8.10 SUMMARY

Many common generalizations and causal claims are based on inductive and statistical arguments. If these arguments are carefully constructed using scientific methods of experimental verification, it may take specialized statistical knowledge to evaluate them properly.[13] However, many of the most common generalizations and causal claims can be very effectively questioned and criticized without any specialized knowledge of statistical techniques, or at least any more than is given in this chapter. The first question to ask is, What is the evidence? If the evidence given is based on a sample, then it can be questioned whether the sample is inadequate or biased. If vague terms are used or there is an evident lack of access to data, questions relating to the fallacies of meaningless and unknowable statistics can be raised. If the survey that provided the evidence for a claim was based on a question asked to a sample of respondents, it may be reasonable to inquire into the precise wording of the questions.

In general, any vague terms used in a precise statistical claim should be questioned. The burden of proof should be on the arguer who advanced the statistical claim to offer a clear definition. Some terms, however, are so vague and so open to interpretation and controversy that, if they are used in a statistical claim, they must be very carefully defined, and these definitions must be defended as reasonable. If such definitions or defenses are not forthcoming, the statistical argument must be regarded as weak or open to criticism.

Whether a failure to offer clear enough definitions is so hopeless that it can justifiably be said to commit the error of meaningless statistics is a question of judgment for the context of dialogue in each particular case. But the two hallmarks of this error are (1) the use of an extremely vague term subject to broad interpretation and (2) no attempt to define the term clearly or to justify a definition. When these failures in a particular argument are so bad that it is highly implausible that any precise, justifiable definition could be given that would be consistent with the exact statistical figure given, then a critic is justified in alleging an error of meaningless statistics. Similarly, the error of unknowable statistics occurs when the practical impossibility of gathering evidence to support a statistical claim establishes that no defense of the claim could be plausibly made.

Finally, if the argument is one that goes from correlation to caus-

---

13 I thank Hatem Howlader, Jan Kmenta, and Günter Weiss for reading this chapter and suggesting many improvements of formulation to represent more accurately or be consistent with correct developments in the field of statistics. These friendly statisticians also pointed out several books and articles that turned out to be very useful.

ation, it may be reasonable to ask many kinds of questions. How many instances of the correlation were determined? Can we be assured that the causal relation goes in the direction indicated? Is there some third factor, a common cause, that might account for the correlation? Could the causal relationship be indirect – mediated through other causal variables? Could the causal relationship be limited to certain cases? As each criticism is dealt with successfully in the particular case at issue, the plausibility of the argument from correlation to causation is strengthened.

Generally speaking, correlation and causation are two different kinds of relationships. Correlation is a symmetrical relationship, meaning that, whenever A is correlated with B, B will always be correlated with A. However, causation is not generally a symmetrical relation, for there are many cases when A causes B, but B does not cause A. Yet causation is not totally asymmetrical either, for there are some instances when A causes B, and B causes A. This can happen in the feedback relationship between two variables that we encountered in our analysis of arguing in a circle in section 2.7. For example, in a particular case it might be that emigration of families from an area causes a slump in the building trade in that area, while at the same time it may also be true that the slump in the building trade is causing emigration of families from the area. Here the two variables are not causally independent of each other, so there is a circular relationship between them.

Generally, then, correlation and causation are different types of relationships, and you cannot argue directly or conclusively from correlation to causation or vice versa. Correlation is established by observing how often a type of event occurs or does not occur when another type of event occurs or does not occur. Once instances of correlations are observed and reported, the statistician can draw inferences about them. Causality, by contrast, is a relationship that links two events, or types of events, in a practical way such that the occurrence of the one event is affected by the occurrence of the other in a particular situation.

Even though causation and correlation are fundamentally different, you can argue, in a suitably careful and circumspect manner, from one to the other. The problem of dealing with *post hoc* argumentation is to know how to construct and evaluate such arguments without committing specific basic errors or lapses in your argument.

In evaluating a particular case of causal conclusion advanced by a proponent, it may be difficult to know, or to establish conclusively, that any, or all, of the relevant critical questions have been satisfactorily answered according to the obligation of proof appropriate for the context of dialogue. However, if there seems to be plausible doubt that any of them is met in a particular case, an initial burden of proof is on the respondent to ask the right critical questions and thereby challenge the causal conclusion put forward by the proponent. If the question is reasonable, according to the given evidence and knowledge of the case in dispute, the burden of proof is thereby shifted onto the proponent to give reasons why each premise challenged can reasonably be accommodated by evidence. Only in extreme cases, however, may it be justifiably said that a *post hoc* fallacy has been committed, for instance, when no adequate response has been given or is forthcoming, and the arguer dogmatically insists that his causal conclusion cannot be challenged or questioned in the discussion. Such a refusal to meet the obligations of answering reasonable questions and to give arguments for one's claim violates the negative rules of persuasion dialogue given in Chapter 1.

In this chapter it has been shown how characteristic types of gaps can occur in statistical and causal arguments, which should invite relevant questions by the reasonable respondent to the argument. When a clear gap is left open, then the respondent's question may indicate that an error or bias has occurred. However, errors can be rectified, and the reasonable respondent should not leap too quickly to accuse one who has left such a gap of having committed a fallacy; for, as we have often emphasized, an allegation of fallacy is a very serious criticism of an argument. Only when the critic can show that the gap cannot plausibly be filled should the arguer be reasonably accused of having committed a fallacy in his argument from correlation to causation or statistical argument. Only if an argument is so weak or bad that any possible defense of it appears hopeless, and no response to relevant critical questions is given, should the argument be condemned as fallacious.

The basic problem with arguing from correlation to causation is that it may be possible that the correlation is simply due to coincidence or to some link other than a causal relationship. Hence in a scientific inquiry, a serious effort must be made to answer each of the seven critical questions, using careful experimental methods of investigation. In working to rule out error, tests may have to be repeated. Study of a control group is another important step in this work. Careful use of random procedures for selecting test subjects may help to rule out bias.

In this chapter we have not tried to set out complete criteria for a good scientific method in gathering data. Our goal has been the more modest one of giving a critical reasoner some basic tools for reasonably questioning the evidential basis of common statistical claims and generalizations that play such an important role in everyday arguments.

9

Natural language argumentation

All the arguments and disputes we have been concerned with have been conducted and evaluated in the medium of natural language. But in natural language, words are vague and ambiguous. Words are most often not defined very precisely and are therefore subject to the interpretation of the disputants in an argument. And since words in an argument may be interpreted in different ways or according to different standards of precision, they can be used in a fashion that is friendly to the case of the arguer and unfriendly to the case of the person to whom the argument is directed. Words can be used as weapons in argument.

When an Israeli border town is bombed, the newspapers in Israel describe the event as a terrorist attack. But Arab sources describe the same event as an action taken by freedom fighters in defense of their rights. However, when an Arab city is bombed, its inhabitants describe the event as a terrorist attack, unlike the Israelis, who describe it as a defensive strike against terrorists. The same group of individuals, in each instance, are described as "terrorists" by one side and "freedom fighters" by the other side. Now neither of these contentious terms has been defined, so they are subject to wide and various interpretations in a particular situation. For this reason, it is appropriate to question whether the two terms are being used in such a way that any action by the other side is routinely classified as that of "terrorists," and any action by one's own side is classified as that of "freedom fighters." In effect, the words are used as weapons, like guns and bombs.

This aggressive and one-sided use of words in argument is not consistent with the aims of reasonable dialogue. It is a way of preempting or stifling reasonable dialogue. The program of this chapter is to study the most important problems and strategies in argument related to the sophistical deployment of vague and ambiguous terms in natural language.

239

A term is said to be *ambiguous* if it has more than one meaning. For example, the term 'bank' is ambiguous. It could mean 'savings bank' in one context, but it could also mean 'river bank' in another context. In many arguments we may get into no trouble even if a word is ambiguous, for the context of the dialogue may make it clear which meaning is meant. For example, if I were to say, 'I just went to the bank and deposited a check into my savings account', the context would make it clear which way the term 'bank' should plausibly be taken.

It is when the context does not clearly disambiguate that we can get into trouble with ambiguous terms. If Smith tells his wife to meet him at the bank at three o'clock, there might be doubt, in some contexts, whether he means the river bank or the savings bank. In such a case, Smith might be taken to task for not being sufficiently clear.

A term is said to be *vague* if there exist borderline cases in which it is not clear whether the term correctly applies. For example, the term 'rich' is vague. If a man says he has one hundred thousand dollars in total assets, some would say he is rich. But if the conversation takes place among a group of billionaires during a meeting of the Oil Magnates Club, such a man would not be called rich.

There is no exact cutoff point at which a person may be definitely said to pass from being not rich to rich. Of course, one could stipulate an exact point by saying, for example, that any person who has a million dollars or more is rich and nobody with less than that amount is rich. But such a precise definition could be open to reasonable dispute or question. Why? Because the term 'rich' is vague.

In some contexts of dialogue, it can be useful to give a precise definition of a vague term. But unless a good reason can be given for selecting a particular cutoff point, the precise definition may be of no use for the purposes of reasonable argument. Vagueness is all-pervasive in natural language, and it is neither possible nor useful to eliminate all vague terms from every argument.

Because we are continually discovering or inventing new things, terms that were not vague or ambiguous can become so. For example, the meaning of the term 'death' used to be clear enough. Death was defined as the irreversible cessation of breathing and blood circulation. But with the advent of technology to continue artificial breathing and blood circulation even after the irreversible destruction of the brain, a new definition of 'death' had to be considered. Or at any rate, new standards for the determination of death in borderline cases had to be considered. The problem was posed by the fact that these borderline cases were not previously known to exist. So the term 'death', applied to a person, had to be made more precise in order to deal with the developments in medicine.

This continual increase in the clarification of terms is true of the sciences, as well as the law and other nonscientific fields. With plant taxonomy in biology, for example, a taxon classification category may later be split up into several taxa. So plants that many years ago were considered to be the same may now be classified as several different types of plants. For example, according to Jeffrey (1982, p. 70), the family Saxifragaceae, as circumscribed by Hooker in 1865, is now considered to represent eleven different families of plants.

In short, vagueness and ambiguity can never be entirely eliminated. And vagueness and ambiguity are not completely intolerable or always destructive of reasonable argument. But they can lead to failure of communication and other problems in some contexts of argument. Terms need to be defined precisely enough in relation to the specific context of dialogue.

It is the mark of the pedant to use unnecessarily precise definitions of terms in contexts in which this extra precision is not practically useful. In fact, the use of spurious precision can itself be a serious obstacle to good argument. If you see a claim that 75 to 80 percent of all convicted criminals are products of broken homes, you should realize that these figures may reflect a spurious precision; for whether the claim is plausible very much depends on how you define 'broken home'. If no definition is offered, the numerical claim is meaningless. But even if a more precise definition of 'broken home' were attempted, the definition itself might well be open to dispute or question in the context of the issue being argued. In a case like this, the use of precise figures or cutoff points may not necessarily be a sign of justifiable or reasonable argument.

The degree of precision that best serves good argument must be relative to the context of dialogue. The nature of a particular controversy must set the reasonable standard for precision of the definitions of the terms that occur in an argument.

You may be inclined to think that deciding upon the definition of a word is a matter of harmless quibbling, of no serious consequence. But in fact, an adoption of a definition of a term like 'poverty' or 'unemployment' by an organization or government agency can have serious economic consequences for large numbers of people.

Consider the vague term 'farmer'. A hobby farmer who has a few acres that he does not regularly cultivate or depend upon for a living may call himself a farmer. But his neighbors, who have huge grain farms, may not call him a farmer. However, if he wants to call himself a farmer, nobody may care to dispute it. But if the context of argument is a government benefit or income tax exemption that applies only to farmers, his claim may now become subject to considerable dispute. To make the new regulation workable, the government will have to offer a more precise definition of 'farmer' that will clearly rule whether this man is eligible for the benefit. Such definitions are often tied closely to statistical arguments, as Chapter 8 has shown. Governments often base their policies and regulations on statistical findings that are, in turn, based on definitions of key words and concepts. However, in many cases, arguments about these policies may conceal the controversial nature of an underlying definition of a vague term.

Even more curiously, in some cases one side to a dispute or controversy may declare a definition, and the other side may even challenge the first side's right to advance the definition. According to a report, the U.S. Public Health Service published a rule that specified who would qualify as an Indian and therefore be eligible for Indian Health Service benefits. The definition of 'Indian' required that the individual must have one-half or more Indian or Native Alaska ancestry, or have one-quarter or more Indian or Native Alaska ancestry if he resides in a designated health service delivery area. The reaction of the director of the National Indian Health Board, Mr. Jake Whitecrow, was to declare that the government was "infringing on the rights of individual tribes to determine who is eligible to be called a member." The problem here is to decide who should have the right to decide how the term 'Indian' is to be defined in this context.[1]

1 "In Brief: For Access to Health Care, Who Is an Indian and Who Decides," *Hastings Center Report*, Vol. 16, August 1986.

In some contexts of argument, terms can be ambiguous or vague, and no problems may result. In other cases, however, we can get into terrible trouble with vague and ambiguous terms in an argument. Because many words in natural language tend to be vague or ambiguous, there is often room for argument on how a term should best be defined. Indeed, words and phrases are often used, defined, or invented by one party in a dispute in such a manner as to defeat or undermine the other party's side of the dispute. Here the term in question is being used, in effect, as an argument. Therefore, the other side should have a right to reply to, or even to reject, the controversial term.

9.2 LOADED TERMS AND QUESTION-BEGGING LANGUAGE

An argument contains a *loaded term (argumentatively loaded term)* when one of its terms is defined or used in such a way as to defeat or undermine the position of the participant(s) in dialogue to whom the argument is directed. The word *term* is meant here in a broad sense to include both words and phrases. As noted in Section 9.1, the used of loaded terms in argument often takes the form of defining two parallel terms, one of which has connotations of being good or right and the other of which has connotations of being bad or wrong. Then the latter term is applied to the opponent's side of the argument, and the former term is reserved for the proponent's side.

Indeed, in some extreme cases, the opponent himself is defined as coming under the heading of the bad term. When this happens, the use of loaded terms is combined with an *ad hominem* attack. We have already seen a case of this sort. In example 6.8, the leader of a religious group, in effect, defined all his opponents as 'devils' by the following sweeping proclamation:

Example 6.8

The dictionary defines devil as an adversary of God. If you are an opponent of mine, then you would be classified as a devil.

This appears to leave the opponent little room for maneuvers. He may accept the dictionary definition, but if he accepts the application of the term to himself, he has lost the argument.

243

There are really two kinds of problems with the use of loaded definitions in argument from the point of view of the respondent who has to try to deal with them. One is the reasonableness of the definition itself. The other is the reasonableness of the application of the term in question to one's own side of the argument or to the proponent's side. In example 6.8, it is the second problem that appears paramount. Somehow it appears that the opponent against whom the argument is directed has been classified on the devil's side, whether he likes it or not.

A slightly more subtle case of the same type of strategy occurs in the example following:

Example 9.0

A psychologist, commenting on the case in which parents encourage their little girl to play with dolls and their little boy to play with a model construction set, describes the parents' behavior as "gender-prejudiced." He concludes that the parents should try harder to make their behavior gender-neutral. The parents object to this term being applied to them because they say that they feel there are genuine and important differences between boys and girls and, according to their view, respecting these differences may be justifiable rather than "prejudiced" behavior.

In this case, the parents are certainly objecting to the psychologist's argument on the ground that it contains a loaded term that stacks the argument unfairly against their point of view. They evidently do not see the description of their behavior as "prejudiced" as being reasonable, for the use of the term 'prejudiced' implies that their behavior is wrong and that their position in the argument is biased and unreasonable.

What is going on in this type of case seems fairly clear. Terms may be defined or applied in a way that is not neutral with respect to an argument. And how a term is to be defined may itself be an issue subject to argument. Hence to define or use a term in a one-sided, argumentative way can be objectionable.

Words and definitions often have persuasive force in an argument. So you must be careful in argument to watch that the terms are not defined or applied in a way that stacks the argument against your case at the outset. When this happens in reasonable dialogue, it can be appropriate to challenge your opponent's argument on the ground that it contains a loaded term or definition.

So far, things are relatively clear. However, a complication arises because the term 'begging the question' is often used to describe the kind of objection made by the parents in case 9.0. The parents might have objected that the psychologist's use of the phrase 'gender-prejudiced' begs the question. But what could this objection mean, over and above the objection already lodged? According to Section 2.7, begging the question is arguing in a circle. But where is the circle in the psychologist's argument in example 9.0? It seems hard to say, and hence the use of the phrase 'begging the question' has introduced a puzzle.

According to Hamblin (1970, p. 32), the origin of the term 'begging the question' is through the translation of Aristotle's original Greek phrase τὸ ἐν ἀρχῇ αἰτεῖσθαι in turn translated into Latin as *petitio principii*, which means 'beg for that which is in the question at issue.' The meaning of this curious phrase becomes clearer in the context of persuasion dialogue based on a conflict of opinion between two parties. In persuasion dialogue, one party may *ask to be granted* certain premises he needs to build up his case to persuade the other party of his thesis (his conclusion to be established in the dispute). The thesis (conclusion) is the *question* that is to be established by this party through his argument. Hence to include this conclusion within the premises asked to be granted is to *beg the question,* that is, to "beg for" the question (conclusion) that is supposed to be proved. In other words the fault is that of "begging for" something that should be earned through the work of argument.

According to the account given in Section 2.7, begging the question is essentially the same fault in argument as arguing in a circle. However, unfortunately, the phrase 'begging the question' seems to be used in popular tradition, and even in logic textbooks, in various other ways. In some cases, the alleged fault of 'begging the question' is taken to mean the simple lack of evidence in argument. Similarly, the fallacy of question-begging epithet (question-begging appellative, question-begging term) is often used to refer to cases in which a loaded term has been used in argument. But this can be a misnomer because the use of a loaded term in an argument does not necessarily imply that the argument is circular.

This tendency may have been historically encouraged by the treatment of Bentham (1838/1962, p.437), who interpreted the fallacy of begging the question very broadly. Bentham was concerned with appellatives (terms) that can be used in a laudatory (positive), neutral, or vituperative (negative) way in argument. He linked the use of such terms to the fallacy of begging the question by observing that in a certain type of example, the use of a loaded term can be used to disguise an absence of proof for a conclusion:

Example 9.1

This doctrine is heresy.
Therefore, this doctrine must be condemned.

According to Bentham (1838, p. 436f.), this use of a loaded (vituperative) term to classify something can be an instance of the fallacy of begging the question because (1) the conclusion requires to be proved, and (2) the use of the loaded term is meant to cause a respondent to take it that the conclusion has been proved, but (3) the conclusion, in fact, has not been proved.

Now we can see that example 9.1 could, indeed, represent an interesting kind of failure that can occur in argument. But is it an instance of begging the question? The problem is that it is not necessarily a case of begging the question, if we mean circular argument by this phrase, as already proposed.

Consider the point of view of an arguer who has championed the doctrine in question and then is confronted with the argument in example 9.1. What is he to say? Well, of course, he could agree that, if the doctrine is heresy, it should be condemned and accept the validity of the argument. But even so, he might reject the classification of his doctrine as 'heresy'. And therefore, he could reject the argument as an instance of the use of a loaded term. So far, there is no problem. The critic may have every right to make this objection.

But what if he claims that the argument begs the question. How could he support this criticism? He might say that he does not accept the conclusion that the doctrine must be condemned. Therefore, he does not accept the premise that the doctrine is heresy either, because the proponent of the argument has not proved it. This too is a reasonable objection, but it does not show that the argument is circular. It shows only that the argument is weak, that it lacks sufficient evidence to support the premise.

How could the critic support a contention that the argument is an instance of begging the question? One possibility is the following: He could argue that the premise could only be plausible on the prior presumption that the doctrine must be condemned, because 'heresy' is a vituperative (loaded) term for something bad. But the problem is that the proponent of the argument could reasonably reject this contention, arguing that 'heresy' means 'contrary to the accepted teachings of the church', and that he can offer independent evidence that this particular doctrine is contrary to the teachings of the church. He might also concede that heresy is something bad and that therefore 'heresy' is a loaded term. Yet he could argue that the proposition 'This doctrine is heresy' neither requires the prior presumption of, nor is equivalent to, the proposition 'This doctrine must be condemned'. In short, the argument in example 9.1 is not necessarily a case of begging the question, though it may be an instance of a loaded definition.

The problem is that the term 'begging the question' is somewhat confusing because of its unfamiliar and curious etymology, and the fact that it has become widely used in popular speech for many faults or objections in argument other than circular argument. Indeed, according to Professor D. D. Todd (1987), the phrase 'to beg the question' has been commonly used in newspaper articles to refer to the practice of earnestly requesting or demanding that a certain question be raised or answered. This extreme misusage suggests that the phrase is often used in an incorrectly broad manner to refer to something other than arguing in a circle.

In some cases, the problem is a *loaded definition* rather than a loaded term. In this type of case, a definition that tends to preempt or exclude an opponent's side of the case is advanced:

Example 9.2

Black and White are arguing about whether murder is always wrong. White concedes that murder is normally wrong, but argues that it may not be wrong in exceptional cases. For example, if someone had murdered Hitler just before 1939, according to White, it would not have been a morally wrong act. Black argues that it can be established that murder is always morally wrong, based on a premise that he feels is reasonable. Then Black presents his argument: Murder is unjustified killing; therefore, murder is always wrong.

What Black has done here is to define 'murder' as unjustified killing. This move appears to win the argument by proving White's thesis false and by ruling out White's argument based on his counterexample of the case of the hypothetical murder of Hitler; for if murder is unjustified killing, then if White is right that the killing of Hitler would have been justified, it would follow that the killing of Hitler would not have been murder. Hence White's counterexample no longer counts against Black's thesis that murder is always wrong.

How could White reply to Black's strategy? There are two options. He could dispute Black's definition of murder as unjustified killing. Or he could insist that the case of the killing of Hitler would have been murder, no matter how you reasonably define 'murder'. Either way, White would be criticizing Black's argument for its use of a loaded and unacceptable definition.

Could White accuse Black of having used a question-begging definition? To do this he would have to take an additional step. One way he might try to do this is as follows: White might argue that to prove something is unjustified requires the prior presumption that it is morally wrong. He might argue, for example, that 'unjustified' simply means 'morally wrong' and that therefore Black's argument is circular.

Note, however, that Black could dispute this contention. He could argue that 'unjustified' means 'not justified', which means that a justification has not been given. He could argue that this does not necessarily require that the act in question be morally wrong.

So once again, care is needed. Black's definition of murder as unjustified killing can be objected to by White as a loaded definition. But that does not necessarily mean that the definition begs the question.

Why is it that the term 'question begging' is so tempting to apply to cases of a loaded definition in argumentation? The explanation could be that any use of a term or definition that seems to be contrary to one's own side of an argument is often a source of worry that the term in question could be somehow used to beg the question without anyone being clearly aware of what has transpired. A scientific case study may illustrate this kind of concern.

Disputes can arise among scientists on how terms in an area of science should be defined. Recently there have been heated debates about whether the Darwinian theory of evolution is a clear and verifiable scientific theory. New evolutionists have offered criticisms and improvements of the traditional theory of evolution based on new scientific findings in other areas of science like genetics.

These critics are now beginning to question whether the familiar way of classifying animals into mammals, reptiles, amphibians, and so forth, is defensible. A new school of classification called *cladistics* (from the Greek term for branch, *clade*) insists on classifying groups of animals without making prior assumptions about the evolutionary descent of those groups. The Hennig Society is named after the East German entomologist Willi Hennig, who founded cladistics in the 1950s. According to the following account of Begley (1985, p. 81), cladists are agnostic about evolution:

Example 9.3

Unlike evolutionists, they do not take into account which animals might share a common ancestor – something that can be inferred from fossils but never proved. "Fossils are just a bunch of bones at different time levels. [Ancestry is] something you fill in with your mind," says biologist Steve Farris of the State University of New York at Stony Brook, who is also president of the three-year-old Hennig Society. Because cladists care about how many traits various groups of animals share today, not how they got that way, they are agnostic about evolution. Says Farris, "You don't have to presuppose evolution to do cladistics."

The cladistic approach to classification results in some differences between their definitions and those of the more traditional evolutionists. For example, crocodiles are grouped with birds instead of lizards because their ankle joints and hearts resemble those of birds more than those of lizards. The traditional evolutionist would link crocodiles and lizards, but separate birds as a different class. However, the cladist would regard birds and crocodiles as the more natural grouping because of the characteristics that they share.

According to Bowler (1984, p. 330), it is the more radical exponents of cladism that maintain that relationships between forms can be established without reference to evolution. These so-called transformed cladists are outspoken critics of Darwinism who argue that the traditional arguments for natural selection are unscientific.

As the quotation from Begley suggests, the concern of the cladist about the traditional approach to taxonomy is that the traditional classifications may beg the question. By allowing assumptions about common descent of groups of animals into the very definitions of the groups, one may be begging the question of which animals share a common ancestor. Why? Because the question of which animals share a common ancestor is inferred from the fossil evidence once the fossils are grouped into certain taxonomic categories. But the prior act of grouping the organisms into these taxonomic categories may, in the traditional approach, be done partly on the basis of which ones are thought to share a common ancestor. Clearly, this procedure presents a real danger of having adopted question-begging language. In this case, the issue of potential circularity is related to the definitions of terms used by biologists. The cladists are not necessarily claiming that the traditional classifications and definitions beg specific conclusions about evolution. But because they are worried about the potential danger of circular reasoning, they try to choose terms that make no specific assumptions about lines of evolutionary descent.

Thus it is not necessarily fallacious to use vague terms, ambiguous terms, or even loaded terms in argument. However, such uses of terms can lead in some cases toward the possibility of question-begging language. That is not the only problem that can arise from argumentative language, however. Other important problems arising from the use of vague and ambiguous terms are the subject of the remainder of this chapter.

9.3 EQUIVOCATION

The traditional fallacy of equivocation is said to occur in an argument when a word or phrase is used ambiguously, shifting into different meanings during the course of the argument. The danger of equivocation is that, if the ambiguous term is taken in one way in one occurrence in the argument and in another way in a second occurrence, the argument could seem to be valid without really being so. The resulting deception is the source of the fallacy.

A simple example may serve to illustrate how equivocation works:

Example 9.4

All stars are in orbit in outer space.
Sarah Flamingo is a star.
Therefore, Sarah Flamingo is in orbit in outer space.

This argument would be said to be an equivocation because the term 'star' is used ambiguously in it. In the first premise, 'star' is most plausibly taken to mean 'distant, luminous celestial body'. But there is a shift of meaning. In the second premise, 'star' would most plausibly be taken to mean 'entertainment celebrity'. Because of this meaning shift, the argument could be taken to be valid when in fact it may not be valid.

If you look at example 9.4, it has the form of a valid argument: Every x has property F; y is an x; therefore, y has property F. This form of argument is deductively valid. But is example 9.4 a valid argument? No, it is not, if the two occurrences of 'star' are disambiguated according to the most plausible interpretations of the premises, as follows:

Example 9.5

All celestial bodies are in orbit in outer space.

Sarah Flamingo is an entertainment celebrity.

Therefore, Sarah Flamingo is in orbit in outer space.

This argument is not valid. According to the most plausible interpretation we have in mind, the premises are true and the conclusion is false.

So now we see how equivocation can work as a fallacy. Example 9.5 is clearly invalid and would not fool anybody. But example 9.4 has a valid form of argument and might therefore convince somebody to accept its conclusion because he had accepted both premises not realizing the ambiguity. An equivocal argument is one that may appear valid but is not valid when disambiguated.

What makes an equivocation work is the contextual shift. We are tugged to interpret 'star' one way in order to make one premise plausibly come out true but tugged another way in the different context of the other premise. By being tugged both ways, we equivocate.

The problem with an equivocal argument is that it is not really a single argument at all. In reality it is a bundle of arguments. The person to whom the argument is offered is presented with too many arguments and is thereby invited to accept confusingly what appears to be a single argument that both is valid and has true premises. In example 9.4, the person to whom the argument is directed is really offered four arguments. Only one of the four, namely example 9.5, has two plausibly true premises. But example 9.5 is an invalid argument. If you interpret 'star' consistently in both premises as

251

meaning the same thing, then you will get an argument that is valid. But the problem is that one of the premises will be false. In short, once you disambiguate, no matter how you do it, you can never get a valid argument with two plausible premises. So example 9.4 is really a cheat. It is not what it purports to be. It looks like you are getting one good argument. But in reality, you are getting four bad arguments.

With some of the previous fallacies, the problem was that an emotional appeal masked the very lack of argument. There, what seemed to be an argument was no argument. Here, what seems to be an argument is, in reality, too many arguments – a bundle of worthless arguments dressed up to look like one good argument.

In some cases equivocation can be associated with the shift of meaning of a relative term as it occurs in different contexts. For example, 'tall' and 'short' are relative terms that shift their meanings in different contexts. A short basketball player may not be a short man. And a tall jockey many not be a tall woman. When such a shift in the meaning of a relative term occurs in two or more different propositions in an argument, an equivocation may occur:

Example 9.6

An elephant is an animal.

A gray elephant is a gray animal.

Therefore, a small elephant is a small animal.

Both premises are true in this argument, but the conclusion is false. A small elephant is plausibly taken in most contexts to be a relatively large animal, for example, if you had to transport it from one zoo to another.

The fact that words can shift in meaning as the context of argument changes means that in longer arguments the process of shifting can be more gradual. Changing standards of comparison can be less easily detected when several steps are involved. A simple case is the following classic example. In this case, each individual premise is plausible. But when you put all three premises together, a shift of meaning seems to gradually take place:

Example 9.7

The more you study, the more you know.

The more you know, the more you forget.

252

The more you forget, the less you know.
So why study?

Each of the three premises of this argument can plausibly be interpreted as being true. But if you look at the second and third premises together, you can see a problem. If you learn more and consequently forget more, it does not follow that you know less. Your total increment of knowledge might be greater than before. As you learn more, you may forget more, but it does not follow that, on the whole, you must know less.

The type of gradual equivocation in example 9.7 is developed through a series of gradual steps toward a conclusion, and therefore it could be a shift that may slip by unnoticed. A gradual shift of meanings or standards of precision over several steps in argument could be an error that is harder to catch. In Section 9.9, we will encounter a more subtle example of this phenomenon, and consequently gain a deeper understanding of equivocation.

9.4 ARGUMENTS BASED ON ANALOGY

Often, comparison to a similar situation can be forcefully used as an argument to press for consistency. This type of argument is based on the presumption that practical inconsistency, once alleged in argument, shifts a burden of reply onto the arguer who is accused of failing to be consistent. In this regard, the mechanism of the burden of proof is similar to that of the circumstantial argument against the person. Consider the following example:

Example 9.8

A lawyer for three prison inmates claimed that the law denying all sentenced prisoners the right to vote is irrational. The lawyer argued that the present law does not make sense because it excludes those who are in jail from voting, but allows those who are out on parole or awaiting sentence to vote. He also argued that the law makes no distinction between prisoners convicted for serious crimes and those in prison for minor infractions of the law. The lawyer argued that, if lawmakers want to exclude prisoners from the democratic process, they must ensure that the reason is sufficiently important to override the constitutional right to vote. He concluded that the burden of proof

253

must be on the state to show why prisoners should be denied this fundamental civil right.[2]

In this example, the lawyer's argument uses two comparisons between classes of prisoners to argue that the law is inconsistent, and thereby tries to shift the burden of proof onto the state to defend the current law. The first comparison is between those on parole or awaiting sentence, and the remainder of prisoners not in either of these categories. The first group is allowed to vote and the second is not. The argument is that this practice is not consistent because there is no relevant difference, with regard to the right to vote, between the two groups. The second comparison is between those who have committed serious crimes and those who are in prison for minor infractions. Here there is a relevant difference, according to the lawyer's argument. But the law does not recognize this difference with regard to voting and is therefore once again inconsistent. The lawyer concludes that the present law, excluding all prisoners from voting, is irrational.

The lawyer is using these allegations of inconsistency to argue for changing the present law. Normally, the burden of proof would be on the one who argues for changing an existing practice. However, in this case the lawyer argues that the burden of proof should be on the state to defend the present law because all persons have a constitutional right to vote.

The kind of argument used here is the basis of the wedge argument studied in connection with slippery slope reasoning in Section 9.7. The lawyer is arguing that we already allow convicted persons who are on parole or awaiting sentence the right to vote. To be consistent, then, we should allow other convicted persons who do not happen to be in either of these two situations, the right to vote as well. The argument is that we should treat the two similar cases alike.

The principle of treating similar cases similarly underlies many of the different kinds of arguments and cirticisms studied in the previous chapters. For example, in the case of the *ad hominem* argument in example 6.3, the child's criticism of the parent's inconsistency in smoking while advocating nonsmoking turned on the

---

2 This example is based on information in an article by Paul Moloney, "Voting Right Denial Called Unfair to Prisoners," *Winnipeg Free Press*, March 5, 1986.

presumption that the parent is not treating himself and the child on the same basis. The parent smokes, but then tells the child he should not smoke. The child, by his allegation of circumstantial inconsistency, is in effect accusing the parent of treating similar cases differently.

The requirement of practical consistency means that similar cases should be treated alike, but it allows for a case to be treated differently if a good argument can be given that the two cases are different in a relevant respect. Thus case-by-case consistency is different from logical consistency, as defined in Chapter 5. If two propositions are logically inconsistent, then, if one is true, the other has to be false. But if two cases are not treated consistently, then this means that they are not similar in some respects, although they may be similar in other respects.

Sometimes the best way to argue against an argument based on comparison to another case is to produce yet another case that is also similar, but leads to the opposite conclusion. In example 9.8, the comparison between groups of individuals led the lawyer to the conclusion that convicts should be given the right to vote. However, during the controversy on this issue, the following argument from a parallel case was used to question whether convicts should be given the right to vote:

Example 9.9

In recent mock elections held in high schools, teenagers have shown themselves politically aware and capable of expressing their views in a civilized fashion. On this evidence, it is reasonable to have more confidence in the ability to reason and sense of honesty and fair play of many seventeen-year-olds, and less cause to be vigilant of their motives or integrity than you could say for many of those adults convicted of crimes. "In our haste to create a fair and equitable society for all, does it really make sense to extend the right to vote to criminals and degenerates in our jails but not to our young people? Why should anyone whose birthday falls one day too late be any less entitled to vote than someone else who has been found guilty of committing a crime and has been exiled out of society behind bars?"[3]

The conclusion of this argument seems to question the wisdom of allowing convicts the right to vote. The argument contends that,

3 Roger Young, "Readers Forum: No Vote for Convicts," *Winnipeg Free Press*, March 22, 1986.

if we allow convicted prisoners the right to vote in elections, then, in all consistency, how can we fail to recognize the right of our young people to vote as well?

By raising this question, the argument of example 9.9 suggests that we should not give convicted prisoners the right to vote, at least so long as we have the practice of not allowing minors the right to vote. Here, the use of the comparison to the case of minors leads toward a conclusion opposed to the conclusion of the previous argument based on a comparison of cases used in example 9.8.

An argument that proceeds on the basis of a comparison of two similar cases is called an *argument from analogy*. Arguments from analogy are often extremely powerful forms of persuasion to a particular audience because they can compare an issue to something the audience is very familiar with or has very positive feelings about. Arguments based on analogies are a form of plausible reasoning. Two situations may be similar or dissimilar in indefinitely many respects, which could be cited. But if a relevant similarity is cited, it may be used to shift the burden of proof in an argument.

Arguments that press for consistency by means of a comparison between two cases alleged to be similar are arguments from analogy. It is therefore useful for us to study the argument from analogy.

9.5 ARGUMENTATIVE USE OF ANALOGY

The following example shows the use of analogy in a dispute, a type of dialogue in which the conclusion of the one arguer is opposed to the conclusion of the other:

Example 9.10

President Reagan, in a speech for congressional funds to aid the Contra rebels in Nicaragua, compares the Contras to the American patriots who fought in the War of Independence. A speaker in Congress opposed to sending aid to the Contras compares the situation in Nicaragua to the war in Vietnam.

This example shows an argumentative use of analogy. Reagan's argument operates on the presumption that the patriots in the War of Independence must be accepted as having fought for a good cause that Congress must support. By his analogy, then, Congress should likewise support the cause of the rebels in Nicaragua. The conclusion that Reagan would appear to be arguing for, one may presume, is that Congress should, therefore, grant funds to aid the Contra rebels.

The opposing speaker is evidently arguing for the opposite conclusion. His conclusion is that Congress should not get involved in the situation in Nicaragua, that is, that Congress should not grant funds to support the Contras. The basis of his argument is the comparison between Nicaragua and Vietnam. United States intervention in Vietnam was disastrous. That is the presumption that the opposing speaker's argument operates on, because the present climate of opinion is that U.S. involvement in the Vietnam War led to an expensive, protracted war that the U.S. lost, and the results were politically divisive. It is not a situation that any country would want to repeat. Because the situation in Nicaragua is like that of Vietnam, by the speaker's analogy, his conclusion is that Congress should not get involved in aiding the rebel forces in Nicaragua.

Both speakers have advanced powerful analogies in this debate. Whether one argument is more persuasive than the other will depend on the continuation of the debate. Each can try to support his own analogy by bringing out relevant similarities and to refute his opponent's analogy by citing relevant differences between the two cases.

The argumentation scheme for each side can be represented as follows, in which S_0 represents the situation of the Vietnam War, S_1 represents the situation at the time of the American War of Independence, and S_2 represents the situation in Nicaragua. Also, let A represent the course of action that support be given to the forces fighting against the larger regime. The first argumentation scheme (F_1) represents the form of Reagan's argument, and the second scheme (F_2) is that of the opposing argument:

(F_1) The right thing to do in S_1 was to carry out A.

S_2 is similar to S_1.

Therefore, the right thing to do in S_2 is to carry out A.

(F_2) The wrong thing to do in S_0 was to carry out A.

S_2 is similar to S_0.

Therefore, the wrong thing to do in S_2 is to carry out A.

Notice that, in this dialogue, each of the two analogies is being used argumentatively. This means that the analogy in the premises is used to derive a conclusion to the argument that is based on the analogy in the premises. The first premise says that something applies in one situation. The second premise says that another situation

257

is similar to the first situation. The conclusion is that the thing mentioned in the first premise also applies to the second situation.

An argument from analogy is not necessarily limited to two situations. If several situations can be shown to all share a particular characteristic, then it can be concluded that a new situation also shares that characteristic.

Many texts, for example Copi (1982, p. 389), notice that analogies may be based on similarities among multiple cases, and conclude that all arguments from analogy are essentially inductive in nature. Their thesis is that an argument from analogy starts from a premise that one thing has a certain property, and that a second and third thing, and so forth, all have the property, and reaches the conclusion that some other thing will also *probably* have the same property. However, the thesis that all arguments from analogy are inductive arguments is open to question.

The following example is cited by Copi (1982, p. 390) as an everyday inference by analogy:

Example 9.11

I infer that a new pair of shoes will wear well on the grounds that I got good wear from other shoes previously purchased from the same store.

However, if example 9.11 is treated as an inductive argument, we would have to evaluate it by the standards of that argument as bad. First, it should be criticized as an instance of the fallacy of insufficient statistics, for no information is given on the size of the sample. How many pairs of shoes did I previously buy from this store? Perhaps not enough to justify an inductive generalization. Second, it could be a case of biased statistics. It could well be that the shoes I previously bought from this store were not representative of the pair of shoes I just bought. For example, it could be that all the other shoes I previously bought there had thick soles, whereas this new pair of shoes has thin soles.

Many arguments from analogy that could be reasonable arguments unfortunately have to be evaluated as weak, questionable, or even fallacious if treated as inductive arguments. Why is this so? It is so because many powerful arguments from analogy are plausible arguments rather than inductive arguments.

To see why, look back to argumentation schemes (F_1) and (F_2).

258

The first premise in each of these arguments is based on the presumption that the audience to whom the argument is directed must accept this proposition as basically plausible, given their basic position. The second premise is based upon a perceived similarity between two situations, again an assumption that essentially rests on plausible rather than inductive grounds.

Consider the following everyday type of inference based on analogy:

Example 9.12

Bob has a 1973 Volkswagen Rabbit, and his brakes needed important repair work after he had driven his car for thirty thousand miles. We have just driven our Volkswagen Rabbit for almost thirty thousand miles. The next time we take it in for servicing, we should have the brakes checked.

Here again, if we treat the argument as essentially inductive, it is a weak argument at best, because it could be a case of insufficient or biased statistics. However, it does seem to be a good argument from analogy, for there is some reason to believe that my car and Bob's might be similar in the relevant respect.

You could say with justification that example 9.12 is a sort of *ad ignorantiam* argument. It is like example 2.19, in which there was reason to be cautious about a rifle because we did not know that it was not loaded. Here again, we do not know that the car is unsafe, but, because there are reasonable grounds for caution, it is better to assume that the car might be unsafe. It is reasonable, in other words, to stack the burden of proof high enough against the presumption that the car is safe to justify checking the brakes. So if it is an *ad ignorantiam* argument, it is a reasonable, not a fallacious, instance of it. In this case, then, the argument from analogy does support its conclusion because it is a plausible argument, not because it is an inductively strong argument.

Generally speaking, then, the argumentative use of analogy shifts the burden of proof against an opponent's contention and toward one's own argument in controversial disputes in which inductive evidence is not available and plausible reasoning is the moving force in shifting opinion one way or the other. It is exactly in this context of dialogue that analogy is a powerful basis for argument for a conclusion.

Analogies are often used nonargumentatively, for example, as similes and metaphors to create vivid mental pictures in literature, or to explain something unfamiliar by comparing it to something more familiar:

Example 9.13

The name of the baleen whale is derived from the long flexible plates which hang down from the roof of the whale's mouth, known as baleen or whalebone. The margin of each plate is frayed into a hairlike fringe, and the action of these fringed plates serves as a food strainer.[4]

Most of us have not observed the inside of a whale's mouth, and it is not easy to visualize how the baleen functions or what it is like. The description of the margin of the baleen as a "hairlike fringe" is an analogy that helps us to picture the mouth and to get an idea of how it functions in straining out marine organisms when the whale is feeding. So there we have an analogy, but its use is not argumentative. The author is not using the analogy to shift the burden of proof to his side in an issue of controversy. We cannot pick out a conclusion that he is using the analogy to establish in argument. Rather, the more reasonable interpretation of example 9.13 is that the author is using the simile of hair to help the reader visualize an unfamiliar subject so the whale can be described to him.

When approaching any corpus, the first question is always to ask what the conclusion is, or whether there is a conclusion to be established by the arguer. So in this instance too, at the first point of examining a *corpus* containing an analogy it is good to distinguish carefully whether there is an argument from analogy or whether it is an instance of a nonargumentative analogy.

9.6 CRITICIZING ARGUMENTS FROM ANALOGY

Arguments from analogy are persuasive because they compare two situations, at least one of which is familiar to the audience, and because there is a plausible basis of similarity between the two situations. But exactly what set of propositions comprise a familiar situation? Exactly when are two situations plausibly similar? In a particular case, these may be hard questions to answer very firmly.

---

4 Robert T. Orr, *Marine Mammals of California,* Berkeley and Los Angeles, University of California Press, 1972, p. 11.

Arguments based on analogy may be difficult to either confirm or refute decisively. Yet, as we will see, there are critical questions for the argument based on analogy. Any two situations can continue being compared in a dispute in a potentially unlimited number of ways pro and con. Therefore, the use of an analogy characteristically leaves the dispute open to further argument. What a powerful analogy does, however, is to shift the burden of proof to one side, thereby requiring a response from the other side. When an analogy is challenged by pointing out a dissimilarity, the burden of proof is placed on the defender to respond. If the defender can successfully respond, the burden of proof is once again on the critic to argue for a relevant dissimilarity. In many cases, this pattern of challenge and response can go on for several moves in a sequence of reasonable dialogue without either party clearly getting the upper hand.

Johnson and Blair (1983, p. 100) cite an interesting case in which a reader responded to an article in *Saturday Review*[5] by Thomas Middleton that argued for stricter gun control legislation:

Example 9.14

I wish to protest the article written by Mr. Middleton. Can Mr. Middleton be so naive as to really believe that banning ownership of firearms would significantly reduce murders and robberies? Did banning booze significantly reduce drinking?

This example is a typical argument from analogy. The plausible premise that would be accepted by the average reader is that prohibition did not, in fact, work as a measure to reduce drinking. The analogy or comparison premise is that banning ownership of firearms is similar to banning consumption of alcohol. The conclusion of the argument is that banning ownership of firearms will not work to significantly reduce crimes like murder or robbery.

The first premise, that prohibition did not work, is historically plausible, and would not likely be challenged by the readership to whom this argument was directed. Thus the question is whether the analogy premise is also plausible.

In their evaluation (p. 100), Johnson and Blair argue that the analogy premise fails and that therefore the argument is a case of faulty

5 Paul Curtis, "Gun Control Debated," *Saturday Review,* November 29, 1975, p. 4.

analogy. They argue that it is faulty because the two situations being compared are not similar in the relevant respect required to support the conclusion. Their grounds for this challenge are based on the following cited dissimilarity. Liquor, beer, and wine are easy to make at home, therefore, prohibition was difficult to enforce. However, it would be difficult to manufacture guns secretly, or at home, and easier to police distribution of guns. Hence, they argue, the reasons prohibition failed do not apply to the case of gun control.

Johnson and Blair's challenge to the argument is highly reasonable, but a defender of the argument still has room to respond. It could be argued that there is currently an active trade in illicit arms all over the world, which might be very difficult to effectively control even if owning firearms were made illegal, or more illegal than it is. Also, banning firearms in northern areas, where hunting game is an important source of food and income might be ineffective. Also, it is not as difficult to manufacture a gun at home as one might initially think.

One can easily see, in the case of this interesting analogy, how the dispute might go on in the form of further challenges and responses in a critical discussion. The dispute is by no means trivial and might lead to further interesting dialogue on the subject of gun control. An interesting analogy can be a way of provoking thoughtful discussion on a subject.

There are three basic ways to critically question the argument from analogy. The first way is to question the major premise that asserts that a certain conclusion is plausible or right in the analogous situation presented by the premise. In this case, such a criticism would not be easy to argue persuasively because it is highly plausible (as a matter of conventional wisdom) that prohibition did not work to reduce consumption of alcohol. The second way would be to argue that the analogy premise fails. This means questioning whether the analogy is faulty because the two situations compared are not similar in the relevant respect. This is Johnson and Blair's approach in their analysis of example 9.14 above. The third way would be to propose a counteranalogy. A good example of this type of strategy would be to try to question Reagan's argument from example 9.10 by offering the counteranalogy that the situation in Nicaragua is like the situation in Vietnam. In the present case, for example, a critic might argue that gun control has worked in Britain to significantly reduce armed robberies and other violent crimes in which firearms are used; therefore, banning ownership of firearms would also work in North America. Here, the critic draws a parallel between one situation and another, thus deploying one analogy to criticize the original analogy. By using a possibly better counteranalogy, the critic shifts the burden of proof back onto the original arguer to defend the plausibility of his analogy if he can.

Once an analogy between two cases is conceded, in some cases this concession can be exploited even further by an aggressive arguer by pressing for consistency with yet another case. When such a chain of arguments is set into motion, it is called a slippery slope argument.

9.7 SLIPPERY SLOPE ARGUMENTS

A slippery slope argument gets started when you are led to acknowledge that a difference between two things is not really significant. Once having acknowledged this first step, it may be difficult to deny that the same difference between the second thing and some third thing is likewise not really significant. Once this sort of argument gets started, it can be too late to do anything to stop it decisively. You are on the slippery slope. The argument can be applied over and over, driving you to concede a conclusion that is absurd:

Example 9.15

A man is clocked at fifty-six miles per hour by a radar detection unit of the highway patrol in a fifty-five mile per hour speed limit zone. He argues to the patrolman that he should not get a ticket because the difference in speed of one mile per hour is insignificant: "After all, it's really arbitrary that the agreed-upon speed limit is fifty-five rather than fifty-six isn't it? It's just because fifty-five is a round number that it is chosen as the limit."

What happens if the police officer accepts this argument? Then the next speeder, who is clocked at fifty-seven miles per hour, will argue: "Well, you let Smith off when he was clocked at fifty-six miles per hour. You conceded that one mile per hour doesn't really make a significant difference. By the same criterion, you must let me off without a ticket as well. If you don't, I am going to complain that you are not fair in doing your job. You did a special favor for

Smith in letting him off. If you don't do the same for me, then that is favoritism and special treatment for your friends." Now the police officer is really in trouble, for the next motorist, who is clocked at fifty-eight miles an hour, can use the same argument: "I hear you let Jones off when he was clocked at fifty-seven. Since you admitted that one mile an hour doesn't make any difference, you have to let me off too." And so on, and so on. Ultimately, the poor police officer will have to let any speeder go without a ticket, no matter how fast he was going. Once the word spreads, everyone can demand "equal treatment."

A slippery slope argumentation scheme is a sequence of steps, a chain argument of the following form: First, it is conceded that there is no significant difference between two things A_0 and A_1. And since A_0 is acceptable, A_1 must be acceptable too. But then, because there is the very same relationship between A_1 and yet another thing A_2 as there was between A_0 and A_1, it must be conceded that A_2 is acceptable as well. Each time it is argued that the difference is not significant until, by a sequence $A_0, A_1, \ldots, A_k$, we eventually arrive at some absurd or disastrous result A_k. The inevitable conclusion is that A_k must be acceptable too. In example 9.15, we might eventually reach the point in which a driver clocked at one hundred miles per hour could argue that he should not receive a speeding ticket.

How could the traffic patrolman have critically replied to the first speeder's argument? He could have replied that, although the speed limit of fifty-five might be arbitrary to some degree, that is the exact limit set as uniform policy. And that uniform policy must be applied equally and fairly to all motorists. If a motorist is speeding to the hospital to save a badly injured passenger, then that could be fairly judged as a significantly relevant difference to exempt this driver from the policy in a particular case. So there may be exceptions in special cases. But the claim that a motorist is exceeding the limit by only a small amount may not be a significantly relevant difference between his case and that of the motorist who is driving within the limit. By this type of reply, then, the patrolman could resist the slippery slope argument of the speeder.

In many cases of slippery slope argumentation there is some legitimate room for attack and defense. The reason is that, with any organizational, legal, or social rules and policies, we rightly demand fair policies that apply equally to all persons who come under the

264

rule. But we also require that rules should not be rigidly applied by a thoughtless bureaucracy. If a unique case is reasonably judged to be relevantly different enough to qualify fairly as an exceptional case, then we require that the rule be broken. It is a question of how much one case resembles another.

In realistic argumentation, assessing whether one case is relevantly similar enough to another case may require considerable judgment. This kind of judgment is based on an analogy between the cases. No doubt each case must be judged on its own merits. But the slippery slope enters the picture once an initial judgment is made that two cases are similar. Then, if a third case has no less similarity to the last one, consistency requires that the next step be to accept that third case as well. And once on the slippery slope, there may be no way off.

The slippery slope is a particularly inviting trap when the first steps are the easiest to take. Some steps can be easier to take than others because vague terms can apply more easily in some situations than others. A traditional type of argument exemplifying this variability among different steps in the sequence is called the *sorites* argument. Example 9.16, like all sorites arguments, has two premises: a base premise (B_0) and an inductive premise (I):

Example 9.16

(B_0) Every man who is four feet in height is short.

(I) If you add one-tenth of an inch to a short man's height, he still remains short.

(C) Therefore, every man is short.

In this instance, the base premise is highly plausible. If you apply the inductive premise to the base premise, the result, B_1, is also highly plausible:

(B_1) Every man who is four feet and one-tenth of an inch in height is short.

But the sorites is a species of slippery slope argumentation because, each time you apply the inductive step (I) to the next new premise, B_2, B_3, . . ., B_k, you have to accept the next premise after that. It is typical of slippery slope argumentation that, once you have conceded the first step, then consistency requires that you concede each succeeding step. And you must keep going as long as the purveyor of the slippery slope argument keeps leading you along. But then if you keep going indefinitely, you must concede an absurd conclusion. In example 9.16, you must eventually concede that every man is short.

The sorites is a puzzling argument and has often been thought to be a fallacy or sophistical argument because the premises seem true, the argument seems valid, and yet the conclusion is clearly false. But that appears to be a contradiction, for if the premises of a valid argument are true, then the conclusion must be true.

The sorites argument has traditionally been called the "heap" or "bald man" argument. If you have a heap of sand, and you take one grain away, it is still a heap of sand. You can continue to apply the process, however, and eventually there will no longer be a heap. Or similarly, if you remove one hair from a man's head, he is not bald. But if you keep doing it, then eventually he will cease being not bald. The sorites argument works because terms like 'short', 'heap', and 'bald' are vague. There is not a single precise point x, for example, at which we can say that a man is bald if he has less than x hairs on his head and not bald if he has x or more hairs on his head. Because of this lack of an exact cutoff point, there is no clear step of the slippery slope argument at which the defender can resist applying the inductive step.

The reason the sorites argument is so effective as a tactic of argumentation is that there is a variation in the degree of plausibility with which a vague concept can be applied in different situations. For example, it is highly plausible to claim that a man who is four feet in height is short. It is still highly plausible to say that a man who is five feet in height is short, in most contexts, even though in some contexts – for example, if we are talking about jockeys – the plausibility of the claim may be less. But although it may still be fairly plausible to say that a man who is five foot six is short, this claim has become less plausible than the two earlier ones.

Recognizing this variability, we can see how the sorites argument arts out strong, but then gets weaker in plausibility. When you 'v (I) to (B$_0$) at the first step, the next conclusion (B$_1$) follows deductively valid form of argument *modus ponens*. Since both 'I) are very highly plausible, (B$_1$) must be just as plausible. ·y, (B$_1$) may be a little less plausible than (B$_0$), for in a ·nent, the conclusion is only as plausible as the least Hence, the inductive step (I) must be less plausible than (B_0). And as we go along each step in the chain of *modus ponens* arguments, (I) must become less and less plausible.[6] What this shows is that the conditional (I) is not absolutely true, but rather has a practical legitimacy that can vary in plausibility value at different stages of application to men of different heights. As this conditional is applied over and over, its plausibility value tends to decrease somewhat. And eventually it reaches a range of cases for which its plausibility has become marginal. Hence the sorites argument fails to prove that its conclusion (C) is true. You cannot conclude from it that every man must be short. So we can see that the sorites argument can involve a kind of fallacy or sophism when applied to a particular case.

Why the sorites argument is a particularly powerful scheme of slippery slope argumentation is precisely because of the variability of the inductive premise in different contexts. Applied to the first premise (B_0), the inductive step (I) is highly plausible. It is virtually impossible to resist accepting it as a plausible argument from a practical point of view. But then, it seems, to maintain consistency, the arguer to whom the slippery slope is directed, must continue to accept (I) at each succeeding step. If he refuses, he can be accused of inconsistency. And his problem is that there is no particular, clear point in the sequence at which he can refuse to accept (I). For with vague terms, there is no precise cutoff point at which the term clearly fails to apply. So the slippery slope is like the processes of temptation and seduction. Once it is begun and then set into motion, it becomes progressively harder to stop from going along with it.

The *domino effect argument* is the counteractive use of the possibility or threat of a slippery slope argument to counsel against taking a first step. It is often used as a conservative argument against any new policy or proposal that is untried. For example, it might be argued that, if terminally ill patients are allowed to refuse heroic medical treatment, this might lead to elimination of the unfit. And this, then, eventually might lead to concentration camps and Nazi genocide squads. The domino effect argument is not a positive use of the slippery slope argument but is a kind of defensive argument tactic or critical reply against a slippery slope that might develop. When dealing with the domino argument, it is important to dis-

6 This analysis is based on a solution to the sorites paradox similar to one offered in King (1979).

tinguish between the claim that certain consequences *might* develop and the claim that they *will* develop. The suggestion that they might develop is often used as a scare tactic or strategy of intimidation to try to silence the opposition and prematurely close off the argument.

The slippery slope argument is often premised on exploiting the vagueness of a term in natural language. There is nothing wrong or fallacious about vagueness, in itself. But just as ambiguity is exploited by an equivocation, vagueness is exploited by the slippery slope argument; for when the term deployed in a slippery slope attack is vague, there is no precise cutoff point at which the defender can start to resist deployment of the inductive step by the attacker. To successfully defend against the use of a slippery slope argument, then, one must be careful not to commit oneself to the application of the inductive step right at the base premise until it is seen which way the argument is going and what its ultimate conclusion might be.

The domino effect argument is a mirror image of the sorites argument, and it also involves a series of steps or stages, S_0, S_1, $\ldots$ S_k. Both the sorites argument and the slippery slope argument generally have to do with vagueness of a term, but both of them can also typically involve causal links between the various stages of a sequence. The domino effect argument, for example, is often based on the premise that there is a causal link between S_0 and S_1, and between S_1 and S_2, and so forth until some "horrible" outcome S_k is reached.

Sometimes the causal domino effect argument is reasonable. For example, if a row of dominos is set up close enough to its neighbor, then if the first domino is pushed, the last one in the row will ultimately fall over as well. But where the causal domino effect argument becomes a fallacy is in the context in which the premise that each step *might* cause the next is used to frighten an arguer to conclude that the last, "horrible" step *will* happen unless he refuses to anything that might cause the first step to happen. This type ument can be criticized as inadequate if not enough additional evidence is given to show that what might happen really n, or is likely to happen.

causal type of domino effect is reasonable depends on plausibility of the evidence given to support the osed at each step. The classic case of the domino its use during the Vietnam War era to argue that, if Vietnam fell to the Communists, then neighboring countries like Cambodia would also fall. Then, other adjacent countries would fall until the whole of East Asia would be in Communist hands. This argument was often used as a kind of scare tactic by its exponents, and because not much evidence seemed available to back it up very firmly, it came to be thought of as a fallacious type of argument, in this particular instance.

However, the domino effect argument can be a reasonable argument if enough evidence can be given to make its premises plausible. Only when such evidence has not been given can we say that an instance of the domino effect argument is erroneous, incorrect, or unpersuasive.

In any slippery slope argument, there is an attacker and a defender. In example 9.15 the attacker is the motorist who tries to argue that his case should be the exception to the rule. The police officer tries to defend the applicability of the rule. In this instance, it was the attacker who used the argument incorrectly because his argument did not justify that his case should be treated as an exception. Sometimes the attacker's side of the argument is called the *wedge argument* because it has the effect that, once the defender makes the first exception, he will not be able to resist making more and more exceptions until the rule is overwhelmed and destroyed. So the wedge argument is a countertactic or rebuttal to the domino effect argument.

In trying to counter a slippery slope argument, the defender can use the domino effect response incorrectly or badly if he sticks dogmatically to requiring adherence to the rule in a particular case, even when a reasonably well justified argument for admitting an exception has been made by the attacker. A case in point, here, is the use of the domino effect argument in which the defender tries to use scare tactics instead of plausible evidence to keep the wedge from being driven in. This illicit use of the domino effect argument could also be called the *all hell will break loose* argument, and it has also been called the argument from *rigorism*.

9.8 SUBTLE EQUIVOCATIONS

The examples of equivocation examined in Section 9.3 were simpl
cases of equivocation that would not be likely to seriously decei
alert and thoughtful participants in realistic arguments. Once

269

amibiguity is realized, these simple examples can be easily perceived as equivocal and dismissed as fallacious. However, in a context of discussion, there can be some complicating factors to make equivocation less easy to detect and criticize.

One problem is that in arguments in natural language, the meanings of the words or phrases that occur may themselves be subject to dispute. Consider the following argument, advanced in the context of a dialogue on the morality of law:

Example 9.17
Following the law is obligatory.
Failing to do something obligatory is morally wrong.
Therefore, failing to follow the law is morally wrong.

Anyone to whom this argument is directed might criticize it as committing the fallacy of equivocation, on the following grounds. In the first premise, 'obligatory' means legally obligatory. That is, a citizen has no choice but to follow the letter of the law – laws that apply to everyone alike – and anyone who breaks a law may be subject to penalty. But in the second premise, 'obligatory' means morally obligatory. Because 'obligatory' has shifted its meaning from the one premise to the other, example 9.17 is an equivocation. The only way both premises can be plausibly taken as true is to equivocate.

This criticism seems very reasonable, but what if the proponent of example 9.17 replies to the criticism as follows: "My argument is not an equivocation. It is a perfectly convincing and sound argument, for in it I have identified the class of morally obligatory acts and the class of acts prescribed by law as perfectly equivalent meaning. In fact, I am stipulating that, for the purposes of this ᴵment, 'morally obligatory acts' and 'acts prescribed by law' ᴵean the same thing." Now according to this reply, example ᴵot any longer be fairly considered an instance of the fallacy ᴵion. Or so it seems, for there is no longer any ambiguity ᴵase an equivocation. For this arguer, there is no double ᴵe there can be no shift of meaning from the one ᴵer.

ᴵght question this arguer's right to impose his ᴵrally upon the dispute, or even criticize his

270

definition as loaded or prejudicial. But apart from these possible objections, his reply to the charge of equivocation seems very reasonable. What are we to say now? Is example 9.17 a fallacy of equivocation? To resolve this dilemma we need to probe a little more deeply into the context of the dialogue.

We need to ask what the issue of the dialogue is supposed to be. Let us suppose that the issue is the moral basis of the law. Black, the proponent of example 9.17, is a legal positivist. That is, Black's position is that black-letter law (the statement of the law in "black and white" as it occurs in the current codes or law books) is identical to what the law should be taken to be, at any given time. White has a different position. He feels that the law as written is not always right, and that it can and should be subject to improvements. According to White, then, real law is not the same as black-letter law.

Let us presume that the context of dialogue is that Black and White are opposed in a dispute. Black is set to prove his thesis that failing to follow the law is always morally wrong. White is set to argue for his thesis that failing to follow the law can, in some cases, be morally acceptable. In this context Black has put forward example 9.17 as an argument. Is it a fallacy of equivocation?

To answer this question we have to ask what the purpose of Black's argument should be in the context of the persuasion dialogue on morality of law. Since the dialogue is a dispute, Black's objective should be to argue from premises that White is committed to, in order to derive the conclusion that his own (Black's) thesis is true. Black must try to show by valid arguments that his conclusion follows from propositions that White will accept as plausible. Now the problem with Black's use of example 9.17 for this purpose is that White will accept the two premises as plausible only if 'obligatory' is disambiguated differently in each one.

So the problem with example 9.17, as an argument put forward in the context of reasonable dialogue with White on the issue of the dispute, is that the argument is not practically useful as a means of persuading White. True, from Black's point of view, there may be no ambiguity. From the viewpoint of Black's position as a legal positivist, the argument may be valid and both premises may be acceptable (to Black). But that is not necessarily a completely successful defense against White's objection that the argument is an equivocation.

For White, there is a very real and important distinction to be made between 'morally obligatory' and 'legally obligatory'. Any argument that denies the moral significance of this distinction would beg the question against White's case. Therefore, once White recognizes the ambiguity in the premises of example 9.17, this argument is worthless against his case in reasonable dialogue. Or at any rate, the burden of proof is on Black to show that his definition of the disputed term can be justified. If the premises are interpreted ambiguously, they could both be plausible, but the argument would then be invalid. If the premises are interpreted consistently, then the argument would be valid, but one premise or the other would not be plausible from White's point of view. Either way then, the argument is worthless as a means for Black to carry forward his case against White's position. Therefore, White is justified in criticizing the argument as an equivocation.

However, Black is also justified in his defense against White's charge of equivocation, to some extent, for from the viewpoint of Black's argued position, there is no ambiguity. Who then has the strongest argument? It depends on what the term 'obligatory' really means. In other words, the argument between Black and White has become a verbal dispute about the meaning of a term. In this regard, it is similar to example 9.2.

Sometimes, in a dispute about the meaning of a term in natural language, one side can be shown by appeal to linguistic evidence to have the stronger claim. But in this case, both disputants have some claim to being justified in their usage of 'obligatory,' since this term does appear to be open to different interpretations. However, it seems fair to judge that a heavier burden of proof should be placed on Black's side of the argument, because most of us would be reasonably prepared to concede that there are some acts that are legally obligatory but not morally obligatory and vice versa. The plausibility of White's distinction shifts the burden toward Black.

In this case, equivocation has turned out to be similar, in an important respect, to the question-begging epithet. By aggressively insisting on a meaning of the term 'obligatory' that is friendly to his own side of the argument, Black attempts to block White's side of the argument by refusing to countenance a distinction between the terms 'morally obligatory' and 'legally obligatory'.

Our discussion of example 9.17 shows that a charge of equivocation can reveal serious problems in realistic arguments. Moreover, by filling in a plausible context of dialogue for the argument, it has been possible to see how a realistic criticism of equivocation could be much harder to nail down than you might initially have thought. Definitions of key words in an argument are often open to dispute. Hence the burden of proof is initially on the critic who alleges an equivocation to show that there is an ambiguity used in an illicit way in the argument claimed to be fallacious. But if the charge is substantiated, the burden is then on the defender to reply if he can.

Equivocation can be harder to detect when the shift of meaning takes place gradually over several steps in a longer argument. Standards of precision for vague terms, we have seen, may vary from proposition to proposition. When this sort of shift is more subtle and gradual, then the danger of sliding gradually into a fallacious argument is an even more serious threat to reasonable dialogue. The equivocation by Black in example 9.17 is like the question-begging language studied in Section 9.2. It aggressively defines a term from the point of view of one side of the argument in an attempt to block the opponent's argument. In such a case, the defender against the charge of equivocation may be open to a further criticism of using a loaded definition.

We could say, then, that equivocation is a kind of use of an ambiguous term (or terms) in argument. Sometimes simply revealing the ambiguity is enough critical questioning to refute the argument as a fallacy of equivocation. However, in other cases, the defender of the argument may stick to his guns more resolutely and deny any ambiguity, from the point of view of his position. When this happens, the situation is very much like the case of a loaded definition, in which the arguer may insist on defining a contentious term in a way that supports his own side of the argument and undermines his opponent's side. Or it may even be a case of question-begging language. In such cases, the argument has degenerated into a terminological dispute. This frequently happens in hotly contested arguments on controversial issues, and it can be a bad sign that reasoning is degenerating into a quarrel.

Some terminological disputes can be moderated by appealing to the dictionary, common usage, or plausible interpretations of a term, in order to judge with whom the burden of proof should lie. But in other cases, a terminological dispute can be just as subject to reasonable argument as any other topic of reasonable dialogue. In such a case, it may be no trivial job to get a charge of equivocation to stick. So it is always a good idea when you are criticizing an argument as an instance of equivocation to ask how the argument could be defended against the charge by a determined defender.

9.9 VARIABILITY OF STRICTNESS OF STANDARDS

If vague terms are used in a consistent manner throughout an argument, there may be no logical difficulties or fallacies in the use of these terms. A problem can arise, however, when a vague term occurs more than once in different propositions in an argument, and differing standards of precision are required at each occurrence to make the propositions plausible. The problem that arises in such a case is a special kind of equivocation that is posed through the vagueness of terms in an argument. This is different from the slippery slope type of problem, but exhibits some of the same features.

The context of dialogue for the following example is the question of whether one should get married. Frank takes the traditional view that marriage is an excellent institution or practice that couples should enter into in good faith and seek to preserve by serious efforts. Larry takes the progressive thesis that marriage is no longer practical or relevant in the 1980s and that couples should no longer enter into it or take it seriously. At one point in the dispute, Larry advances the following argument:

Example 9.18

Getting married involves promising to live with a person for the rest of your life. But nobody can safely predict compatibility with another person for life.[7]

Frank then asks, 'Don't we often make promises that we don't keep?' and Larry replies, 'Yes, but the point is that one should not make a promise unless one can safely predict that one will keep it'. Finally, Frank replies, 'So you mean that if two people aren't compatible, they can't live together. So they shouldn't promise to do something they can't do'. Larry concedes that this is exactly what he means, adding, 'I conclude that no one should ever get married'.

7 This example is derived from a similar example in Cederblom and Paulsen (1982, p. 59).

Larry seems to have a logical argument here. How should Frank criticize it? The premises seem plausible and the argument seems valid. As a first step of analysis, let us set out Larry's argument more explicitly, listing the premises and conclusion:

Example 9.19

(1) Getting married involves promising to live with a person for the rest of one's life.
(2) No one can safely predict compatibility with another person for life.
(3) One should not make a promise unless one can safely predict that one will keep it.
(4) If two people aren't compatible, they can't live together.
(5) One should not promise to do something one can't do.
(6) Therefore, nobody should ever get married.

Now if you look at premises (1) to (5) separately, each seems fairly plausible, or at least arguably plausible. But when you put them together, they imply (6) by valid arguments. Premises (2) and (4) together imply that no one can safely predict that two people can live together for life. But together with (3) and (5), this implies that one should not make a promise to live together with someone for life. But then this conclusion, taken together with (1), implies that no one should ever get married. In short, then, Larry appears to have a valid argument for his conclusion, with plausible premises as well. Poor Frank seems to be getting the worst of the argument.

Let us look at the argument more closely. The term 'compatible' occurs in both premise (2) and premise (4). 'Compatible' is a vague term. It could be hard to say exactly when two people have reached the point of being incompatible. Should we say that two people are incompatible if they have occasional disputes or differences of opinion, or do not have much in common? Or should we reserve the term incompatible for cases when there is a deep hatred or bitterness between them, or constant fighting. It seems hard to say. Some couples can tolerate differences and disagreements better than others. We can have higher standards of what qualifies as compatibility, but then, in other contexts, we could equally well adopt more relaxed standards.

275

We could sum up the two extreme possibilities of different sets of strictness in our standards of compatibility as follows:

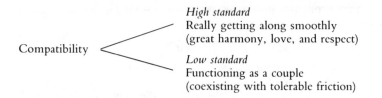

High standard
Really getting along smoothly
(great harmony, love, and respect)

Compatibility

Low standard
Functioning as a couple
(coexisting with tolerable friction)

Now let us look at (4), which states that, if two people can live together, they must be compatible. If we demanded the high standard of compatibility, (4) could plausibly come out false. To make (4) plausible, we have to drop to the low standard of compatibility, for some couples can manage to live together, even during bad periods when you could not really call them 'compatible', according to the high standard.

Now let us look at (2), a premise that also contains the term 'compatible'. Here, the lower your standard of compatibility, the more couples there will be who will qualify as compatible. So if you predict compatibility with the lower standard in mind, the more likely you are to be right that a couple will remain compatible for a longer period. In this case, going for the lower standard makes for more danger that proposition (2) will come out false. The higher your standard of compatibility, the harder it will be to predict that couples will remain compatible for life. To make (2) plausible, we tend to opt for the high standard of compatibility.

But the same sort of ambiguity of strictness of standards affects the term 'safely predict' in premises (2) and (3):

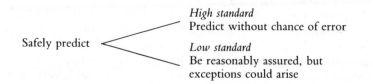

High standard
Predict without chance of error

Safely predict

Low standard
Be reasonably assured, but
exceptions could arise

Premise (3) states that you should not make a promise unless you can safely predict that you will keep it. But only if you interpret 'safely predict' by lower standards does (3) come out as plausible, because promises cannot always be kept in every situation. Perhaps

276

I could not have predicted that I could not keep my promise of being present on my father's birthday. But I had no way of knowing, when I made the promise, that my wife would be ill on the same day as my father's birthday.

On the other hand, if you interpret (2) by the same low standard of 'safely predict', it could most plausibly be interpreted as false, for if your standards of safe prediction are low, then someone who predicts compatibility for life in a reasonable number of cases is much more likely to be right. The low standard for 'safely predict' that makes (3) come out as plausible tends to make (2) come out as implausible. And consistent interpretation of (2) and (3) using the high standard would have the opposite result.

With respect to the two vague terms 'compatible' and 'safely predict' in the argument of example 9.19, the most plausible interpretation of the standard of precision appealed to in one premise is the least plausible interpretation in another premise. The most plausible interpretation of each term at each occurrence is summarized below:

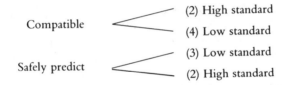

What has gone wrong with the argument of example 9.19 is that the vague terms appeal to different standards of precision in different premises during the course of an extended argument. The result is a kind of ambiguity imposed on the person to whom the argument is directed when he tries to interpret each individual premise as a plausible proposition. So it is a classic case of equivocation, yet one that occurs in a subtle pragmatic context of shifting standards over the course of an argument as it develops in dialogue.

9.10 CONCLUSIONS

In a relatively simple case of equivocation, in which there are only two premises and one ambiguous term that occurs in each, the problem is usually easy to detect. Why? Because once you look at the two premises together, you may perceive that, to make both of them plausible, you must interpret one premise one way, and the other in another way. But if the argument is longer, with several different premises and several ambiguous or vague terms, the shift in meaning may be harder to detect. Why? Because you may not see the two premises next to each other when there is an equivocation between them. There may be several other premises between each of these two premises. In the meantime, you may well have forgotten that a particular word occurred before, in a previous plausible premise, and that you now need to interpret the same word in a different way than before to make the new premise plausible. The longer the argument and the more vague and ambiguous words it contains, the more likely it is that the equivocation may slip by unnoticed.

The trick of an equivocation is that each premise appears individually plausible. It is only when you put two premises together and compare the terms that have occurred in each that the suspicion of equivocation may arise. Thus to deal with realistic cases of equivocation in practical argument, it is necessary to take a global perspective. The critic must scan the whole argument and see if there has been a shift of context that might affect any pair of premises that have been used in the argument.

With all the fallacies of language we have looked at in this chapter, the important thing is to study the whole argument in the context of the dialogue. If there has been a contextual shift, then we may be in trouble with vagueness or ambiguity. Example 9.19 showed how a careful analysis of realistic cases of equivocation may require attention to subtle shifts of standards of accuracy that take place over a longer sequence of argumentation.

Here, as elsewhere in the study of fallacies, a fundamental axiom of reasonable criticism is once again borne out, as remarked upon by Whately (1836, p. 162): "A very *long* discussion is one of the most effective veils of Fallacy; . . . a Fallacy which when stated barely . . . would not deceive a child, may deceive half the world if *diluted* in a quarto volume." In any analysis of an argument, therefore, an important step prior to criticizing the argument is to reconstruct the context of dialogue in order to see what its purpose can be reasonably presumed to be. Otherwise, the evidence to support the claim that the argument contains a fallacy may be incomplete.

As J. L. Mackie (1967, p. 179) put it, "When we suspect a fallacy, our aim must be to discover exactly what the argument is". Mackie adds that the first step in carrying out a reasoned evaluation of an argument is to pick out the main outlines and then go on to examine the more subtle aspects or qualifications of the argument.

Since arguers are often vague, wandering, and inconsistent in what they assert over the course of a discussion, the first important step of analysis is always to determine what the type and goal of the argument is. But precisely in those cases in which the argument is long and a "mass of verbiage," this process of deleting the unimportant details and sorting out and fairly interpreting the main stages can be crucial, and constitutes an important prerequisite of criticism.

Operating on the basis of the principle of charity, when a proposition contains vague or ambiguous terms we naturally want to interpret the proposition in such a way that it comes out as most plausible. That is reasonable and correct. But if we do this in relation to two different propositions in the same argument, we may get into trouble.

With the slippery slope argument, we want to accept the first step, and we are invited to because it is a plausible proposition. But as each step proceeds along the slippery slope, the propositions we are required to accept become less and less plausible. Once we are committed, however, it becomes more difficult to turn back. We are sliding down the slippery slope.

The slippery slope argument becomes a problem, in a particular case, in those middle steps of the application of the vague term in which the inductive step becomes less and less plausible. But the slippery slope argument is such an insidious attack on an arguer's position because, once the defender accepts the first steps, which are highly plausible premises, he appears to become more and more heavily committed to accepting each succeeding step along the way. Hence if he stops and tries to resist the attack in these middle steps, the attacker may accuse him of being inconsistent.

However, each case must be studied on its own merits, because it is possible for the defender to commit a fallacy if the attacker has plausible arguments for overturning a rule or definition of a term, in a particular case, and the defender tries to enforce the rule or definition against a stronger argument. Thus the context of each defense and attack depends on the burden of proof in the context of dialogue. If there is a strong burden of proof behind retaining an established rule or meaning of a term, anyone who argues that their case is a justifiable exception must meet high standards to meet the burden of proof. The cleverness of the slippery slope attack, however, is that it starts out with a highly plausible first premise, and then attacks the defender's position by small degrees.

Similarly with equivocation, we generously interpret an ambiguous term in such a way as to make the proposition in which it occurs plausible. But then at the next step, we can make the next proposition plausible only by accepting a shift of context. It is at this point that the danger of equivocation is present.

The concept of a loaded definition is reminiscent of the concept of a loaded question that we encountered in the context of question-asking fallacies. And indeed, there are some common aspects here. A presupposition of a question is said to be loaded if it automatically prejudices the position of the answerer as soon as he gives any direct answer to the question. Similarly here, a definition in a proposition in somebody's argument may be said to be loaded if assenting to the definition by accepting the proposition in the argument automatically prejudices the position of the person to whom the argument is directed. Loaded definitions are an unduly aggressive way of trying to force an arguer to accept some proposition, whereas in a critical discussion, the arguer should be given the option of accepting the proposition or not. These tactics are violations of the negative rules of persuasion dialogue given in Chapter 1. They are tactics to evade the obligation of proof by trying to bully a respondent into prematurely closing off argumentation. However, an argument that contains a loaded definition is not necessarily a fallacious argument. Similarly, you recall, a loaded question is not necessarily fallacious in every instance.

In general, the concept of a loaded definition and the concept of a question-begging epithet are two distinct types of criticisms. The latter is a stronger type of criticism. As we saw in the case of the loaded term in example 9.0, it does not necessarily follow that the parents are claiming that the psychologist's argument is fallacious or contains a question-begging epithet. It could be possible that the psychologist might have various independent arguments based on evidence from psychology for viewing the parents' behavior, in this case, as an instance of "gender-prejudiced behavior." And it could well be, for all the parents know or have claimed so far, that the psychologist's arguments for this view do not depend on or are equivalent to his conclusion that the parents should try harder to make their behavior more gender-neutral. If this is possible, then it shows that the parents can object to the psychologist's argument on the grounds that it contains a loaded definition without necessarily claiming that his argument must contain a question-begging epithet. Of course, the parents could conceivably go on to claim that the psychologist's argument does contain a question-begging epithet by building up a more extensive analysis and refutation of the psychologist's argument. But they need not do so in order to criticize or question the loaded definition.

To say that an argument contains a loaded definition is to say that a term in the argument is defined or used in such a way as to tend to be prejudicial against the position of the person to whom the argument is directed. However, an argument containing a question-begging epithet is so strongly loaded against the position of the person against whom it is directed that it can be shown to have required presumptions that exclude or negate that person's possibility of proving his thesis in the issue under contention. To prove that an argument is an instance of the unfair use of question-begging language, then, a critic has to do more than to show that the definition is loaded. He has to show that the premise containing the term or clause in question is so tightly connected to the conclusion of the argument to be proven by the one who advances the argument that there is a vicious circle in the argument.

Arguments and criticisms arising out of vagueness and ambiguity of terms in natural language can be difficult and frustrating at times. A precise definition may not be agreed upon because a term is inherently controversial, and even if a precise definition is advanced by one side, the other side may think that such a definition is prejudicial to their point of view. Likewise with analogies, two cases may be similar or dissimilar in one respect or another, but whether the feature cited is relevant may be open to dispute. Hence, in many cases, the best one can hope for is a criticism that will reasonably shift the burden of proof. Often, plausible reasoning is the best standard one can reasonably hope to achieve in natural language argumentation. But often, that is a high enough standard to conclude a successful argument in a critical discussion, inquiry, or negotiation.

Bibliography

Alter, Jonathan, "Round Up the Usual Suspects," *Newsweek*, March 25, 1985, 69.

Apostel, L., "Towards a General Theory of Argumentation," in *Argumentation: Approaches to Theory Formation*, ed. E. M. Barth and J. L. Martens, Amsterdam, Benjamins, 1982, 93–122.

Aqvist, Lennart, *A New Approach to the Logical Theory of Interrogatives*, Uppsala, Filosofiska Studier, 1965.

Aristotle, *Topica et sophistici elenchi*, trans. W. A. Pickard-Cambridge, ed. W. D. Ross, New York, Oxford University Press, 1958.

Bailey, F. G., *The Tactical Uses of Passion*, Ithaca, N.Y., Cornell University Press, 1983.

Barth, E. M., and Krabbe, E. C. W., *From Axiom to Dialogue; A Philosophical Study of Logics and Argumentation*, Berlin, de Gruyter, 1982.

Barth, E. M., and Martens, J. L., "*Argumentum ad Hominem:* From Chaos to Formal Dialectic," *Logique et Analyse*, 77–8, 1977, 76–96.

Bateson, L., "The Message 'This is Play'," in *Group Processes: Transactions, of the Second Conference*, ed. B. Schaffner, New York, Josiah Macy Jr. Foundation, 1956, 145–242.

Begley, Sharon, 'Science Contra Darwin,' *Newsweek*, April 8, 1985, 80–81.

Belnap, Nuel D., and Steel, Thomas B., Jr., *The Logic of Questions and Answers*, New Haven, Conn., Yale University Press, 1976.

Bentham, Jeremy, *The Book of Fallacies*, vol. 2 of *The Works of Jeremy Bentham*, ed. John Bowring, New York, Russell & Russell, 1962 (originally published in 1838).

Bickel, Peter J., Hammel, Eugene A., and O'Connell, William J., "Sex Bias in Graduate Admissions: Data from Berkeley," in *Statistics and Public Policy*, ed. William B. Fairley and Frederick Mosteller, Reading, Mass., Addison-Wesley, 1977. First printed in *Science, 187*, 1975, 398–404.

Bowler, Peter J., *Evolution: The History of an Idea*, Berkeley and Los Angeles, University of California Press, 1984.

Brinton, Alan, "A Rhetorical View of the Ad Hominem," *Australasian Journal of Philosophy, 63*, 1985, 50–63.

Campbell, Stephen K., *Flaws and Fallacies in Statistical Thinking*, Englewood Cliffs, N. J., Prentice-Hall, 1974

Cederblom, Jerry, and Paulsen, David W., *Critical Reasoning*, Belmont, Calif., Wadsworth, 1982.

Clements, Colleen D., and Ciccone, Richard, "Ethics and Expert Witnesses," *Bulletin of the American Academy of Psychiatry and Law*, 12, 1984, 127–36.

Cohen, David, *The Crucial 10% that Really Counts for Trial Victories*, Englewood Cliffs, N.J., Executive Reports, 1973.

Copi, Irving M., *Introduction to Logic*, 6th ed., New York, Macmillan, 1982.

Croxton, Frederick E., and Cowden, Dudley J., *Applied General Statistics*, 2nd ed., Englewood Cliffs, N.J., Prentice-Hall, 1955.

Damer, T. Edward, *Attacking Faulty Reasoning*, Belmont, Calif., Wadsworth, 1980.

de Kruif, Paul, *Men Against Death*, New York, Harcourt Brace, 1932.

DeMorgan, Augustus, *Formal Logic*, London, Taylor & Walton, 1847.

Epstein, Richard L., "Relatedness and Implication," *Philosophical Studies*, 36, 1979, 137–73.

Fischer, David Hackett, *Historians' Fallacies*, New York, Harper & Row, 1970.

Fisher, Alan C., and North, Wendy, "Cancer Survival Rates: What the Media Haven't Told You," *American Council on Science and Health News & Views*, 7, 1986, 1–7.

Freedman, David, Pisani, Robert, and Purves, Roger, *Statistics*, New York, Norton, 1978.

Gevarter, William B., *An Overview of Artificial Intelligence and Robotics*, NASA Technical Memorandum 855838, Houston, NASA Headquarters, Scientific and Technical Information Branch, 1983.

Giere, Ronald N., *Understanding Scientific Reasoning*, New York, Holt, Rinehart & Winston, 1979.

Govier, Trudy, "*Ad Hominem*: Revising the Textbooks," *Teaching Philosophy*, 6, 1983, 13–24.

A Practical Study of Argument, Belmont, Calif., Wadsworth, 1985.

Problems in Argument Analysis and Evaluation, Dordrecht, Foris, 1987.

Graham, Michael H., "Impeaching the Professional Expert Witness by a Showing of Financial Interest," *Indiana Law Journal*, 53, 1977: 35–53.

Grice, H. Paul, "Logic and Conversation," in *The Logic of Grammar*, ed. Donald Davidson and Gilbert Harman, Encino, Calif., Dickenson, 1975, 64–75.

Hamblin, C. L., *Fallacies*, London, Methuen & Co., 1970.

Harrah, David, "The Logic of Questions," in *Handbook of Philosophical Logic*, vol. 2, ed. D. Gabbay and F. Guenther, Dordrecht, Reidel, 1984, 715–64.

Hinman, Lawrence M., "The Case for *Ad Hominem* Arguments," *Australasian Journal of Philosophy*, 60, 1982, 338–45.

Hintikka, Jaakko, *The Semantics of Questions and the Questions of Semantics*, Acta Philosophica Fennica, vol. 28, Amsterdam, North-Holland, 1976.

"The Logic of Information-Seeking Dialogues: A Model," in *Konzepte der Dialektik*, ed. Werner Becker and Wilhelm K. Essler, Frankfurt am Main, Klostermann, 1981, 212–31.

"What is the Logic of Experimental Inquiry?" *Synthese*, *74*, 1988, 173–90.

Hooke, Robert, *How to Tell the Liars from the Statisticians*, New York, Dekker, 1983.

Huff, Darrel, *How to Lie with Statistics*, New York, Norton, 1954.

Imwinkelried, Edward J., *Scientific and Expert Evidence*, New York, Practicing Law Institute, 1981.

"Science Takes the Stand: The Growing Misuse of Expert Testimony," *The Sciences*, *26*, 1986, 20–5.

Jeffrey, C., *An Introduction to Plant Taxonomy*, 2nd ed., Cambridge University Press, 1982.

Johnson, Ralph H., and Blair, J. Anthony, *Logical Self-Defense*, Toronto, McGraw-Hill Ryerson, 1983.

Johnstone, Henry W., Jr., *Validity and Rhetoric in Philosophical Argument*, University Park, Pa., Dialogue Press of Man and World, 1978.

Jones, Andrew, J. I., *Communication and Meaning*, Dordrecht, Reidel, 1983.

Kielkopf, Charles, "Relevant Appeals to Force, Pity and Popular Pieties," *Informal Logic Newsletter*, *2*, 1980, 2–5.

King, John L., "Bivalence and the Law of Excluded Middle," *American Philosophical Quarterly*, *16*, 1979, 17–25.

Krabbe, Erik C. W., "Formal Systems of Dialogue Rules," *Synthese*, *63*, 1985, 295–328.

Locke, John, *An Essay Concerning Human Understanding*, ed. John W. Yolton, 2 vols., London, Dent, 1961 (originally published in 1690).

Lorenzen, Paul, *Normative Logic and Ethics*, Mannheim, Hochschultashenbücher, 1969.

Mackie, J. L., "Fallacies," *The Encyclopedia of Philosophy*, vol. 3, ed. Paul Edwards, New York, Macmillan, 1967, 169–79.

Mann, William C., "Dialogue Games: Conventions of Human Interaction," *Argumentation* 2, 1988, to appear.

Manor, Ruth, "A Language for Questions and Answers," *Theoretical Linguistics*, *6*, 1979, 1–21.

"Dialogues and the Logics of Questions and Answers," *Linguistische Berichte*, *73*, 1981, 1–28.

Moore, Christopher W., *The Mediation Process*, San Francisco, Jossey-Bass, 1986.

Moore, David S., *Statistics: Concepts and Controversies*, San Francisco, Freeman, 1979.

Newton-Smith, W. H., *Logic: An Introductory Course*, London, Routledge & Kegan Paul, 1985.

Rescher, Nicholas, *Plausible Reasoning*, Assen, Van Gorcum, 1976.
Dialectics, Albany, State University of New York Press, 1977.

Sanders, Robert S., *Cognitive Foundations of Calculated Speech*, Albany, State University of New York Press, 1987.

Seligman, Daniel, "We're Drowning in Phony Statistics," *Fortune*, November 1961, 146–71.

Sell, Peter S., *Expert Systems: A Practical Introduction*, London, Macmillan Press, 1985.

Shepherd, Robert Gordon, and Goode, Erich, "Scientists in the Popular Press," *New Scientist, 76,* 1977, 482–4.

Simon, H. A., "Spurious Correlation: A Causal Interpretation," *Journal of the American Statistical Association, 49,* 1954, 467–92.

Sperber, Dan, and Wilson, Deidre, *Relevance,* Cambridge, Mass., Harvard University Press, 1986.

Stebbing, L. Susan, *Thinking to Some Purpose,* Harmondsworth, Penguin Books, 1939.

Todd, D. D., "Begging the Question," *Globe and Mail* (Letters to the Editor), February 24, 1987, 6.

Trankell, Arne, *Reliability of Evidence,* Stockholm, Beckmans, 1972.

van der Meij, Hans, *Questioning,* The Hague, Selecta Reeks, 1986.

van Eemeren, Frans H., "Dialectical Analysis as a Normative Reconstruction of Argumentative Discourse," *Text, 6,* 1986, 1–16.

van Eemeren, Frans H., and Grootendorst, Rob, *Speech Acts in Argumentative Discussions,* Dordrecht, Foris, 1984.

van Eemeren, Frans H., Grootendorst, Rob, and Kruiger, Tjark, *Handbook of Argumentation Theory,* Dordrecht, Foris, 1987.

van Eemeren, Frans H., Grootendorst, Rob, Blair, J. Anthony, and Willard, Charles A., eds., *Argumentation: Across the Lines of Discipline,* Dordrecht, Foris, 1987.

Argumentation: Perspectives and Approaches, Dordrecht, Foris, 1987.

Argumentation: Analysis and Practices, Dordrecht, Foris, 1987.

Walton, Douglas N., "Why Is the *Ad Populum* a Fallacy?" *Philosophy and Rhetoric, 13,* 1980, 264–78.

"The Fallacy of Many Questions," *Logique et Analyse, 95–6,* 1981, 291–313.

Topical Relevance in Argumentation, Amsterdam, Benjamins, 1982.

Logical Dialogue-Games and Fallacies, Lanham, Md., University Press of America, 1984.

"New Directions in the Logic of Dialogue," *Synthese, 63,* 1985a, 259–74.

Arguer's Position: A Pragmatic Study of Ad Hominem *Attack, Criticism, Refutation, and Fallacy,* Westport, Conn., Greenwood, 1985b.

Informal Fallacies, Philadelphia, Benjamins, 1987.

"Burden of Proof," *Argumentation, 2,* 1988, 81–102.

Weber, O. J., "Attacking the Expert Witness," *Federation of Insurance Counsel Quarterly, 31,* 1981, 299–313.

Whately, Richard, *Elements of Logic,* New York, Jackson, 1836.

Elements of Rhetoric, ed. Douglas Ehninger, Carbondale, Southern Illinois University Press, 1963 (reprint of the seventh British edition, published in 1846).

Wilson, Patrick, *Second-Hand Knowledge: An Inquiry into Cognitive Authority,* Westport, Conn., Greenwood, 1983.

Woods, John, and Walton, Douglas, "*Argumentum Ad Verecundiam,*" *Philosophy and Rhetoric, 7,* 1974, 135–53.

"*Ad Baculum,*" *Grazer Philosophische Studien, 2,* 1976, 133–40.

"*Post Hoc, Ergo Propter Hoc,*" *Review of Metaphysics, 30,* 1977, 569–93.

"The Fallacy of *Ad Ignorantiam*," *Dialectica, 32,* 1978, 87–99.

"Equivocation and Practical Logic," *Ratio, 21,* 1979, 31–43.

Argument: The Logic of the Fallacies, Toronto, McGraw-Hill Ryerson, 1982.

Fallacies; Selected Papers 1972–1987, Dordrecht, Foris, 1988.

Wright, Richard A., and Tohinaka, Ken, *Logical Thinking,* Englewood Cliffs, N.J., Prentice-Hall, 1984.

Younger, Irving, "A Practical Approach to the Use of Expert Testimony," *Cleveland State Law Review, 31,* 1982, 1–42.

Zeide, Janet S., and Leibowitz, Jay, "Using Expert Systems: The Legal Perspective," *IEEE Expert, 2,* Spring 1987, 19–21.

Zeisel, Hans, *Say It with Figures,* 5th ed., New York, Harper & Row, 1968.

Index

action-seeking, dialogue, 8–9
ad baculum, 93–101, 106–107
ad hominem, 4, 20–1, 88, 127, 134–71, 254
  loaded terms, 243
ad ignorantiam, 43–9, 56, n65, 259
  burden of proof, 47
ad populum, 105–7
ad verecundiam, 172–97
  administrative authority, 174
  argumentation scheme, 192–7
  cognitive authority, 174–5, 176–7
  common errors, 178–81
  critical questions, 194–7
  evaluating expert authority, 184–9
  expert testimony, 181–4
  interpreting expert opinion, 189–92
  knowledge base, 193
advertising
  ad populum appeal in, 84–7
  overt, pictorial appeals to pity, 103–5
agenda
  defined, 72
  for a discussion, 71–5
Alter, Jonathan, 139, 186
ambiguity and vagueness, 240–3, 269–70, 280–1
analogy
  arguments based on, 253–6
  burden of proof, 254
  criticizing arguments from, 260–3
  use of, 256–60
  used as similes and metaphors, 260
appeals
  to emotion, 82–107
  to force, 93–7
    ad baculum, 93–101
  to pity, 101–5
    ad misericordiam, 101–2
    overt, pictorial, 103–5
  to popularity
    argumentum ad populum, 84–90
    problems with, 90–1

Aqvist, Lennart, n27
argument(s), *see also argumentum:* fallacy
  analogy, *see* analogy
  appeals to emotion, 82–107
  burden of proof, 47–8, 49–52, 58–9
  causal strengthening, 228–34
  collective terms, 128–30
  components, 9–11
  on controversial subjects, 25
  criticisms of irrelevance, 75–7
  deductively valid, *see* deductively valid arguments
  defined, 114
  distributive terms, 128–30
  domino effect, 267–9
  enthymeme, 115
  fallacies in, 19–23
  fallacious, 62
  from ignorance, 43–9
  inductive, *see* inductive
  irrelevant premises, 76–7, 78
  irrelevant shift in argument (red herring), 77
  issue 60–1
  loaded terms, 243–50, 280–1
  MP, *see* MP
  natural language, 239–81
  plausible, 15–16
  from popularity, 87–90
  post hoc, 212–15
  pragmatic aspects, 115
  reasonable, 23–4
  reasoned dialogue, 1–26
  relevance in, 60
  from rigorism, 269
  rules in criminal law, 47, 65–6
  semantic aspects, *see* semantic(s)
  slippery slope, 263–9, 279
    sorites argument, 265–66
  thesis, 60
  threat, 100–1

arguments (*cont.*)
truth in, 14–15
types, 3–9
vagueness and ambiguity, 240–3,
269–70, 281
valid, *see* valid arguments
valid forms of, 117–21
argumentative dialogue
component, 9–11
types, 3–9
argumentum, see also fallacy
ad baculum, 20
ad hominem, 20–1, 134–71
abusive, 134, 135–40, 151
cases, 168–71
circumstantial, 134, 141–9, 151,
157–8
critical questions, 163–5
poisoning the well, or bias-imputing, 134–5, 149–54
replying to a personal attack, 159–
62
rules of persuasion dialogue,
138
tu quoque, 135, 147–8, 159–60
types of error to check, 165–8
ad ignorantiam, 22, 43–9
burden of proof, 47
ad misericordiam, 20
ad populum, 20, 84–7, 95
ad verecundiam, 21, 172–97
dialogue, 192
Aristotle, 63–4, 245

Bailey, F. G., 92–3
Bailor, John, 233–4
Barth, E. M., n5, n143
Bateson, L., 126
Begley, Sharon, n227, 249
Belnap, Nuel D., n27
Bentham, Jeremy, 245–6
bias, 198–238
ad hominem, 134–5, 149–54
due to defining variables, 220–4
imputing (poisoning the well), 134–
5, 149–54
in statistics, 206–8
Bickel, Peter J., 220
Binkley, Robert, n149
Blair, J. Anthony, 76–7, 261–3
Bowler, Peter J., 249
Brothers, Joyce, 200–1

burden of proof
ad ignorantiam, 47
analogy, 254
basic rule of, 59
causal argument, 231
loaded question, 49–52
persuasion dialogue, 12–14
reasonable dialogue, 47–8, 58–9, 77–
8, 272
shifts in, 17, 156, 159–61, 166, 177–
8
slippery slope argument, 279–80
statistical claim, 235

Campbell, Stephen K., 206, 207, 209
capital punishment, 91–2
causal
argument, 230–1
relationship, 236
post hoc errors, 215–22
two-place, 225
causality, 228, 236
Cerf, Christopher, 21
Chrétien, Jean, 32–4
cladistics, 249
Clark, Ronald W., n179
Cohen, David, 190
Coleman, Fred, n99
conjunction, 125–6
contradiction, 124–6
valid arguments, 128
Copi, Irving M., n94, 258
criticism(s)
ad baculum, 100–1
argument, 25–6
of biased statistics, 207–8
circumstantial, 158
defeasible, 159
impartial, 24
of irrelevance, 60–81
loaded definition, 280–1
personal, 157, 165; *see also* ad hominem, argumentum
post hoc, 224–8
question–answer relevance, 67–71
question–begging epithet, 280–1
reasonable dialogue, 39–40
vagueness and ambiguity, 240–3,
269–70, 281
cumulative dialogue, 7
Cuomo, Mario M., 169
Curtis, Paul, n261

Damer, T. Edward, 218
debate, 24
    forensic, 4, 10
    House of Commons, 32–3
deductively valid arguments, 14–15,
    110
De Kruif, Paul, 232
DeMorgan, Augustus, n189
Dershowitz, Alan A., 187
dialogue
    action-seeking, 8–9
    argumentative, 3–11
    bargaining, 7–8
    critical discussion, see persuasion
        dialogue
    cumulative, 7
    defined, 3
    dialectical shift, 150
    disputes, 60
    educational, 9
    forensic debate, 4, 10
    information-seeking, 8
    issue in, 60
    negotiation, 7–8
        interest-based conflict, 8
    personal quarrel, 3–4, 10,
        24
    persuasion, see persuasion dialogue
    question–answer relevance, 67–
        71
    questioning in, 38–9
    reasonable, see reasonable dialogue
    relevance in, 68–9
    rules of, 10–11
    setting an agenda for discussion, 71–
        5
    stages of, 9–11, 17–19
    steps in analysis, 42–3
disjunctive complex question, 41
disjunctive syllogisms, see DS
double bind, 126–7
DS (disjunctive syllogisms), 118–19,
    131
Dyson, John, n175

educational dialogue, 9
Einstein, Albert, 179
enthymeme, 115
Epstein, Richard L., n67
equivocation, see fallacy
ESP, 48–9
evidence, 235

fallacies, 198–238
    informal, 16–23, 24–25
    logical (appeals to emotion), 82–3
    in questions, 29
    sophistici elenchi, 17
Fallacy, see also argument, argumentum
    ad baculum, 93–101, 106–7
    ad hominem, 4, 127, 145–6, 165
    ad ignorantiam, 43–9, 56, n65
    ad populum, 84–7, 89, 90, 93, 105–7
    begging the question, 22–3, 245–6
    black and white, 40
    of composition, 23, 129–30
        part–whole relationships, 129
    of division, 129–30
    equivocation, 22, 250–3, 274, 277–8
        subtle, 269–74
    of ignoratio elenchi, 19–20, 61–6, 75–
        6, 77, 79–80
    ad misericordiam, 101–2
    of insufficient statistics, 258
    of many (complex) questions, 19,
        29, 35–9
    analysis, 42–3
    post hoc, ergo propter hoc, 21–2, 212–
        15
    criticisms, 224–8
    errors, 213, 215–232
    slippery slope, 23
    straw man, 22
Fineman, Howard, n137
Fischer, David Hackett, n210, 215–16,
    223
Fitzgerald, Karen, n227
forensic debate, see debate
Freedman, David, n208
Frum, Barbara, 70–1

Gallup, Poll, 211–12
Giere, Ronald N., n208
Goode, Erich, 185–6
Govier, Trudy, 78, n134, n157
Graham, Michael H., 183–4
Greenspan, Alan, 187
Grice, H. Paul, n9
Grootendorst, Rob, n5, n6, n7, n9
Gross, Walter, n21
Grunberger, R., 94

Hailey, Arthur, 76–7
Hamblin, C. L., 14, n17, n83, 102
Hammel, Eugene A., 220

Harrah, David, n27, n28
Hennig, Willi, 249
Himmelstein, David, 233–4
Hintikka, Jaakko, n5, n6, n32
House of Commons, 32–3, 151–2
HS (hypothetical syllogism), 118, 120, 131
Huff, Darrel, 216–17
Hyer, Marjorie, n211
hypothetical syllogism, *see* HS

ignoratio elenchi, 19–20, 61–6, 75–6, 79–80; *see also* irrelevance
ad misericordiam, 101–2
failure of relevance, 77
impartiality
attack on arguer's, 149–54
criticism, 24
Imwinkelried, Edward, J., 181–2
inconsistency, 108, 124–8, 133, 156, 254
circumstantial, 145, 148–9, 158–9, 165–6
conjunction, 125–6
contradiction, 124–6
logical, 145–6
negation, 125
in propositions, 124
inductive
arguments, 198–9, 258
errors, 198–238
invalid arguments, 121–4 MP, 122
irrelevance
allegations of, 61–4
criticisms of, 60–81
in a regulated dialogue, 72–3
varieties of, 75–7
global, 64–7, 74, 78
local, 78
in premises, 76, 78
shift in argument (red herring), 77

Johnson, Ralph H., 76–7, 261–3
Johnston, Lynn, n176
Johnstone, Henry W., Jr., n141, n157
Jones, Andrew, J. I., 126–7

Krabbe, Erik C. W., n5

loaded terms, 243–50, 280–1
Locke, John, 172–3
logic
formal, 132
rule for conditional, 121

logical
constants, 131
inconsistency, 145–6
pragmatics, 1–3
semantics, 1–3
theory, 1

McIntosh, Dave, n2
Manor, Ruth, n58
Martens, J. L., n143
Martin, Paul, 76–7
Middleton, Thomas, 261
modus operandi, 101
modus ponens, see MP
modus tollens, see MT
Moloney, Paul, n254
Moore, Christopher W., 8, 73–4, 208, 210
Morganthau, Tom, n137
MP *(modus ponens),* 110, 113, 118, 120, 131
invalid arguments, 122
sorites argument, 266
MT *(modus tollens),* 118, 120, 131
Mulroney, Brian, 33

natural language argumentation, 239–81
ambiguity and vagueness, 240–3, 269–70
analogy, *see* analogy
equivocation, 250–3, 274, 277–8
subtle, 269–74
loaded terms and question-begging language, 243–50, 280–1
slippery slope arguments, 263–9, 279
variability of strictness of standards, 274–81
Navasky, Victor, 21
negation, 125
negotiation dialogue, 7–8
bargaining, 7–8
interest-based conflict, 8
Newman, Cardinal, 153
Nixon, Richard, 136–7, 167
North, Wendy, n210, 223

O'Connell, William J., 220
opposition, 12–13
Orr, Robert T., n260

personal attack in argumentation, *see*
   ad hominem
persuasion dialogue, 5–7
   argumentum ad verecundiam, 192
   asymmetrical, 11–12
   begging the question, 52–3
   blunders, 16
   burden of proof, 12–14
   external proof, 5–6
   informal fallacies, 16
   inquiry, 7
   internal proof, 5
   normative model, 16
   rhetoric, 82
   rules, 11–16
      ad hominem, 138
      negative, 16–19
      positive, 16
   symmetrical, 12–14
petitio principii, 245
Pisani, Robert, n208
plausible argument, 15–16
post hoc, see fallacy
pragmatic(s)
   aspects, 115
   logical, 1–3
Pravda, 95
prejudice, 244, 280
premise(s), 109
   ad baculum, 100
   enthymematic, 115
   irrelevance in, 76–8
presuppositions, 28–31
   analysis, 42
   disjunction, 55
   of a question, 54–5, 280
   questioning, 35–9
   unwelcome commitments, 31
principle of charity, 114
proof
   burden of, *see* burden of proof
   external, 5–6
   internal, 5
   obligation of, 237
propositions, 58–9
   ad baculum, 100
   circumstantially inconsistent, 148–9
   conclusion, 109
   conditional, 119–21
   conjunction, 125–6
   connectives, 108–31
   contradiction, 124–6
   disjunctive, 119

   defined, 120
   globally irrelevant, 64
   inconsistent set of, 124–6
   negation, 125
   premises, *see* premise(s)
   semantic core, 114
   threat, 100–1
   unwelcome, 56–7
   invalid arguments, 110–13
   warning, 100–1
Purves, Roger, n208

quarrel, 24
   personal, 3–4, 10
question(s)
   aggressive, 32–3, 55–6
   analysis, 42
   –answer relevance, 67–71
   and answers in dialogue, 27–59
   circular sequences, 53–4
   begging the, 22–3, 52–9
   fallacy of, 246
   loaded terms and, 243–50, 280–1
   petitio principii, 245
   direct answer, 28
   analysis, 43
   fallacious, 29
   House of Commons, 32–3
   indirect answer, 28
   loaded, 31, 35–9, 59, 280–1
   analysis, 42
   of many (complex), 19, 29, 31–9
   disjunctive, 41
   presuppositions, 28–31, 54–5, 280
   reasonableness
   analysis, 43
   replying to a question with, 49–52
   whether-, 27, 40, 54
   why-, 27, 41–2, 54, 55
   yes–no-, 27, 29–30, 54–5

Reagan, Ronald, 256–7, 262
reasonable dialogue, 39–43
   breach of procedures, 100
   burden of proof, 47–8, 58–9, 77–8,
      272
   criticism, 39–40
   one-sided use of words, 239
   prejudice, 244, 280
   replying to a question with a ques-
      tion, 52
   rhetoric, 82
red herring, 77

relevance, *see also* irrelevance
  failure of, 77
  global, 78, 270
  local, 78
  probative (pertinence), 78–9
  subject–matter–relatedness, 78
Rescher, Nicholas, n12, n15
Reuther, Walter, 92–3
rhetoric
  personal, 82
  popular, 82
rigorism, 269
Roberts, Oral, 97
rules
  of cooperativeness, 11
  in criminal law, 47, 65–6
  dialogue, 10–11
  in persuasion dialogue, 10–19, 138
  of informativeness, 11
  of relevance, 11

Seligman, Daniel, n200, 201–2
semantic(s)
  core, 114
  defined, 1–3
  terms, 128
  validity as, concept, 114–17
Shepherd, Robert Gordon, 185–6
sophistici elenchi, 17
sorites argument, 265–66
Sperber, Dan, n67
statistics
  bias, 222–4, 258
  burden of proof, 235
  fallacy of insufficient, 258
  insufficient and biased, 206–8
  meaningless and unknowable, 200–4
  sampling procedures, 205–6
Stebbing, L. Susan, 68–70
Steel, Thomas B., Jr., n27
Steinem, Gloria, 187
syllogisms
  disjunctive, *see* DS
  hypothetical, *see* HS
symmetrical dispute, 65
  weakly opposed, or asymmetrical,
    dispute, 65–6

Todd, D. D., 247
Tohinaka, Ken, 78
Trankell, Arne, 214
truth in arguments, 14–15

uniform substitution, n118

vagueness and ambiguity, 240–3, 269–
  70, 274
valid arguments, 108–33
  composition and division, 128–31
  contradiction, 128
  deductively, 14–15, 110
  defined, 115–16
  identifying, 110–14
  inconsistency, *see* inconsistency
  logical constants, 131
  proposition, 109–10
    conclusion, 109
    premises, 109
  sequences of, 110
validity
  deductive, 108–10
  logical constants, 128–9
  as a semantic concept, 114–17
van Eemeren, Frans H., n5, n6, n7, n9

Walton, Douglas N., n5, n7, n12, n13,
  n36, n44, n59, 79, n83, n85, n98,
  n130, n141, n157, n188
Weber, O. J., 183
Whately, Richard, 50
Whitecrow, Jake, 242
Will, George F., n137
Wilson, Deidre, n67
Wilson, Jack, n2
Woods, John n5, n44, n130
Woodward, Kenneth L., 169
Woolhandler, Steffie, 233–4
Wright, Richard A., 78

Young, Roger, n255
Younger, Irving, 182–3

Zeisel, Hans, 218